For BILLY GRAHAM, *The Living Story* has been a source of "renewed interest and inspiration" in the "age-abiding truth of the Scriptures."

This modern yet reverent retelling of the Biblical accounts of Christ and His Church will be a wonderful enrichment of the life and faith of any reader, as it brings to him this great story in today's language.

PREFACE

It is thrilling (in this book) to read the Word
with the sense of the eternal coupled with a
style that reads much like today's news-
papers. I have read here with renewed interest and inspiration the age-abiding truths
of the Scriptures as though they had come to
me direct from the Lord. I pray that your
reading them will deepen your spiritual life
and give you a new understanding of the
Scriptures.

Billy Graham

THE
LIVING STORY
Of Christ
and His Church

Selections from *Living Letters, Living Gospels* and *Living Prophecies*

**Paraphrased from the Scriptures
by
KENNETH TAYLOR**

PYRAMID BOOKS   **NEW YORK**

THE LIVING STORY

A PYRAMID BOOK

Published by arrangement with Tyndale House Publishers

Tyndale House edition published November, 1966
Pyramid edition published November, 1966

PYRAMID BOOKS are published by Pyramid Publications,
Inc., 444 Madison Avenue, New York, New York 10022, U.S.A.

CONTENTS

INTRODUCTION

Everyone likes a good story. And when an exciting story is *true*, enjoyment mounts with the tension.

Such a story is the ages-old story of Jesus Christ. Followers of Christ carried the story throughout the world. Some of them were killed because they insisted the story was absolutely true and that Jesus was the only Way to the one, true God.

The story has been translated into more than a thousand languages, and every year millions of people buy copies of it. Yet, many people hardly know the story, partly because old translations do not use the up-to-date language of today. That is the reason for this version of the story of Jesus.

The Living Story is a paraphrase, or careful rephrasing, of the story of Jesus as found in the New Testament of the Holy Bible. The paraphraser, Kenneth Taylor, used copies of the original Greek texts first written by Jesus' early followers: Luke, Paul, James and John. The books included in *The Living Story* describe Jesus' life on earth, the astonishing deeds of His first-century followers, the sublime statements of Christianity's greatest ambassador—Paul—the down-to-earth signs of true Christian faith and the wonders of Jesus' future return as King of all the earth.

The books are selected from three paraphrased volumes, *Living Letters, Living Prophecies* and *Living Gospels,* to present clearly the greatest story ever told about the greatest life ever lived.

THE
LIVING
STORY

of Christ
and
His Church

Luke

CHAPTER 1

Dear Friend who loves God:

1, 2   Several biographies of Christ have already been written using as their source material the reports circulating among us from the early disciples and other eyewitnesses.

3   However, it occurred to me that it would be well to recheck all these accounts from first to last and after thorough investigation to pass this summary on to you

4   So that you may be reassured of the truth of all you were taught.

*   *   *   *   *

5   My story begins with a Jewish priest, Zacharias, who lived when Herod was king of Judea. Zacharias was a member of the Abijah division of the Temple service corps. (His wife Elizabeth was also a member of the priest tribe of the Jews, being a descendant of Aaron.)

6   Zacharias and Elizabeth were godly folk, careful to obey all of God's laws—in spirit as well as in letter.

7   But they had no children, for Elizabeth was barren; and now they were very old.

8, 9   One day as Zacharias was going about his work in the Temple—for his division was on duty that week— the honor fell to him by lot to enter the inner sanctuary and burn incense before the Lord.

10   Meanwhile, a great crowd stood outside in the Temple court, praying as they always did during that part of the service when the incense was being burned.

11, 12   Zacharias was in the sanctuary when suddenly an angel appeared, standing to the right of the altar of incense! Zacharias was startled and terrified.

13 But the angel said, "Don't be afraid, Zacharias! For I have come to tell you that God has heard your prayer, and your wife, Elizabeth, will bear you a son! And you are to name him John!

14 You will both have great joy and gladness at his birth, and many will rejoice with you.

15 For he will be one of the Lord's great men. He must never touch wine or strong drink—and he will be filled with the Holy Spirit, even from before his birth!

16 And he will persuade many a Jew to turn to the Lord his God.

17 He will be a man of rugged* spirit and power, like Elijah, the prophet of old; and he will precede the coming of the Messiah, preparing the people for His arrival. He will teach them to love the Lord, just as their ancestors did, and to live as godly men."

18 Zacharias said to the angel, "But this is impossible! I'm an old man now, and my wife is also well along in years."

19 Then the angel said, "I am Gabriel! I stand in the very presence of God. It was He who sent me to bring you this good news!

20 And now because you haven't believed me, you are to be stricken silent, unable to speak until the child is born. For my words will certainly come true at the proper time!"

21 Meanwhile, the crowds outside were waiting for Zacharias to come out, and wondered why he was taking so long.

22 When he finally appeared, he couldn't speak to them; and they realized from his gestures that he must have seen a vision in the Temple.

23 He then fulfilled the remaining days of his Temple duties and returned home.

24 Soon afterwards Elizabeth his wife became pregnant, and went into seclusion for five months.

25 "How kind the Lord is," she exclaimed, "to take away my disgrace of having no children!"

26 The following month God sent the angel Gabriel to Nazareth, a village in Galilee,

27 To a virgin, Mary, engaged to be married to a man named Joseph, a descendant of King David.

* Asterisks indicate an implied word or phrase

28   Gabriel appeared to her and said, "Congratulations, favored lady! The Lord is with you!"

29   Confused and disturbed, she tried to think what he could mean.

30   "Don't be frightened, Mary," the angel said, "for God has decided to wonderfully bless you!

31   Very soon now, you will become pregnant and have a baby boy, and you are to name Him 'Jesus.'

32   He shall be very great and shall be called the Son of God. And the Lord God shall give Him the throne of His ancestor David.

33   And He shall reign over Israel forever; His Kingdom shall never end!"

34   Mary asked the angel, "But how can I have a baby? I am a virgin."

35   The angel replied, "The Holy Spirit shall come upon you, and the power of God shall overshadow you; so the baby born to you will be utterly holy—the Son of God.

36   Furthermore, six months ago your cousin Elizabeth—'the barren one,' they called her—became pregnant in her old age!

37   For every promise from God shall surely come true."

38   Mary said, "I am the Lord's servant, and I am willing to do whatever He says. May everything come true as you have told me." And then the angel disappeared.

39   A few days later Mary hurried to the highlands of Judea

40   To the town where Zacharias lived, to visit Elizabeth.

41   At the sound of Mary's greeting, Elizabeth's child leaped within her and she was filled with the Holy Spirit!

42   She gave a glad cry and exclaimed to Mary, "You are favored by God above all other women, and your child is destined for God's mightiest praise.

43   What an honor this is, that the mother of my Lord should visit me!

44   When you came in and greeted me, the instant I heard your voice, my baby moved in me for joy!

45   You believed that God would do what He said; that is why He has given you this wonderful blessing."

46   Mary responded, "Oh, how I praise the Lord!

47   How I rejoice in God my Savior!

48   For He took notice of His lowly servant girl, and now generation after generation forever shall call me blest of God!

49   For He; the mighty Holy One, has done great things to me.

50   His mercy goes on from generation to generation to all who reverence Him.

51   How powerful is His mighty arm! How He scatters the proud and haughty ones!

52   He has torn princes from their thrones and exalted the lowly.

53   He has satisfied the hungry hearts and sent the rich away with empty hands.

54   And how He has helped His servant Israel! He has not forgotten His promise to be merciful.

55   For He promised our fathers—Abraham and his children—to be merciful to them forever."

56   Mary stayed with Elizabeth about three months and then went back to her own home.

57   By now Elizabeth's waiting was over, for the time had come for the baby to be born—and it was a boy!

58   The word spread quickly to her neighbors and relatives of how kind the Lord had been to her, and everyone rejoiced.

59   When the baby was eight days old, all the relatives and friends came for the circumcision ceremony. They all assumed the baby's name would be Zacharias, after his father.

60   But Elizabeth said, "No! He must be named John!"

61   "What?" they exclaimed. "There is no one in all your family by that name!"

62   So they asked the baby's father, talking to him by gestures.

63   He motioned for a piece of paper and to everyone's surprise wrote, "His name is JOHN!"

64   Instantly Zacharias could speak again, and he began praising God!

65   Wonder fell upon the whole neighborhood, and the news of what had happened spread through the Judean hills.

66 And everyone who heard about it thought long thoughts and asked, "I wonder what this child will turn out to be? For the hand of the Lord is surely upon him in some special way."

67 Then his father Zacharias was filled with the Holy Spirit and gave this prophecy:

68 "Praise the Lord, the God of Israel, for He has come to visit His people and has redeemed them.

69 He is sending us a Mighty Savior from the royal line of His servant David

70 Just as He promised through His holy prophets long ago—

71 Someone to save us from our enemies, from all who hate us;

72, 73 He has been merciful to our ancestors, yes, to Abraham himself, by remembering His sacred promise to him

74 And by granting us the privilege of serving God fearlessly, freed from our enemies,

75 And by making us holy and acceptable, ready to stand in His presence forever.

76 And you, my little son, shall be called the prophet of the glorious God, for you will prepare the way for the Messiah.

77 You will tell His people how to find salvation by forgiveness of their sins.

78 All this will be because the mercy of our God is very tender, and heaven's dawn is about to break upon us.

79 To give light to those who sit in darkness and death's shadow, and to guide us to the path of peace."

80 The little boy greatly loved God and when he grew up he lived out in the lonely wilderness until he began his public ministry to Israel.

CHAPTER 2

About that time Caesar Augustus, the Roman Emperor, decreed that a census should be taken throughout the nation.

2 (This census was taken when Quirinius was governor of Syria.)

3 Everyone was required to return to his ancestral home for the registration.

4 And because Joseph was a member of the royal line, he had to go to Bethlehem in Judea, King David's ancient home—journeying there from the Galilean province of Nazareth.

5 He took with him Mary, his fiancée, who was obviously pregnant by that time.

6 And while they were there, the time came for her baby to be born;

7 And she gave birth to her first child, a son. She wrapped Him in a blanket and laid Him in a manger, because there was no room for them in the village inn.

8 That night some shepherds were in the fields outside the village, guarding their flocks of sheep.

9 Suddenly an angel appeared among them, and the landscape shone bright with the glory of the Lord. They were badly frightened,

10 But the angel reassured them. "Don't be afraid!" he said. "I bring you the most joyful news ever announced, and it is for everyone!

11 The Savior—yes, the Messiah, the Lord—has been born tonight in Bethlehem!

12 How will you recognize Him? You will find a baby wrapped in a blanket, lying in a manger!"

13 Suddenly, the angel was joined by a vast host of others—the armies of heaven—praising God:

14 "Glory to God in the highest heaven," they sang, "and peace on earth for all those pleasing Him."

15 When this great army of angels had returned again to heaven, the shepherds said to each other, "Come on! Let's go to Bethlehem! Let's see this wonderful thing that has happened, which the Lord has told us about."

16 They ran to the village and found their way to Mary and Joseph. And there was the baby, lying in the manger!

17 The shepherds told everyone what had happened and what the angel had said to them about this child.

18 Everyone who heard the shepherds' story expressed astonishment,

19 But Mary quietly treasured all these things in her heart and often thought about them.

20   Then the shepherds went back to their fields and flocks again, praising God for the visit of the angels and because they had seen the child, just as the angel had told them they would.

21   Eight days later at the baby's circumcision ceremony, He was named Jesus, the name given Him by the angel before He was even conceived.

22   When the time came for Mary's purification offering at the Temple, as required by the laws of Moses after the birth of a child, His parents took Him to Jerusalem to present Him to the Lord,

23   For in these laws God had said, "If a woman's first child is a boy, he shall be dedicated to the Lord."

24   At that time Jesus' parents also offered their sacrifice for purification—"either a pair of turtledoves or two young pigeons" was the legal requirement.

25   That day a man named Simeon, who lived in Jerusalem, was in the Temple. He was a good man, very devout, filled with the Holy Spirit and constantly expecting the Messiah to come soon.

26   For the Holy Spirit had revealed to him that he would not die until he had seen Him—God's anointed King.

27   The Holy Spirit had impelled him to go to the Temple that day; and so, when Mary and Joseph arrived to present the baby Jesus to the Lord in obedience to the law,

28   Simeon was there and took Him in his arms, praising God.

29, 30, 31   "Lord," he said, "now I can die content! For I have seen Him as You promised me I would! I have seen the Savior You have given to the world!

32   He is the Light that will shine upon the nations, and He will be the glory of Your people Israel!"

33   Joseph and Mary just stood there, marveling at what was being said about Jesus.

34, 35   Simeon blessed them but then said to Mary, "A sword shall pierce your soul, for this child shall be rejected by many in Israel, and this to their undoing. But He will be the greatest joy of many others.

And the deepest thoughts of many hearts shall be revealed."

*   *   *   *   *

36, 37 Anna, a prophetess, was also there in the Temple that day. She was the daughter of Phanuel, of the Jewish tribe of Asher, and was very old, for she had been a widow for 84 years following seven years of marriage. She never left the Temple but stayed there night and day, worshiping God by praying, and often going without food.

38 She came along just as Simeon was talking with Mary and Joseph, and she also began thanking God and publicly proclaiming the Messiah's arrival to everyone in Jerusalem who had been awaiting the coming of the Savior.

39 When Jesus' parents had fulfilled all the requirements of the Law of God, they returned home to Nazareth in Galilee.

40 There the child became a strong, robust lad and was known for wisdom beyond His years; and God poured out His blessings on Him.

*   *   *   *   *

41, 42 When Jesus was 12 years old, He accompanied His parents to Jerusalem for the annual Passover Festival, which they attended each year.

43 After the celebration was over, they started home to Nazareth, but Jesus stayed behind in Jerusalem. They didn't miss Him the first day,

44 For they assumed He was with friends among the other travelers. But when He didn't show up that evening, they started to look for Him among their relatives and friends.

45 When they couldn't find Him, they went back to Jerusalem to search for Him.

46 Three days later they finally discovered Him in the Temple, sitting among the teachers of Law, discussing deep questions with them

47 And amazing everyone with His understanding and answers.

48 His parents didn't know what to think when they saw Him sitting there (with those great men). "Son!" His mother said to Him, "Why have You done this to us? Your father and I have been frantic, searching for You everywhere."

49 "But why did you need to search?" He asked. "Didn't you realize that I would be here in My Father's House?"

50 But they didn't understand what He meant.

51 Then he returned to Nazareth with them and was obedient to them; and His mother stored away all these things in her heart.

52 So Jesus grew both tall and wise, and was loved by God and man.

CHAPTER 3

In the fifteenth year of the reign of the Emperor, Tiberius Caesar, a message came from God to John (the son of Zacharias), as he was living out in the deserts (Pilate was governor over Judea at that time; Herod, over Galilee; his brother Philip, over Iturea and Trachonitis; Lysanias, over Abilene; and Annas and Caiaphas were the Jewish High Priests.)

3 Then John went from place to place on both sides of the Jordan River, preaching that people should be baptized to show that they had turned to God and away from their sins, in order to be forgiven.

4 In the words of Isaiah the prophet, John was "a voice shouting from the barren wilderness, 'Prepare a road for the Lord to travel on! Widen the pathway before Him!

5 Level the mountains! Fill up the valleys! Straighten the curves! Smooth out the ruts.

6 And then all mankind shall see the Savior sent from God.' "

7 Here is a sample of John's preaching to the crowds that came for baptism: "You brood of snakes! You are trying to escape hell without truly turning to God! That is why you want to be baptized!

8 First go and show by the way you live that you really have repented. And don't think you are safe because you are descendants of Abraham. That isn't enough! God can produce children of Abraham from these desert stones!

9 The axe of God's judgment is poised over you, ready to sever your roots and cut you down. Yes, every tree

that does not produce good fruit will be chopped down and thrown into the fire."

10 The crowd replied, "Just what do you want us to do?"

11 "If you have two coats," he replied, "give one to the poor. If you have extra food, give it away to those who are hungry."

12 Even tax collectors—notorious for their corruption —came to be baptized and asked, "How shall we prove to you that we have abandoned our sins?"

13 "By your honesty," he replied. "Make sure you collect no more taxes than the Roman* government requires you to."

14 "And us," asked some soldiers, "what about us?" John replied, "Don't extort money by threats and violence; don't accuse anyone of what you know he didn't do; and be content with your pay!"

15 Everyone was expecting the Messiah to come soon, and eager to know whether or not John was He. This was the question of the hour, and it was discussed everywhere.

16 John answered the question by saying, "I baptize only with water; but someone is coming soon who has far higher authority than mine; in fact, I am not worthy of being His slave. He will baptize you with fire —with the Holy Spirit.

17 He will separate chaff from grain, and burn up the chaff with eternal fire and store away the grain."

18 He used many such warnings as he announced the Good News to the people.

19, 20 (But after John had publicly criticized Herod, governor of Galilee, for marrying Herodias, his brother's wife, and for many other wrongs he had done, Herod put John in prison, thus adding this sin to all his many others.)

21 Then one day Jesus Himself joined the crowds being baptized by John! And after He was baptized, and was praying, the heavens opened,

22 And the Holy Spirit in the form of a dove settled upon Him, and a voice from heaven said, "You are My much loved Son, yes, My delight."

23 Jesus was about 30 years old when He began His public ministry. He was known as the son of Joseph.

Joseph's father was Heli;
24 Heli's father was Matthat;
Matthat's father was Levi;
Levi's father was Melchi;
Melchi's father was Jannai;
Jannai's father was Joseph;
25 Joseph's father was Mattathias;
Mattathias' father was Amos;
Amos' father was Nahum;
Nahum's father was Esli;
Esli's father was Naggai;
26 Naggai's father was Maath;
Maath's father was Mattathias;
Mattathias' father was Semein;
Semein's father was Josech;
Josech's father was Joda;
27 Joda's father was Joanan;
Joanan's father was Rhesa;
Rhesa's father was Zerubbabel;
Zerubbabel's father was Shealtiel;
Shealtiel's father was Neri;
28 Neri's father was Melchi;
Melchi's father was Addi;
Addi's father was Cosam;
Cosam's father was Elmadam;
Elmadam's father was Er;
29 Er's father was Jesus;
Jesus' father was Eliezer;
Eliezer's father was Jorim;
Jorim's father was Matthat;
Matthat's father was Levi;
30 Levi's father was Symeon;
Symeon's father was Judas;
Judas' father was Joseph;
Joseph's father was Jonam;
Jonam's father was Eliakim;
31 Eliakim's father was Melea;
Melea's father was Menna;
Menna's father was Mattatha;
Mattatha's father was Nathan;
Nathan's father was David;
32 David's father was Jesse;
Jesse's father was Obed;

Obed's father was Boaz;
Boaz' father was Salmon;
Salmon's father was Nahshon;

33 Nahshon's father was Aminadab;
Aminadab's father was Admin;
Admin's father was Arni;
Arni's father was Hezron;
Hezron's father was Perez;
Perez' father was Judah;

34 Judah's father was Jacob;
Jacob's father was Isaac;
Isaac's father was Abraham;
Abraham's father was Terah;
Terah's father was Nahor;

35 Nahor's father was Serug;
Serug's father was Reu;
Reu's father was Peleg;
Peleg's father was Eber;
Eber's father was Shelah;

36 Shelah's father was Cainan;
Cainan's father was Arphaxad;
Arphaxad's father was Shem;
Shem's father was Noah;
Noah's father was Lamech;

37 Lamech's father was Methuselah;
Methuselah's father was Enoch;
Enoch's father was Jared;
Jared's father was Mahalaleal;
Mahalaleal's father was Cainan;

38 Cainan's father was Enos;
Enos' father was Seth;
Seth's father was Adam;
Adam's father was God.

CHÀPTER 4

And Jesus, full of the Holy Spirit, now left the Jordan River and was urged by the Spirit out into the barren wastelands of Judea, where Satan tempted Him for 40 days. He ate nothing all that time, and was very hungry.

3 Satan said, "If you are God's Son, tell this stone to become a loaf of bread."

4 But Jesus replied, "It is written in the Scriptures, 'Other things in life are more important than bread!' "

5 Then Satan took Him to a place where he revealed to Jesus all the kingdoms of the world in a moment of time.

6, 7 And the Devil told Him, "I will give You all these splendid kingdoms and their glory—for they are mine to give to anyone I wish—if You will only get down on Your knees before me and worship me."

8 Jesus replied, "We must worship God, and Him alone. So it is written in the Scriptures."

9, 10 Then Satan took Him to Jerusalem to a high roof of the Temple and said, "If you are the Son of God jump off! For the Scriptures say that God will send His angels to guard You

11 And to keep You from crashing to the pavement below!"

12 Jesus replied, "The Scriptures also say, "Don't experiment with God's patience!' "

13 When the Devil had ended all the temptations, he left Jesus for a while and went away.

14 Then Jesus returned to Galilee, full of the Holy Spirit's power. Soon He became well known throughout all that region

15 For his sermons in the synagogues; everyone praised Him.

16 When He came to the village of Nazareth, His boyhood home, He went, as usual, to the synagogue on Saturday, and stood up to read the Scriptures.

17 The book of Isaiah the prophet was handed to Him, and He opened it to the place where it says:

18, 19 "The Spirit of the Lord is upon Me; He has appointed Me to preach Good News to the poor; He has sent Me to announce that captives shall be released and the blind shall see, that the downtrodden shall be freed from their oppressors, and that God is ready to give blessings to all who come to Him."

20 Then He closed the book and handed it back to the attendant and sat down, while everyone in the synagogue gazed at Him intently.

21 Then He added, "These Scriptures came true today!"

22 All who were there spoke well of Him and were amazed by the beautiful words that fell from His lips. "How can this be?" they asked. "Isn't this Joseph's son?"

23 Then He said, "Probably you will quote Me that proverb, 'Physician, heal yourself'—meaning, 'Why don't you do miracles here in your home town as you did in Capernaum?'

24 But I solemnly declare to you that no prophet is accepted in his own home town!

25, 26 For example, remember how Elijah, the prophet, used a miracle to help the widow of Zarephath—a foreigner from the land of Sidon. There were many Jewish widows needing help in those days of famine, for there had been no rain for three and one-half years and hunger stalked the land; yet Elijah was not sent to them.

27 Or think of the prophet Elisha, who healed Naaman, a Syrian, rather than the many Jewish lepers needing his help."

28 As He made these remarks, the people in the synagogue were filled with sudden fury;

29 And jumping up, they mobbed Him and took Him to the edge of the hill on which the city was built, to push Him over the cliff.

30 But He walked away through the crowd and left them.

31 Then He returned to Capernaum, a city in Galilee, and preached there in the synagogue every Saturday.

32 Here, too, the people were amazed at the things He said! For He spoke as one who knew the truth, instead of quoting the opinions of others as His authority.

33 Once as He was teaching in the synagogue, a man possessed by a demon began shouting at Jesus,

34 "Go away! We want nothing to do with You, Jesus of Nazareth. You have come to destroy us! I know who You are—the Holy Son of God!"

35 Jesus cut him short. "Be silent!" He told the demon. "Come out!" The demon threw the man to the floor as the crowd watched, and then left him without hurting him further.

36 Amazed, the people asked, "What is in this man's words that even demons obey Him?"

37 The story of what He had done spread like wild-fire throughout the whole region.

38 After leaving the synagogue that day, He went to Simon's home where He found Simon's mother-in-law very sick with a high fever. "Please heal her," everyone begged.

39 Standing at her bedside, He spoke to the fever, rebuking it, and immediately her temperature returned to normal and she got up and prepared a meal for them!

40 As the sun went down that evening, all the villagers who had sick people in their homes, no matter what their diseases were, brought them to Jesus; and the touch of His hands healed every one!

41 Some were possessed by demons; and the demons came out at His command, shouting, "You are the Son of God!" But He stopped them and told them to be silent, because they knew He was the Christ.

42 Early the next morning He went out into the desert. The crowds searched for Him everywhere, and when they finally found Him, they begged Him not to leave them, but to stay at Capernaum.

43 But He replied, "I must preach the Good News of the Kingdom of God in other places, too, for that is why I was sent."

44 So He continued to travel around, preaching in synagogues throughout Judea.

CHAPTER 5

One day as He was preaching on the shore of Lake Gennesaret, great crowds pressed in on Him to listen to the Word of God.

2 He noticed two empty boats standing at the water's edge, while the fishermen washed their nets.

3 Stepping into one of the boats, Jesus asked Simon (its owner) to push out a little into the water, so that He could sit in the boat and speak to the crowds from there.

4 When He had finished speaking, He said to Simon, "Now go out where it is deeper and let down your nets and you will catch a lot of fish!"

5 "Sir," Simon replied, "we worked hard all last

night and didn't catch a thing! But if You say so, we'll try again."

6　And this time their nets were so full that they began to tear!

7　A shout for help brought their partners in the other boat, and soon both boats were filled with fish and on the verge of sinking!

8　When Simon Peter realized what had happened, he fell to his knees before Jesus and said, "Oh, sir, please leave us, for I'm too much of a sinner for You to have around."

9　For he was awestruck by the size of their catch, as were the others with him,

10　And his partners too—James and John, the sons of Zebedee.

Jesus replied, "Don't worry! From now on you'll be fishing for the souls of men!"

11　And as soon as they landed, they left everything and went with Him.

12　One day when He was in a certain village, a man with an advanced case of leprosy was there. When he saw Jesus he fell to the ground before Him, face downward in the dust, begging to be healed. "Sir," he said, "if You only will, You can clear me of every trace of my disease."

13　Jesus reached out and touched the man and said, "Oh course I will! Be healed!" And the leprosy left him instantly!

14　Then Jesus instructed him to go at once, without telling anyone what had happened, and be examined by the Jewish priest. "Offer the sacrifice Moses' law requires for lepers who are healed," He said. "This will prove to everyone that you are well."

15　Now the report of His power spread even faster, and vast crowds came to hear Him preach and to be healed of their diseases.

16　But He often withdrew to the wilderness for prayer.

17　One day while He was teaching, some Jewish religious leaders and teachers of the Law were sitting nearby. (It seemed that these men showed up from every village in all Galilee and Judea, as well as from Jerusalem!) And the Lord's healing power was upon Him.

18, 19 Then—look! Some men came carrying a paralyzed man on a sleeping mat. They tried to push through the crowd to Jesus but couldn't reach him. So they went up on the roof above him, took off some tiles and lowered the sick man down into the middle of the crowd, still on his sleeping mat, right in front of Jesus!

20 Seeing their faith, Jesus said to the man, "My friend, your sins are forgiven!"

21 "Who does this fellow think He is?" the Pharisees and teachers of the Law exclaimed among themselves. "This is blasphemy! Who but God can forgive sins?"

22 Jesus knew what they were thinking, and He replied, "Why is it blasphemy?

23 Which is easier for Me to do, to say I have forgiven his sins, or to actually heal him?

24 Now I will prove My authority to forgive sin by demonstrating My power to heal disease." Then He said to the paralyzed man, "Get up, roll up your sleeping mat and go on home!"

25 And immediately, as everyone watched, the man jumped to his feet, picked up his mat and went home praising God!

26 Everyone present was gripped with awe and fear. And they praised God, remarking over and over again, "We have seen strange things today."

27 Later on, as He left the town, He saw a tax collector—with the usual reputation for cheating—sitting at a collection booth. The man's name was Levi. Jesus said to him, "Come and be one of My disciples!"

28 So Levi left everything, sprang up and went with him.

29 Soon Levi held a reception in his home, with Jesus as the guest of honor. Many of Levi's fellow tax collectors and other guests were there.

30 But the Pharisees and teachers of the Law complained bitterly to Jesus' disciples about His eating with such notorious sinners.

31 Jesus answered them, "It is the sick who need a doctor, not those in good health!

32 My purpose is to invite sinners to turn from their sins, not to spend My time with those who think themselves already good enough."

33 Their next complaint was that Jesus' disciples were feasting instead of fasting! "John the Baptist's disciples are constantly going without food and praying," they declared, "and so do the disciples of the Pharisees. Why are yours wining and dining?"

34 Jesus asked, "Do happy men fast? Do wedding guests go hungry while celebrating with the groom?

35 But the time will come when the bridegroom will be killed; then they won't want to eat!"

36 Then Jesus told them a story: "No one tears up unshrunk cloth to make patches for old clothes, for the new garment is ruined and the old one isn't helped when the patch tears out again!

37 And no one puts new wine into old wineskins, for the new wine bursts the old skins, ruining the skins and spilling the wine!

38 New wine must be put into new wineskins.

39 But no one after drinking the old wine seems to want the fresh and the new! 'The old ways are best,' they say."

CHAPTER 6

One Sabbath as Jesus and His disciples were walking through some grainfields, they were breaking off the heads of wheat, rubbing off the husks in their hands and eating.

2 But some Pharisees said, "That is illegal. Your disciples are harvesting grain, and it is against the Jewish law to work on the Sabbath."

3 Jesus replied, "Don't you read the Scriptures? Didn't you ever read what King David did when he and his men were hungry?

4 He went into the House of God and took the shewbread, the special bread that was placed before the Lord, and ate it—illegal as this was—and shared it with others."

5 And Jesus added, "I am master even of the Sabbath."

6 On another Sabbath He was in the synagogue teaching, and a man was present whose right hand was deformed.

7 The teachers of the Law and the Pharisees watched

closely to see whether He would heal the man that day, since it was the Sabbath! For they were eager to find some charge to bring against Him.

8   How well He knew their thoughts! But He said to the man with the deformed hand, "Come and stand here where everyone can see." So he did.

9   Then Jesus said to the Pharisees and teachers of the Law, "I have a question for you. Is it right to do good on the Sabbath day, or to do harm? To save life, or to destroy it?"

10   He looked around at them one by one and then said to the man, "Reach out your hand." And as he did, it became completely normal again!

11   At this, the enemies of Jesus were wild with rage, and began to plot His murder.

*   *   *   *   *

12   One day soon afterwards He went out into the mountains to pray, and prayed all night.

13   At daybreak He called together His followers and chose twelve of them to be the inner circle of His disciples. (They were appointed as His "apostles," or, "missionaries.")

14, 15, 16   Here are their names:
       Simon (He also called him Peter),
       Andrew (Simon's brother),
       James,
       John,
       Philip,
       Bartholomew,
       Matthew,
       Thomas,
       James (the son of Alphaeus),
       Simon (also called "Zealotes"),
       Judas (son of James),
       Judas Iscariot (who later betrayed Him).

17, 18   When they came down from the slopes of the mountain they stood with Jesus on a large, level area, surrounded by many of His followers who were, in turn, surrounded by the crowds. For people from all over Judea and from Jerusalem and from as far north as the seacoasts of Tyre and Sidon had come to hear Him or to be healed. And He cast out many demons.

19 Everyone was trying to touch Him, for when they did, healing power went out from Him and they were cured.

20 Then He turned to His disciples and said, "What happiness there is for you who are poor, for the Kingdom of God is yours!

21 What happiness there is for you who are now hungry, for you are going to be satisfied! What happiness there is for you who weep, for the time will come when you shall laugh with joy!

22 What happiness it is when others hate you and exclude you and insult you and smear your name because you are Mine!

23 When that happens, rejoice! Yes, jump for joy! For you will have a great reward awaiting you in heaven! And you will be in good company—the ancient prophets were treated that way too!

24 But, oh, the sorrows that await the rich! For they have had their happiness down here.

25 They are fat and prosperous now, but a time of awful hunger is before them. Their careless laughter now, means sorrow then.

26 And what sadness is ahead for those praised by the crowds—for *false* prophets have *always* been praised!

27 Listen, all of you! Love your *enemies!* Do *good* to those who hate you!

28 Pray for the happiness of those who curse you; implore God's blessing on those who hurt you.

29 If someone slaps you on the cheek, let him slap the other too! If someone demands your coat, give him your shirt besides!

30 Give what you have to anyone who asks you for it; and when things are taken away from you, don't worry about getting them back.

31 Treat others as you want them to treat you.

32 Do you think you deserve credit for merely loving those who love you? Even the godless do that!

33 And if you only do good to those who do you good —is that so wonderful? Even sinners do that much!

34 And if you only lend money to those whom you

expect to repay you, what good is that? Even the most wicked will lend to their own kind for full return!

35 No! Love your *enemies!* Do good to *them!* Lend to *them!* And don't be concerned about the fact that they won't repay! Then your reward from heaven will be very great, and you will truly be acting as sons of God: for He is kind to the *unthankful* and to those who are *very wicked.*

36 Try to show as much compassion as your Father does.

37 Never criticize or condemn—or it will all come back on you! Go easy on others; then they will do the same for you!

38 For if you give, you will get! Your gift will return to you in full and overflowing measure, pressed down, shaken together to make room for more, and running over. Whatever measure you use to give—large or small —will be used to measure what is given back to you."

39 Here are some of the story-illustrations Jesus used in His sermons: "What good is it for one blind man to lead another? He will fall into a ditch and pull the other down with him.

40 How can a student know more than his teacher? But if he works hard, he may learn as much.

41 And why quibble about the speck in someone else's eye—his little fault—when a board is in your own?

42 How can you think of saying to him, 'Brother, let me help you get rid of that speck in your eye,' when you can't see past the board in yours? Hypocrite! First get rid of the board, and then perhaps you can see well enough to deal with his speck!

43 A tree from good stock doesn't produce scrub fruit nor do trees from poor stock produce choice fruit.

44 A tree is identified by the kind of fruit it produces. Figs never grow on thorns, or grapes on bramble bushes!

45 A good man produces good deeds from a good heart. And an evil man produces evil deeds from his hidden wickedness. Whatever is in the heart overflows into speech.

46 So why do you call Me 'Lord' when you won't obey Me?

47 But all those who come and listen and obey Me

48 Are like a man who builds a house on a strong

foundation laid upon the underlying rock. When the waters rise and break against the house, it stands firm, for it is strongly built.

49 But those who listen and don't obey are like a man who builds a house without a foundation! When the floods sweep down against that house, it crumbles into a heap of ruins."

CHAPTER 7

When Jesus had finished His sermon, He went back into the city of Capernaum.

2 Just at that time the highly prized slave of a Roman* army captain was sick and near death.

3 When the captain heard about Jesus, he sent some respected Jewish elders to Him to ask Him to come and heal his slave.

4 So they came and began pleading earnestly with Jesus to come with them and help the man. They told Him what a wonderful person the captain was. "If anyone deserves your help, it is he," they said,

5 "For he loves the Jews and even paid personally for building us a synagogue!"

6, 7 Jesus went with them; but just before arriving at the house, the captain sent some friends to say, "Sir, don't inconvenience yourself by coming to my home, for I am not worthy of any such honor or even to come and meet You. Just speak a word from where You are, and my servant boy will be healed!

8 I know, because I am under the authority of my superior officers, and I have authority over my men. I only need to say 'Go!' and they go; or 'Come!' and they come; and to my slave, 'Do this or that,' and he does it. So just say, 'Be healed!' and my servant will be well again!"

9 Jesus was amazed! Turning to the crowd He said, "Never among all the Jews in Israel have I met a man with faith like this!"

10 And when the captain's friends returned to his house, they found the slave completely healed!

11 Not long afterwards Jesus went with His disciples

to the village of Nain, with the usual vast crowd at His heels.

12 As He approached the village gate, a funeral procession was coming out. The boy who had died was the only son of his widowed mother, and following along with her were many mourners from the village.

13 When the Lord saw her, His heart overflowed with sympathy. "Don't cry!" He said.

14 Then, as He walked over to the coffin and touched it, the bearers stopped. And He said, "Laddie, come back to life again!"

15 The boy sat up and began to talk to those around him! And Jesus gave him back to his mother.

16 Then a great fear swept the crowd, and they exclaimed with praises to God, "A mighty prophet has risen among us," and, "We have seen the hand of God at work today."

17 The report of what He did that day raced from end to end of Judea and out across the borders into the surrounding country.

18 The disciples of John the Baptist soon heard of all that Jesus was doing. When they told John about it,

19 He sent two of his disciples to Jesus to ask Him, "Are You really the Messiah? Or shall we keep on looking for Him?"

20, 21 The two disciples found Jesus while He was curing many sick people of their various diseases, healing the lame and the blind and casting out evil spirits. So they asked Him John's question.

22 And this was His reply: "Go back to John and tell him all you have seen and heard here today: how those who were blind can see! The lame are walking without a limp! The lepers are completely healed! The deaf can hear again! The dead come back to life! And the poor are hearing the Good News!

23 And tell him, 'Happy is the one who does not lose his faith in Me.'"

24 After they left, Jesus talked to the crowd about John. "Who is this man you went out into the Judean wilderness to see?" He asked. "Did you find him weak as grass, moved by every breath of wind?

25 Did you find him dressed in expensive clothes?

No! Men who live in luxury are found in palaces, not out in the wilderness!

26 But did you find a prophet? Yes! And more than a prophet!

27 He is the one to whom the Scriptures refer when they say, 'Look! I am sending My messenger ahead of You, to prepare the way before You!'

28 In all humanity there is no one greater than John! And yet the least citizen of the Kingdom of God is greater than he!"

29 And all who heard John preach—even the most wicked of them—agreed that God's requirements were right, and were baptized by him.

30 All, that is, except the Pharisees and teachers of Moses' Law. They rejected God's plan for them and refused John's baptism.

31 "What can I say about such men? With what shall I compare them?

32 They are like a group of children who complain to their friends, 'You don't like it if we play "wedding" and you don't like it if we play "funeral" '!

33 For John the Baptist used to go without food and never took a drop of liquor all his life, and you said, 'He must be crazy!'

34 But I eat My food and drink My wine, and you say, 'What a glutton Jesus is! And He drinks! And has the lowest sort of friends!'

35 But I am sure you can always justify your inconsistencies!"

36 One of the Pharisees asked Jesus to come to his home for lunch, and Jesus accepted the invitation. As they sat down to eat,

37 A woman of the streets—a prostitute—who had heard He was there, brought an exquisite flask filled with expensive perfume,

38 And going in, she knelt behind Him at His feet, weeping until His feet were wet with her tears; and she wiped them off with her hair and kissed them and poured the perfume on them.

39 When Jesus' host, a Pharisee, saw what was happening and who the woman was, he said to himself, "This proves that Jesus is no prophet, for if God had

really sent Him, He would know what kind of woman this one is!"

40   Then Jesus spoke up and answered his thoughts! "Simon," He said to the Pharisee, "I have something to say to you."

"All right, Teacher," Simon replied, "go ahead."

41   Then Jesus told him this story: "A man loaned money to two people—$5,000 to one and $500 to the other.

42   But neither of them could pay him back, so he kindly forgave them both, letting them keep the money! Which do you suppose loved him most after that?"

43   "I suppose the one who owed him the most," answered Simon. "Correct," Jesus agreed.

44   Then He turned towards the woman and said to Simon, "Look! See this woman kneeling here! When I entered your home, you didn't bother to offer Me water to wash the dust from My feet, but she has washed them with her tears and wiped them with her hair!

45   You refused Me the customary kiss of greeting, but she has kissed My feet again and again from the time I first came in.

46   You neglected the usual courtesy of olive oil to anoint My head, but she has covered My feet with rare perfume.

47   Therefore her sins—and they are many—are forgiven, for she loved Me much; but one who is forgiven little, shows little love!"

48   And He said to her, "Your sins are forgiven!"

49   Then the other men at the table said to themselves, "Who does this man think He is, going around forgiving sins?"

50   And Jesus said to the woman, "Your faith has saved you; go in peace."

CHAPTER 8

Not long afterward He began a tour of the cities and villages of Galilee* to announce the coming of the Kingdom of God, and He took His twelve disciples with Him.

2   Some women from whom He had cast out demons

or healed went along too; among them were Mary Magdalene (Jesus had cast seven demons out of her),

3 Joanna, Chuza's wife (Chuza was King Herod's business manager and was in charge of his palace and domestic affairs), Susanna, and many others who were contributing from their private means to the support of Jesus and His disciples.

4 One day He gave this illustration to a large crowd that was gathering to hear Him—while many others were still on the way, coming from other towns.

5 "A farmer went out to his field to sow grain. As he scattered the seeds on the ground, some of it fell on a footpath and it was trampled on; and the birds came and ate it as it lay exposed.

6 Other seeds fell on shallow soil with rock beneath. These seeds began to grow, but soon withered and died for lack of moisture.

7 Other seeds landed in thistle patches, and the young plants were soon choked out.

8 Still others fell on fertile soil; these grew and produced a crop 100 times as large as he had planted." (As He was giving this illustration He said, "If anyone has listening ears, use them now!")

9 His apostles asked Him what the story meant.

10 He replied, "God has granted you to know the meaning of these parables, for they tell a great deal about the Kingdom of God. But these crowds hear the words and do not understand, just as the ancient prophets predicted.

11 This is its meaning: The seed is God's message to men.

12 The hard path where some seed fell represents the hard hearts of those who hear the words of God, but then the devil comes and steals the words away and prevents people from believing and being saved.

13 The stony ground represents those who enjoy listening to sermons, but somehow the message never really gets through to them and doesn't take root and grow. They know the message is true, and sort of believe for awhile; but when the hot winds of persecution blow, they lose interest.

14 The seed among the thorns represents those who listen and believe God's words but whose faith after-

wards is choked out by worry and riches and the responsibilities and pleasures of life. And so they are never able to help anyone else to believe the Good News.

15 But the good soil represents honest, good-hearted people. They listen to God's words and cling to them and steadily spread them to others who also soon believe."

*   *   *   *   *

16 (Another time He asked*), "Who ever heard of someone lighting a lamp and then covering it to keep it from giving light? No, lamps are mounted in the open where they can be seen.

17 This illustrates the fact that someday everything (in men's hearts) shall be brought to light and made plain to all.

18 So be careful how you listen; for whoever has, to him shall be given more; and whoever does not have, even what he thinks he has shall be taken away from him.

*   *   *   *   *

19 Once when His mother and brothers came to see Him, they couldn't even get into the house where He was teaching, because of the crowds.

20 When Jesus heard they were standing outside and wanted to see Him,

21 He remarked, "My mother and My brothers are all those who hear the message of God and obey it!"

*   *   *   *   *

22 One day about that time, when He and His disciples were in a boat, He said, "Let's go across to the other side of the lake.

23 On the way He lay down for a nap, and while He was sleeping, the wind began to rise. A fierce storm developed that threatened to swamp them, and they were in real danger.

24 They went over and woke Him up, screaming, "Master, Master, we are sinking!" He woke up and told

the storm, "Quiet down," and wind and waves subsided, and all was calm!

25 Then He asked them, "Where is your faith?" And they were filled with awe and fear of Him and said to one another, "Who is this man, that even the winds and waves obey Him?"

26 So they arrived at the other side, in the Gerasene country across the lake from Galilee.

27 As He was climbing out of the boat, a man from the city of Gadara came to meet Him. This man had been demon-possessed for a long time. Homeless and naked, he lived in a cemetery among the tombs.

28 As soon as he saw Jesus, he shrieked and fell down before Him, screaming, "What do You want with me, Jesus, Son of God Most High? Please, I beg You, oh, don't torment me!"

29 For Jesus was already commanding the demon to leave him. This demon had often taken control of the man, so that even when he was shackled with chains, he simply broke them apart and rushed out into the desert, completely controlled by the demon.

30 "What is your name?" Jesus asked the demon. "Legion," they replied—for the man was filled with thousands* of them!

31 They kept begging Him not to order them into the Bottomless Pit.

32 A herd of pigs was feeding on the mountainside nearby, and the demons pled with Him to let them enter into the pigs. And Jesus said they could.

33 So they left the man and went into the pigs, and immediately the whole herd rushed down the mountainside and fell over a cliff into the lake below, where they drowned.

34 The herdsmen rushed away to the nearby city, spreading the news as they ran.

35 A crowd came out to see for themselves what had happened and saw the man who had been demon-possessed sitting quietly at Jesus' feet, clothed and sane! And the whole crowd was badly frightened.

36 Then those who had been there told how the demon-possessed man had been healed.

37 And everyone begged Jesus to go away and leave them alone (for a deep wave of fear had swept over

them). So He returned to the boat and left, crossing back
to the other side of the lake.

38 The man who had been demon-possessed begged
to go too, but Jesus said no.

39 "Go back to your family," He told him, "and
tell them what a wonderful thing God has done for you."
So he went all through the city telling everyone about
Jesus' mighty miracle.

40 On the other side of the lake the crowds received
Him with open arms, for they had been waiting for
Him.

41 And now a man named Jairus, a leader of a Jewish synagogue, came and fell down at Jesus' feet and
began to beg Him to come to his home,

42 For his only child, a little girl twelve years old,
was dying. Jesus went with him, pushing through the
crowds.

43, 44 As they went, a woman came up behind
and touched Him for healing, for she had been slowly
bleeding for twelve years, and could find no cure (though
she had spent everything she had on doctors). But the
instant she touched the edge of His robe, the bleeding
stopped.

45 "Who touched Me?" Jesus asked. Everyone denied it, and Peter said, "Master, so many are crowding
against You. . . ."

46 But Jesus said, "No, it was someone who deliberately touched Me, for I felt healing power go out from
Me."

47 When the woman realized that Jesus knew, she
began to tremble and fell down before Him and told
why she had touched Him and that she was now well.

48 He said to her, "Daughter, your faith has healed
you! Go in peace."

49 While He was still talking with her, a messenger
arrived from the Jairus home with the news that his
little girl was dead. "She's gone," they told her father;
"there is no use troubling the Teacher now."

50 But when Jesus heard what they were saying,
He said to the father, "Don't be afraid! Just trust Me,
and she will be all right."

51 When they arrived at the house, Jesus wouldn't

let anyone into the room with Him except Peter, James and John, and the little girl's father and mother.

52 The home was filled with mourning people, but He said, "Stop the weeping! She isn't dead; she is only asleep!"

53 This brought scoffing and laughter, for they all knew she was dead.

54 He took her by the hand and called, "Get up, little girl!"

55 And at that moment her life returned and she jumped up! And He told them to give her something to eat!

56 Her parents were overcome with happiness, but Jesus insisted that they not tell anyone the details of what had happened.

CHAPTER 9

One day Jesus called together His twelve apostles and gave them authority over all demons—power to cast them out—and to heal all diseases.

2 Then He sent them away to tell everyone about the coming of the Kingdom of God and to heal the sick.

3 "Don't even take along a walking stick," He instructed them, "nor a beggar's bag, nor food, nor money! Not even an extra coat!

4 Be a guest in only one home at each village.

5 If the people of a town won't listen to you when you enter it, turn around and leave, shaking its dust from your feet as you go, to show God's anger."

6 So they began their circuit of the villages, preaching the Good News and healing the sick.

7 When reports reached Herod, the governor, of Jesus' miracles, he was worried and puzzled, for some were saying, "This is John the Baptist come back to life again,"

8 And others, "It is Elijah or some other ancient prophet risen from the dead." These rumors were circulating all over the land.

9 "I beheaded John," he said, "so who is this man, about whom I hear such strange stories?" And he tried to see Him.

10   After the apostles returned and reported to Jesus on all they had done, He slipped quietly away with them to the city of Bethsaida.

11   But the crowds found out where He was going, and followed. And He welcomed them, teaching them again about the Kingdom of God, and curing those who were ill.

12   Late in the afternoon all twelve of the disciples came and urged Him to send the people away to the nearby villages and farms to find food and lodging for the night. "For there is nothing to eat here in this deserted spot," they said.

13   But Jesus said, "You feed them!"

"Why, we have only five loaves of bread and two fish among the lot of us," they protested; "or are You expecting us to go and buy enough for this whole mob?"

14   For there were about 5,000 men there! "Just tell them to sit down on the ground in groups of about fifty each," Jesus replied.

15   So they did.

16   Jesus took the five loaves and two fish and looked up into the sky and gave thanks for the food. Then He broke off pieces for His disciples to set before the crowd.

17   Everyone ate and ate, and twelve basketsful of scraps were picked up afterwards!

*   *   *   *   *

18   One day while He was alone praying, His disciples were nearby, and He asked them, "Who are the people saying I am?"

19   They told Him some thought He was John the Baptist, and others, Elijah, or one of the other ancient prophets risen from the dead.

20   Then He asked them, "Who do you think I am?" Peter replied, "The Messiah—the Christ of God!"

21   But He gave them strict orders not to speak of this to anyone.

22   For I must suffer much," He said, "and be rejected by the Jewish leaders—the elders, chief priests, and teachers of the Law—and be killed; and three days later I will come back to life again!"

23   Then He said to all, "Anyone who wants to

follow Me must put aside his own desires and conveniences and carry his cross with him everyday and *keep close to Me!*

24 Whoever insists on keeping his life will lose it, but whoever loses his life for My sake will save it.

25 And what profit is there in gaining the whole world when it means forfeiting one's self?

26 When I, the Man of Glory, come in My glory and in the glory of the Father and the holy angels—I will be ashamed then of all who are ashamed of Me and My words now.

27 But this is the simple truth—some of these men standing here right now will not die until they have seen the Kingdom of God!"

28 Eight days later He took Peter, James and John with Him into the hills to pray.

29 And as He was praying, His face began to shine, and His clothes became dazzling white and blazed with light.

30 Then two men appeared and began talking with Him—Moses and Elijah!

31 They were splendid in appearance, glorious to see; and they were speaking of His death at Jerusalem, to be carried out in accordance with God's plan.

32 Peter and the others had been very drowsy and had fallen asleep. Now they woke up and saw Jesus covered with brightness and glory, and the two men standing with Him.

33 As Moses and Elijah were starting to leave, Peter, all confused and not even knowing what he was saying, blurted out, "Master, this is wonderful! We'll put up three shelters—one for You and one for Moses and one for Elijah!"

34 But even as he was saying this, a bright cloud formed above them; and terror gripped them as it covered them.

35 And a voice from the cloud said, *"This* is My Son, My Chosen One; listen to *Him."*

36 Then, as the voice died away, Jesus was there alone with His disciples. They didn't tell anyone what they had seen until long afterwards.

37 The next day as they descended from the hill, a huge crowd met Him,

38   And a man in the crowd shouted to Him, "Teacher, this boy here is my only son,

39   And a demon keeps seizing him, making him scream; and it throws him into convulsions, so that he foams at the mouth; it is always hitting him and hardly leaves him alone.

40   I begged Your disciples to cast out the demon, but they couldn't."

41   "O you stubborn, faithless people," Jesus said (to His disciples*), "How long should I put up with you? Bring him here."

42   While the boy was coming, the demon knocked him to the ground and threw him into a violent convulsion. But Jesus ordered the demon to come out, and healed the boy and handed him over to his father.

43   Awe gripped the people as they saw this display of the power of God. Meanwhile, as they were exclaiming over all the wonderful things He was doing, Jesus said to His disciples,

44   "Listen to Me and remember what I say. I, the Son of Mankind, am going to be betrayed."

45   But the disciples didn't know what He meant, for their minds had been sealed, and they were afraid to ask Him.

46   Now came an argument among them as to which of them would be greatest (in the coming Kingdom*)!

47   But Jesus knew their thoughts, so He stood a little child beside Him

48   And said to them, "Anyone who takes care of a little child like this is caring for Me! And whoever cares for Me is caring for God, who sent Me. Your care for others is the measure of your greatness."

49   His disciple John came to Him and said, "Master, we saw someone using Your name to cast out demons! And we told him not to. After all, he isn't in our group."

50   But Jesus said, "You shouldn't have done that! For anyone who is not against you is for you!"

51   As the time drew near for His return to heaven, He moved steadily onward towards Jerusalem with an iron will.

52   One day He sent messengers ahead to reserve rooms for them in a Samaritan village.

53   But they were turned away! The people of the

village refused to have anything to do with them because they were headed for Jerusalem!

54 When the word came back of what had happened, James and John said to Jesus, "Master, shall we order fire down from heaven to burn them up?"

55 But Jesus turned and rebuked them,

56 And they went on to another village.

57 As they were walking along, someone said to Jesus, "I will always follow You, no matter where You go."

58 But Jesus replied, "Remember, I don't even own a place to lay My head. Foxes have dens to live in and birds have nests, but I, the Man from Heaven, have no earthly home at all."

59 Another time, when He invited a man to come with Him and be His disciple, the man agreed—but wanted to wait until his father's death.

60 Jesus replied, "Let those without eternal life concern themselves with things like that. Your duty is to come and preach the coming of the Kingdom of God to all the world."

61 Another said, "Yes, Lord, I will come, but first let me ask permission of those at home."

62 But Jesus told him, "Anyone who lets himself be distracted from the work I plan for him is not fit for the Kingdom of God."

CHAPTER 10

The Lord now chose 70 other disciples and sent them on ahead in pairs to all the towns and villages He planned to visit later.

2 These were His instructions to them: "Plead with the Lord of the harvest to send out more laborers to help you, for the harvest is so plentiful and the workers so few!

3 Go now, and remember that I am sending you out as lambs among wolves!

4 Don't take any money with you, or a beggar's bag, or even an extra pair of shoes. And don't waste time along the way.

5 Whenever you enter a home, give it your blessing.

6 If it is worthy of the blessing, the blessing will stand; if not, the blessing will return to you.

7 When you enter a village, don't shift around from home to home; but stay in one place, eating and drinking without question whatever is set before you. And don't hesitate to accept hospitality, for the workman is worthy of his wages!

8, 9 If a town welcomes you, follow these two rules:

(1) Eat whatever is set before you.

(2) Heal the sick; and as you heal them, say, 'The Kingdom of God is very near you now.'

10 But if a town refuses you, go out into its streets and say,

11 'We wipe the dust of your town from our feet as a public announcement of your doom. Never forget how close you were to the Kingdom of God!'

12 Even wicked Sodom will be better off than such a city on the Judgment Day.

13 What horrors await you, you cities of Chorazin and Bethsaida! For if the miracles I did for you had been done in the cities of Tyre and Sidon, their people would have sat in deep repentance long ago, clothed in sackcloth and throwing ashes on their heads to show their remorse.

14 Yes, Tyre and Sidon will receive less punishment on the Judgment Day than you.

15 And you people of Capernaum, what shall I say about you? Will you be exalted to heaven? No, you shall be brought down to hell."

16 Then He said to the disciples, "Those who welcome you are welcoming Me. And those who reject you are rejecting Me. And those who reject Me are rejecting God, who sent Me."

17 When the 70 disciples returned, they joyfully reported to Him, "Even the demons obey us when we use Your name."

18 "Yes," He told them, "I saw Satan falling from heaven as a flash of lightning!

19 And I have given you authority over all the power of the Enemy, and to walk among serpents and scorpions and to crush them! Nothing shall injure you!

20 However, the important thing is not that demons

obey you, but that your names are registered as citizens of heaven!"

21　Then He was filled with the joy of the Holy Spirit and said, "I praise You, O Father, Lord of heaven and earth, for hiding these things from the intellectuals—the worldly wise—and for revealing them to those who are as trusting as little children. Yes, thank You, Father, for that is the way You wanted it.

22　I am the Agent of My Father in everything; and no one except the Father really knows the Son, and no one knows the Father except the Son and those to whom the Son chooses to show Him."

23　Then, turning to the twelve disciples, He said quietly, "How privileged you are to see what you have seen!

24　Many a prophet and king of old has longed for these days; to see and hear what you have seen and heard!"

25　One day an expert on Moses' laws came to test Jesus' orthodoxy by asking Him this question: "Teacher, what does a man need to do to live forever in heaven?"

26　Jesus replied, "What does Moses' law say about it?"

27　"It says," he replied, "that you must love the Lord your God with all your heart, and with all your soul, and with all your strength, and with all your mind. And you must love your neighbor just as much as you love yourself."

28　"Right!" Jesus told him. *"Do* this and *you* shall live!"

29　The man wanted to justify (his lack of love for some kinds of people), so he asked, "Which neighbors?"

30　Jesus replied with an illustration: "A Jew going on a trip from Jerusalem to Jericho was attacked by bandits. They stripped him of his clothes and money and beat him up and left him lying half dead beside the road.

31　By chance a Jewish priest came along; and when he saw the man lying there, he crossed to the other side of the road and went by.

32　A Jewish Temple-assistant did the same thing; he, too, left him lying there.

33 But a despised Samaritan came along; and when he saw him, he felt deep pity for him.

34 Kneeling beside him, the Samaritan soothed his wounds with medicine and bandaged them. Then he put the man on his donkey and walked along beside him till they came to an inn. He nursed him through the night,

35 And the next day he handed the innkeeper two twenty-dollar bills and told him to take care of the man. 'If his bill runs higher than that,' he said, 'I'll pay the difference the next time I am here.'

36 Now which of these three would you say was a neighbor to the bandits' victim?"

37 The man replied, "The one who showed him some pity."

Then Jesus said, "Yes, now go and do the same."

38 As Jesus and the disciples continued on their way to Jerusalem,* they came to a village where a woman named Martha welcomed them into her home.

39 Her sister Mary sat spellbound on the floor, listening to Jesus as He talked.

40 But Martha was the jittery type, and was worrying over the big dinner she was preparing. She came to Jesus and said, "Sir, doesn't it seem unfair to You that my sister just sits there while I do all the work? Make her come and help me."

41 But the Lord said to her, "Martha, dear friend, you are so upset over all these details!

42 There is really only one thing worth your concern. Mary has chosen it—and I won't take it away from her!"

CHAPTER 11

Once when Jesus had been out praying, one of His disciples came to Him as He finished and said, "Lord, teach us a prayer to recite,* just as John taught one to his disciples."

2 And this is the prayer He taught them: "Father, may Your name be honored for its holiness; send Your Kingdom soon!

3 Give us our food day by day,

4 And forgive our sins—for we have forgiven those

who sinned against us. And don't allow us to be tempted."

5, 6   Then, teaching them more about prayer, He used this illustration: "Suppose you went to a friend's house at midnight, wanting to borrow three loaves of bread! You would shout to him, 'A friend of mine has just arrived for a visit and I've nothing to give him to eat.'

7   He would call down from his bedroom, 'Please don't ask me to get up! The door is locked for the night and we are all in bed. I just can't help you this time!'

8   But I'll tell you this—though he won't do it as a friend, if you keep knocking long enough he will get up and give you everything you want—just because of your persistence!

9   And so it is with prayer—keep on asking, and you will keep on getting; keep on looking, and you will keep on finding; knock, and the door will be opened!

10   Everyone who asks, receives; all who seek, find; and the door is opened to everyone who knocks.

11   You men who are fathers—if your boy asks for bread, do you give him a stone? If he asks for fish, do you give him a snake?

12   If he asks for an egg, does he get a scorpion from you? Of course not!*

13   And if even sinful persons like yourselves give children what they need, don't you realize that your heavenly Father will do at least as much, and give the Holy Spirit to those who ask for Him?"

14   Once when Jesus cast out a demon from a man who couldn't speak, his voice returned to him again. Most of the crowd was enthusiastic,

15   But some said, "No wonder He can cast them out. He gets His power from Satan, the king of demons!"

16   Others asked for something to happen in the sky to prove His claim of being the Messiah.

17   He knew the thoughts of each of them, so He said, "Any kingdom filled with civil war is doomed, so is a home filled with argument and strife.

18   Therefore, if Satan is fighting against himself by empowering Me to cast out his demons, as you are saying, how can his kingdom survive?

19   And if I am empowered by Satan, what about your own followers? For they cast out demons! Do you

think this proves they are possessed by Satan? Ask *them* if you are right!

20   But if I am casting out demons because of power from God, it proves that the Kingdom of God has arrived!

21   For when Satan, strong and full-armed, guards his palace, it is safe—

22   Until someone stronger and better armed attacks and overcomes him and strips him of his weapons and carries off his belongings!

23   Anyone who is not for Me is against Me; if he isn't helping Me, he is hurting My cause.

24   When a demon is cast out of a man, it goes to the deserts, searching there for rest; but finding none, it returns to the person it left

25   And finds its former home all swept and clean.

26   Then it goes and gets seven other demons more evil than itself, and they all enter the man. And so the poor fellow is seven times* worse off than he was before."

27   As He was speaking, a woman in the crowd called out, "God bless Your mother—the womb from which You came, and the breasts that gave You suck!"

28   He replied, "Yes, but even more blessed are all who hear the Word of God and put it into practice."

29, 30   As the crowd pressed in upon Him, He preached them this sermon: "These are evil times, with evil people. They keep asking for some strange happening in the skies (to prove I am the Messiah*), but the only proof I will give them is a miracle like that of Jonah, whose experiences proved to the people of Nineveh that God had sent him. My similar experience will prove that God has sent Me to these people.

31   And at the Judgment Day the Queen of Sheba shall arise and point her finger at this generation, condemning it, for she went on a long, hard journey to listen to the wisdom of Solomon; but one far greater than Solomon is here (and the people pay no attention).*

32   The men of Nineveh, too, shall arise and condemn this nation, for they repented at the preaching of Jonah; and someone far greater than Jonah is here (and it won't listen).*

*   *   *   *   *

33　No one lights a lamp and hides it! Instead he puts it on a lampstand to give light to all who enter the room.

34　Your eye lights up your inward being.

A pure eye lets sunshine into your soul. A lustful eye shuts out the light and plunges you into darkness.

35　So watch out that the sunshine isn't blotted out.

36　If you are filled with light within, with no dark corners, then the outside will be radiant too, as though a floodlight is beamed upon you."

37, 38　As He was speaking, one of the Pharisees asked Him home for a meal. When Jesus arrived, He sat down to eat without first performing the ceremonial washing required by Jewish custom. This greatly surprised His host.

39　Then Jesus said to him, "You Pharisees wash the outside, but inside you are still unclean—full of greed and wickedness!

40　Fools! Didn't God make the inside as well as the outside?

41　Purity is best demonstrated by generosity!

42　But woe to you Pharisees! For though you are careful to tithe even the smallest part of your income, you completely forget about justice and the love of God. You should tithe, yes, but you should not leave these other things undone!

43　Woe to you Pharisees! For how you love the seats of honor in the synagogues and respectful greetings from everyone as you walk through the markets!

44　Yes, awesome judgment is resting upon you! For you are like hidden graves in a field. Men pass by you with no knowledge of the corruption nearby."

45　"Sir," said an expert in religious law who was standing there, "You have insulted my profession, too, in what You just said."

46　"Yes," said Jesus, "the same horrors await you! For you crush men beneath impossible religious demands—demands that you yourselves would never think of trying to keep!

47　Woe to you! For you are exactly like your ancestors who killed the prophets long ago.

48　Murderers! You agree with your fathers that

what they did was right—you would have done the same
yourselves.

49 This is what God says about you: 'I will send
prophets and apostles to you, and you will kill some of
them and chase away the others';

50 And you of this generation will be held responsible
for the murder of God's servants from the founding of
the world—

51 From the murder of Abel to the murder of Zecha-
riah who perished between the altar and the sanctuary.
Yes, it will surely be charged against you.

52 Woe to you, experts in religion! For you hide
the truth from the people; you won't accept it for yourselves, and you prevent others from having a chance to
believe it."

53, 54 The Pharisees and legal experts were furious; and from that time on they plied Him fiercely with
a host of questions, trying to trap Him into saying something for which they could have Him arrested.

CHAPTER 12

Meanwhile the crowds grew until thousands upon thousands were milling about and crushing each other. He
turned now to His disciples and warned them, "More than
anything else, beware of these Pharisees and the way they
pretend to be good when they aren't.

2 But such hypocrisy cannot be hidden forever.
Though they conceal it now, it will be exposed.

3 And for you also it is true that whatever you have
said in the dark shall be heard in the light, and what you
have whispered in the inner rooms shall be broadcast
from the housetops for all to hear!

4 Dear friends, don't be afraid of these who want to
murder you! They can only kill the body; they have no
power over your souls.

5 But I'll tell you whom to fear—fear God who has the
power to kill and then cast into hell.

6 What is the price of five sparrows? A couple of
pennies? Not much more than that! Yet God does not
forget a single one of them.

7 And He knows the number of hairs on your head!

Never fear, you are far more valuable to Him than a whole flock of sparrows!

8 And I assure you of this: I, the Man from Heaven, will publicly honor you in the presence of God's angels if you publicly acknowledge Me here on earth as your Friend.

9 But I will deny before the angels those who deny Me here among men.

10 (Yet those who speak against Me may be forgiven—while those who speak against the Holy Spirit shall never be forgiven.)

11 And when you are brought to trial before these Jewish rulers and authorities in the synagogues, don't be concerned about what to say in your defense,

12 For the Holy Spirit will give you the right words even as you stand there."

13 Then someone called from the crowd, "Sir, please tell my brother to divide my father's estate with me."

14 But Jesus replied, "Man, who made Me a judge over you to decide such things as that?

15 Beware! Don't always be wishing for what you don't have."

16 Then He gave an illustration: "A rich man had a fertile farm that produced fine crops.

17 In fact, his barns were full to overflowing—he couldn't get everything in. He thought about his problem

18 And finally exclaimed, 'I know—I'll tear down my barns and build bigger ones! Then I'll have room enough!

19 And I'll sit back and say to myself, "Friend, you have enough stored away for years to come. Now take it easy! Wine, women and song for you!"

20 But God said to him, 'Fool! Tonight you die. Then who will get it all?'

21 Yes, every man is a fool who gets rich on earth but not in heaven."

22 Then turning to His disciples He said, "Don't worry about whether you have enough food to eat or clothes to wear.

23 For life consists of far more than food and clothes.

24 Look at the ravens—they don't plant or harvest or have barns to store away their food, and yet they get along all right—for God feeds them. And you are far more valuable to Him than birds!

25 And besides, what's the use of worrying? What good does it do? Will it add a single day to your life? Of course not.

26 And if it can't even do such little things as that, what's the use of worrying over bigger things?

27 Look at the lilies! They don't toil and spin, and yet Solomon in all his glory was not robed as well as they are.

28 And if God provides clothing for the flowers that are here today and gone tomorrow—don't you suppose He will provide clothing for you, you doubters?

29 And don't worry about food—what to eat and drink; don't worry at all that God will provide it for you.

30 All mankind scratches for its daily bread. But your heavenly Father knows your needs.

31 He will always give you all you need from day to day if you will make the Kingdom of God your primary concern.

32 So don't be afraid, little flock. For it gives your Father great happiness to give you the Kingdom.

33 Sell what you have and give to those in need. This will fatten your purses in heaven! And the purses of heaven have no rips or holes in them! Your treasures there will never disappear; no thief can steal them; no moth can destroy them!

34 Wherever your treasure is, there your heart and thoughts will be also!

35 Be prepared—all dressed and ready—

36 For your Lord's return from the wedding feast. Then you will be ready to open the door and let Him in the moment He arrives and knocks.

37 There will be great joy for those who are ready and waiting for His return. He, Himself, will seat them and put on a waiter's uniform and serve them as they sit and eat!

38 He may come at nine o'clock at night—or even at midnight. But whenever He comes, there will be joy for His servants who are ready!

39 Everyone would be ready for Him if they knew the exact hour of His return—just as they would be ready for a thief if they knew when he was coming!

40 So be ready all the time! For I, the Man of Glory, will come when least expected."

41 Peter asked, "Lord, are You talking just to us or to everyone?"

42, 43, 44 And the Lord replied, "I'm talking to any faithful, sensible man whose master gives him the responsibility of feeding the other servants regularly. If his master returns and finds that his servant has done a good job, there will be a reward—his master will put him in charge of all he owns.

45 But if the man begins to think, 'My Lord won't be back for a long time,' and begins to whip the men and women he is supposed to protect, and spends his time at drinking parties and in drunkenness—

46 Well, his Master will return without notice and remove him from his position of trust and assign him to the place of the unfaithful.

47 He will be severely punished, for though he knew his duty, he refused to do it.

48 But anyone who is not aware that he is doing wrong will be punished only lightly. Much is required from those to whom much is given, for their responsibility is greater.

49 I have come to bring fire to the earth, and, oh, that My task were completed!

50 There is a terrible baptism ahead of Me, and how I am pent up until it is accomplished!

51 Do you think I have come to give peace to the earth? *No!* Rather, strife and division!

52 From now on families will be split apart, three in favor of Me, and two against Me—or perhaps the other way around.

53 A father will decide one way about Me; his son, the other; mother and daughter will disagree; and the decision of an honored mother-in-law will be spurned by her daughter-in-law."

54 Then He turned to the crowd and said, "When you see clouds beginning to form in the west, you say, 'Here comes a shower.' And you are right.

55 When the south wind blows, you say, 'Today will be a scorcher.' And it is.

56 Hypocrites! You interpret the sky well enough, but you refuse to notice the warnings all around you about crises ahead.

57 Why do you refuse to see for yourselves what is right?

58 If you meet your accuser on the way to court, try to settle the matter before it reaches the judge, lest he sentence you to jail;

59 In which case you won't be free again until the last penny is paid in full."

CHAPTER 13

About this time He was informed that Pilate had butchered some Jews from Galilee as they were sacrificing at the Temple in Jerusalem.

2 "Do you think they were worse sinners than other men from Galilee?" He asked. "Is that why they suffered?

3 No! Don't you know that you also will perish unless you leave your evil way and turn to God?

4 And what about the 18 men who died when the tower of Siloam fell on them? Were they the worst sinners in Jerusalem?

5 No! You will perish, too, unless you repent."

6 Then He used this illustration: "A man planted a fig tree in his garden and came again and again to see if he could find any fruit on it, but he was always disappointed.

7 Finally he told his gardener to cut it down. 'I've waited three years and have not found a single fig!' he said. 'Why bother with it any longer? It's taking up space we can use for something else.'

8 'Give it one more chance,' the gardener answered. 'Leave it another year, and I'll give it special attention and plenty of fertilizer.

9 If we get figs next year, fine; if not, I'll cut it down.' "

*   *   *   *   *

10 One Sabbath as He was teaching in a synagogue,

11 He saw a seriously handicapped woman who had been bent double for 18 years and was unable to straighten herself and stand upright.

12 Calling her over to Him, Jesus said, "Woman, you are healed of your sickness!"

13 He touched her, and instantly she could stand straight! How she praised and thanked God!

14 But the local Jewish leader in charge of the synagogue was very angry about it because Jesus had healed her on the Sabbath day. "There are six days of the week to work," he shouted to the crowd. "Those are the days to come for healing, not on the Sabbath!"

15 But the Lord replied, "You hypocrites! You work on the Sabbath! Don't you untie your cattle from their stalls on the Sabbath and lead them out for water?

16 And is it wrong for Me, just because it is the Sabbath day, to free this Jewish woman from Satan's 18 years of bondage?"

17 This shamed His enemies. But the rest of the people rejoiced at the wonderful things He did.

18 Now He began teaching them again about the Kingdom of God: "What is the Kingdom like?" He asked. "How can I illustrate it?

19 It is like a tiny mustard seed planted in a garden; soon it grows into a tall bush, and the birds live among its branches. . . .

20, 21 It is like yeast kneaded into dough, which works unseen until it has risen high and light."

22 He went from city to city and village to village, teaching as He went, always pressing onward toward Jerusalem.

23 Someone asked Him, "Will only a few be saved?" And He replied,

24, 25 "The door to heaven is narrow. Work hard to get in, for the truth is, many will try to enter, but when the head of the house has locked the door, it will be too late. Then if you stand outside knocking and pleading, 'Lord, open the door for us,' He will reply, 'I do not know you.'

26 'But we ate with You, and You taught in our streets,' you will say.

27 And He will reply, 'I tell you, I don't know you. You can't come in here, guilty as you are. Go away.'

28 And there will be great weeping and gnashing of teeth as you stand outside and see Abraham, Isaac, Jacob and all the prophets within the Kingdom of God—

29 For people will come from all over the world to take their places in the Kingdom of God.

30   And note this: some who are despised now will be greatly honored then; and some who are highly thought of now will be least important then."

31   A few minutes later some Pharisees said to Him, "Get out of here if You want to live, for King Herod is after You!"

32   "Go tell that fox," Jesus said, "that I will keep on casting out demons and doing miracles of healing today and tomorrow; and the third day I will reach my destination.

33   Yes, today, tomorrow, and the next day! For it wouldn't do for a prophet of God to be killed except in Jerusalem!

34   O Jerusalem, Jerusalem! The city that murders the prophets! The city that stones those sent to help her! How often I have wanted to gather your children together, even as a hen protects her brood under her wings, but you wouldn't let Me.

35   And now—now your house is left desolate. And you will never again see Me until you say, 'Welcome to Him who comes in the name of the Lord.' "

CHAPTER 14

One Sabbath as He was in the home of one of the Jewish council members, the Pharisees were watching Him like hawks to see if He would heal a man who was present, suffering from dropsy.

3   Jesus said to the Pharisees and legal experts standing around, "Well, is it within the Law to heal a man on the Sabbath day, or not?"

4   And when they refused to answer, Jesus took the sick man by the hand and healed him and sent him away.

5   Then He turned to them, "Which of you doesn't work on the Sabbath? If your cow falls into a pit, don't you proceed to get it out at once?"

6   Again they had no answer.

*   *   *   *   *

7   When He noticed that everyone who came to the

dinner was trying to sit near the head of the table, He gave them this advice:

8   "If you are invited to a wedding feast, don't always head for the best seat. For if someone more respected than you shows up,

9   The host will bring him to your place and say, 'Let this man sit here instead.' And you, embarrassed, will have to take whatever seat is left at the foot of the table!

10   Do this instead—start at the foot; and when your host sees you, he will come and say, 'Friend, we have a better place than this for you!' Thus you will be honored in front of all the other guests!

11   For everyone who tries to honor himself shall be humbled; and he who humbles himself shall be honored."

12   Then He turned to His host. "When you put on a dinner," He said, "don't invite friends, brothers, relatives and rich neighbors! For they will return the invitation!

13   Instead, invite the poor, the crippled, the lame and the blind.

14   Then at the resurrection of the godly God will reward you for inviting those who can't repay you."

15   Hearing this, a man sitting at the table with Jesus exclaimed, "What a privilege it would be to get into the Kingdom of God!"

16   But Jesus replied with this illustration; "A man prepared a great feast and invited many to come.

17   When all was ready, he sent his servant around to notify the guests that it was time for them to come.

18   But then they all began making excuses. One said he had just bought a field and wanted to inspect it, and he asked to be excused.

19   Another said he had just bought five pair of oxen and wanted to try them out.

20   Another had just been married and for that reason couldn't come.

21   The servant returned and reported to his master what they had said. His master was angry and told him to go quickly into the streets and alleys of the city and to invite the beggars, crippled, lame and blind.

22   But even after he had done this, there was still room!

23   'Well then,' said his master, 'go out into the country lanes and out behind the hedges and urge anyone you find to come, so that the house will be full.

24   For none of those I invited first will get even the smallest taste of what I had prepared for them.'"

* * * * *

25   Great crowds were following Him. He turned around and addressed them as follows:

26   "Anyone who wants to be My follower must love Me far more than he does his own father, mother, wife, children, brothers or sisters—yes, more than his own life —otherwise he cannot be My disciple.

27   And no one can be My disciple who does not carry his own cross and follow Me.

28   But don't begin until you count the cost.* For who would begin construction of a building without first getting estimates and then checking to see if he has enough money to pay the bills?

29   Otherwise he might only complete the foundation before running out of funds. And then how everyone would laugh!

30   'See that fellow there?' they would mock. 'He started that building and ran out of money before it was finished!'

31   Or what king would ever dream of going to war without sitting down first with his counselors and discussing whether his army of 10,000 is strong enough to defeat the 20,000 men who are marching against him?

32   If the decision is negative, then while the enemy troops are still far away, he will send a truce team to discuss terms of peace.

33   So no one can become My disciple unless he first sits down and counts his blessings—and then renounces them all for Me!

34   What good is salt that has lost its saltiness?

35   Flavorless salt is fit for nothing—not even for fertilizer. It is worthless and must be thrown out. Listen well, if you would understand My meaning."

CHAPTER 15

D ishonest tax collectors and other notorious sinners were all gathering to listen to Jesus' sermons;

2 And the Jewish religious leaders and the experts on Jewish law complained because He was associating with such people—even eating with them!

3, 4 So Jesus used this illustration: "If you had 100 sheep and one of them strayed away and was lost in the wilderness, wouldn't you leave the 99 others to go and search for the lost one until you found it?

5 And then you would joyfully carry it home on your shoulders.

6 When you arrived you would call together your friends and neighbors to rejoice with you because your lost sheep was found.

7 Well, in the same way heaven will be happier over the one lost sinner who returns to God than over the 99 others who haven't strayed away!

8 Or take another illustration: A woman has ten valuable silver coins and loses one. Won't she light a lamp and look in every corner of the house and sweep every nook and cranny until she finds it?

9 And then won't she call in her friends and neighbors to rejoice with her?

10 In the same way there is joy in the presence of the angels of God when one sinner repents."

To further illustrate the point, He told them this story:

11 "A man had two sons.

12 When the younger told his father, 'I want my share of your estate now, instead of waiting until you die!' his father agreed to divide his wealth between his sons.

13 A few days later this younger son packed all his belongings and took a trip to a distant land, and there wasted all his money on parties and prostitutes.

14 About the time his money was gone, a great famine swept over the land, and he began to starve.

15 He persuaded a local farmer to hire him, and the farmer sent him out into the fields to feed pigs.

16 But even so, the boy became so hungry he gladly

would have eaten the pods he was feeding the swine. And no one gave him anything.

17   When he finally came to his senses, he said to himself, 'At home even the hired men have food enough and to spare, and here I am, dying of hunger!

18   I will go home to my father and say, "Father, I have sinned against both heaven and you,

19   And am no longer worthy of being called your son. Please take me on as a hired man." '

20   So he returned home to his father. And while he was still a long distance away, his father saw him coming and was filled with loving pity and ran and embraced him and kissed him.

21   His son said to him, 'Father, I have sinned against heaven and you, and am not worthy of being called your son. . . .'

22   But his father said to the slaves, 'Quick! Bring the finest robe in the house and put it on him. And a jeweled ring for his finger; and shoes!

23   And kill the calf we have in the fattening pen. We must celebrate with a feast,

24   For this son of mine was dead and has returned to life! He was lost and is found!' So the party began.

25   Meanwhile the older son was in the fields working; when he returned home, he heard dance music coming from the house.

26   He asked one of the servants what was going on.

27   'Your brother is back,' he was told, 'and your father has killed the calf we were fattening and has prepared a great feast to celebrate his coming home again unharmed.'

28   The older brother was angry and wouldn't go in. His father came out and begged him.

29   But he replied, 'All these years I've worked hard for you and never once refused to do a single thing you told me to; and in all that time you never gave me even one young goat for a feast with my friends.

30   Yet when this son of yours comes back after spending your money on prostitutes, you celebrate by killing the finest calf we have on the place.'

31   'Look, dear son, his father said to him, 'you and I are very close, and everything I have is yours.

32 But it is right to celebrate. For he is your brother; and he was dead and has come back to life!

He was lost and is found!"

CHAPTER 16

J esus now told this story to His disciples: "A rich man hired an accountant to handle his affairs, but soon a rumor went around that the accountant was thoroughly dishonest.

2 So his employer called him in and said, 'What's this I hear about your stealing from me? Get your report in order, for you are to be dismissed.'

3 The accountant thought to himself, 'Now what? I'm through here, and I haven't the strength to go out and dig ditches, and I'm too proud to beg.

4 I know just the thing! And then I'll have plenty of friends to take care of me when I leave!'

5, 6 So he invited each one who owed money to his employer to come and discuss the matter. He asked the first one, 'How much do you owe him?' 'My debt is 850 gallons of olive oil,' the man answered. 'Here is your agreement to pay him the 850 gallons,' the accountant told him. 'Tear it up and write another one for half that much!'

7 'And how much do you owe him?' he asked the next man. 'A thousand bushels of wheat,' was the reply. 'Here,' the accountant said, 'take your note and replace it with one for only 800 bushels!'

8 The rich man had to admire the rascal for being so shrewd. And it is true that the citizens of this world are more clever (in dishonesty*) than the godly are.

9 But shall I tell you to act that way to buy friendship through cheating? Will this ensure your entry into an everlasting home in heaven?

10 NO!* For unless you are honest in small matters, you won't be in large. If you cheat even a little, you won't be honest with greater responsibilities.

11 And if you are untrustworthy about worldly wealth, who will trust you with the true riches of heaven?

12 And if you are not faithful with other people's

money, why should you be entrusted with money of your own?

13 For neither you nor anyone else can serve two masters. You will hate one and show loyalty to the other, or else, the other way around—be enthusiastic about one and despise the other. You cannot serve both God and money."

14 The Pharisees, who dearly loved their money, naturally scoffed at all this.

15 Then He said to them, "You wear a noble, pious expression in public, but God knows your evil hearts. Your pretense brings you honor from the people, but it is an abomination in the sight of God.

16 Until John the Baptist began to preach, the Old Testament laws and the messages of the prophets were your guides. But John introduced the Good News that the Kingdom of God would come soon. And now eager multitudes are pressing in.

17 But that doesn't mean the Law has lost its force in even the smallest point. It is as strong and unshakable as heaven and earth.

18 So anyone who divorces his wife and marries someone else commits adultery, and anyone who marries a divorced woman commits adultery."

* * * * *

19 "There was a certain rich man," Jesus said, "who was splendidly clothed and lived each day in mirth and luxury.

20 One day Lazarus, a diseased beggar, was laid at his door.

21 As he lay there longing for scraps from the rich man's table, the dogs would come and lick his open sores.

22 Finally the beggar died and was carried by the angels to be with Abraham in the place of the righteous dead. The rich man also died and was buried.

23 And his soul went into hell. There, in torment, he saw Lazarus in the far distance with Abraham.

24 'Father Abraham,' he shouted, 'have some pity. Send Lazarus over here if only to dip the tip of his finger in water and cool my tongue, for I am in anguish in these flames.'

25 But Abraham said to him, 'Son, remember that during your lifetime you had everything you wanted, and Lazarus had nothing. So now he is here being comforted and you are in anguish.

26 And besides, there is a great chasm separating us, and anyone wanting to come to you from here is stopped at its edge; and no one over there can cross to us.'

27 Then the rich man said, 'O Father Abraham, then please send him to my father's home—

28 For I have five brothers—to warn them about this place of torment so that they won't come here when they die.'

29 But Abraham said, 'The Scriptures have warned them again and again. Your brothers can read them any time they want to.'

30 The rich man replied, 'No, Father Abraham, they won't bother to read them. But if someone is sent to them from the dead, then they will turn from their sins.'

31 Then Abraham said, 'If they won't listen to Moses and the prophets, they won't listen even if someone rises from the dead.' "

CHAPTER 17

T here will always be temptations to sin," Jesus said one day to His disciples, "but woe to the man who does the tempting.

2, 3 If he were thrown into the sea with a huge rock tied to his neck, he would be far better off than facing the punishment in store for those who harm these little children's souls. I am warning you!

Rebuke your brother if he sins, and forgive him if he is sorry.

4 Even if he wrongs you seven times every day and each time turns again and asks forgiveness, forgive him."

* * * * *

5 One day the apostles said to the Lord, "We need more faith; tell us how to get it."

6 "If your faith were only the size of a mustard seed," Jesus answered, "it would be large enough to uproot that mulberry tree over there and send it hurtling into the sea! Your command would bring immediate results!

7-9 When a servant comes in from plowing or taking care of sheep, he doesn't just sit down and eat, but first prepares his master's meal and serves him his supper before he eats his own. And he is not even thanked, for he is merely doing what he is supposed to do!

10 Just so, if you merely obey Me, you should not consider yourselves worthy of praise! For you have simply done your duty!"

* * * * *

11 As they continued onward toward Jerusalem, they reached the border between Galilee and Samaria.

12 And entered a village. Ten lepers stood at a distance

13 Crying out, "Jesus, Sir, have mercy on us!"

14 He glanced at them and said, "Go to the Jewish priest and show him that you are healed!" And as they were on their way, their leprosy disappeared!

15 One of them came back to Jesus, shouting, "Glory to God, I am healed!"

16 He fell flat on the ground in front of Jesus, face downward in the dust, thanking Him for what He had done. (This man was a despised* Samaritan.)

17 Jesus asked, "Didn't I heal ten men? Where are the nine?

18 Does only this foreigner return to give glory to God?"

19 And Jesus said to the man, "Stand up and go; your faith has made you well."

* * * * *

20 One day the Pharisees asked Jesus, "When will the Kingdom of God begin?" Jesus replied, "The Kingdom of God isn't ushered in with visible signs!

21 You won't be able to say, 'It has begun here in this place or there in that part of the country.' For the Kingdom of God is within you."

22. Later He talked about this again with His disciples. "The time is coming when you will long for Me to be with you even for a single day, but I won't be here," He said.

23 "Reports will reach you that I have returned and that I am in this place or that; don't believe it or go out to look for Me.

24 For when I return, you will know it beyond all doubt! It will be as evident as the lightning that flashes across the skies.

25 But first I must suffer terribly and be rejected by this whole nation.

26 (When I return)* the world will be (as indifferent to the things of God) as the people were in Noah's day.

27 They ate and drank and got married—everything was as usual right up to the day Noah went into the ark and the flood came and destroyed them all.

28 The world will be as it was in the days of Lot, when people went about their daily business—eating and drinking, buying and selling, farming and building—

29 Until the day Lot left Sodom and fire and brimstone rained down from heaven and destroyed them all.

30 Yes, it will be 'business as usual' right up to the hour of My return.

31 Those away from home that day must not return to pack; those in the fields must not return to town—

32 Remember what happened to Lot's wife!

33 Whoever clings to his life shall lose it, and whoever loses his life shall save it.

34 That night two men will be asleep in the same room, and one will be taken away and the other left.

35, 36 Two women will be working together at household tasks, and one will be taken, the other left; and so it will be with men working side by side in the fields."

37 "Lord, where will they be taken to?" the disciples asked.

Jesus replied, "Where the bodies are, the vultures gather!"

CHAPTER 18

One day Jesus told His disciples a story to illustrate their need for constant prayer and to show them that they must keep praying until the answer comes!

2 "There was a city judge," He said, "a very godless man, who had great contempt for everyone.

3 A widow of that city came to him frequently to appeal for justice against a man who had harmed her.

4, 5 The judge ignored her for a while, but eventually she got on his nerves. 'I fear neither God nor man,' he said to himself, 'but this woman bothers me. I'm going to see that she gets justice, for she is wearing me out with her constant nagging!' "

6 Then the Lord said, "If even an evil judge can be worn down like that,

7 Don't you think that God will surely give justice to His people who plead with Him day and night?

8 Yes! He will answer them quickly! But the question is: When I, the Son of Mankind, return, how many will I find who have faith and are praying?"

9 Then He told this story to some who boasted of their virtue and scorned everyone else:

10 "Two men went to the Temple to pray. One was a proud, self-righteous Pharisee, and the other a cheating tax collector.

11 The proud Pharisee 'prayed' this prayer: 'Thank God, I am not a sinner like everyone else, especially like that tax collector over there! For I never cheat, I don't commit adultery,

12 I go without food twice a week, and I give to God a tenth of everything I earn.'

13 But the corrupt tax collector stood at a distance and dared not even lift his eyes to heaven as he prayed, but beat upon his chest in sorrow, exclaiming, 'God, be merciful to me, a sinner.'

14 I tell you, this sinner, not the Pharisee, returned home forgiven! For the proud shall be humbled, but the humble shall be honored."

*   *   *   *   *

15 One day some mothers brought their babies to Him to touch and bless. But the disciples told them to go away.

16, 17 Then Jesus called the children over to Him and said to the disciples, "Let the little children come to Me! Never send them away! For the Kingdom of God belongs to men who have trusting hearts as these little children do. And anyone who doesn't have their kind of faith will never get within the Kingdom's gates!"

*   *   *   *   *

18 Once a Jewish religious leader asked Him this question: "Good sir, what shall I do to get to heaven?"

19 "Do you realize what you are saying when you call me 'good'?" Jesus asked him. "Only God is truly good, and no one else.

20 But as to your question, you know what the ten commandments say—don't commit adultery, don't murder, don't steal, don't lie, honor your parents, and so on."

21 The man replied, "I've obeyed every one of these laws since I was a small child."

22 Jesus said, "There is still one thing you lack! Sell all you have and give the money to the poor—it will become treasure for you in heaven—and come, follow Me."

23 But when the man heard this, he went sadly away, for he was very rich.

24 Jesus watched him go and then said to His disciples, "It is so hard for the rich to enter the Kingdom of God!

25 It is easier for a camel to go through the eye of a needle than for a rich man to enter the Kingdom of God."

26 Those who heard Him say this exclaimed, "If it is as hard as that, how can anyone be saved?"

27 He replied, "God can do what men can't!"

28 And Peter said, "We have left our homes and followed You."

29 "Yes," Jesus replied, "and everyone who has done as you have, leaving home, wife, brothers, parents, or children for the sake of the Kingdom of God,

30   Will be repaid many times over now, as well as receive eternal life in the world to come."

*   *   *   *   *

31   Gathering The Twelve around Him He told them, "As you know, we are going to Jerusalem. And when we get there, all the predictions of the ancient prophets concerning Me will come true.

32   I will be handed over to the Gentiles to be mocked and treated shamefully and spat upon,

33   And lashed and killed. And the third day, I will rise again."

34   But they didn't understand a thing He said. He seemed to them to be talking in riddles.

35   As they approached Jericho, a blind man was sitting beside the road, begging from travelers.

36   When he heard the noise of a crowd going past, he asked what was happening.

37   He was told that Jesus from Nazareth was going by,

38   So he began shouting, "Jesus, Son of David, have mercy on me!"

39   The crowds ahead of Jesus tried to hush the man, but he only yelled the louder, "Son of David, have mercy on me!"

40   When Jesus arrived at the spot, He stopped. "Bring the blind man over here," He said.

41   Then Jesus asked the man, "What do you want?" "Lord," he pleaded, "I want to see!"

42   And Jesus said, "All right, begin seeing! Your faith has healed you!"

43   And instantly the man could see, and followed Jesus, praising God. And all who saw it happen praised God too.

CHAPTER 19

As Jesus was passing through Jericho,
A man named Zacchaeus, one of the most influential Jews in the Roman tax-collecting business (and of course a very rich man),

3　Tried to get a look at Jesus, but he was too short to see over the crowds.

4　So he ran ahead and climbed into a sycamore tree beside the road to see Him, and watched from there.

5　When Jesus came by He looked up at Zacchaeus and called him by name! "Zacchaeus," he said, "Quick! Come down! For I am going to be a guest in your home today!"

6　Zacchaeus climbed down hurriedly and took Jesus to his house in great excitement and joy.

7　But the crowds were displeased. "He has gone to be the guest of a notorious sinner," they grumbled.

8　Meanwhile Zacchaeus stood before the Lord and said, "Sir, from now on I will give half my wealth to the poor, and if I find I have overcharged anyone on his taxes, I will penalize myself by giving him back four times as much!"

9, 10　Jesus told him, "This shows* that salvation has come to this home today. This man was one of the lost sons of Abraham, and I, the Son of Mankind, have come to search for and save such souls as his."

11　And because Jesus was nearing Jerusalem, He told a story to correct the impression that the Kingdom of God would begin right away.

12　"A nobleman living in a certain province was called away to the distant capital of the empire to be crowned king of his province.

13　Before he left he called together ten assistants (his slaves), and gave them each $2,000 to invest while he was gone.

14　But some of his people hated him and sent him their declaration of independence, stating that they had rebelled and would not acknowledge him as their king.

15　Upon his return he called in the men to whom he had given the money, to find out what they had done with it, and what their profits were.

16　The first man reported a tremendous gain—ten times as much as the original amount!

17　'Fine!' the king exclaimed. 'You are a good man. You have been faithful with the little I entrusted to you, and as your reward, you shall be governor of ten cities.'

18　The next man came with his report of a large gain—five times the original amount.

19 'All right!' his master said. 'You can be governor over five cities.'

20 But another brought back only the money with which he had started. 'I've kept it safe,' he said,

21 'Because I was afraid (you would demand my profits*), for you are a hard man to deal with, taking what isn't yours and even confiscating the crops that others plant!'

22 'You vile and wicked slave,' the king roared. 'Hard, am I? That's exactly how I'll be toward you! If you knew so much about me and how tough I am,

23 Then why didn't you deposit the money in the bank so that at least I could get some interest on it?'

24 Then turning to the others standing by he ordered, 'Take the money away from him and give it to the man who earned the most.'

25 'But, sir,' they said, 'he has enough already!'

26 'Yes,' the king replied, 'but it is always true that those who have, get more, and those who have little, soon lose even that.

27 And now about these enemies of mine who revolted—bring them in and execute them before me.' "

28 After telling this story, Jesus went on towards Jerusalem, walking along ahead of His disciples.

29 As they came to the towns of Bethphage and Bethany, on the Mount of Olives, He sent two disciples ahead

30 With instructions to go to the next village. As they entered they were to look for a donkey tied beside the road. It would be a colt, not yet broken for riding. "Untie him," Jesus said, "and bring him here.

31 And if anyone asks you what you are doing, just say, 'The Lord needs him.' "

32 They found the colt as Jesus said,

33 And sure enough, as they were untying it, the owners demanded an explanation. "What are you doing?" they asked. "Why are you untying our colt?"

34 And the disciples simply replied, "The Lord needs him!"

35 So they brought the colt to Jesus and threw some of their clothing across its back for Jesus to sit on.

36, 37 Then the crowds spread out their robes along the road ahead of Him, and as they reached the place where the road started down from the Mount of Olives, the whole procession began to shout and sing as they walked along, praising God for all the wonderful miracles Jesus had done.

38 "God has given us a King!" they exulted. "Long live the King! Let all heaven rejoice! Glory to God in the highest heavens!"

39 But some of the Pharisees among the crowd said, "Sir, rebuke your followers for saying things like that!"

40 He replied, "If they kept quiet, the stones along the road would burst into cheers!"

41 But then as they came closer to Jerusalem and He saw the city ahead, He began to cry.

42 "Eternal peace was within your reach and you have turned it down," He wept, "and now it is too late.

43 Your enemies will pile up earth against your walls and encircle you and close in on you,

44 And crush you to the ground, and your children within you; your enemies will not leave one stone upon another—for you have rejected the opportunity God offered you."

45 Then He entered the Temple and began to drive out the merchants from their stalls,

46 Saying to them, "The Scriptures declare, 'My Temple is a place of prayer; but you have turned it into a den of thieves.' "

47 After that He taught daily in the Temple, but the chief priests and other religious leaders and the business community were trying to find some way to get rid of Him.

48 But they could think of nothing, for He was a hero to the people—they hung on every word He said.

CHAPTER 20

One of those days when He was teaching and preaching the Good News in the Temple, He was confronted by the chief priests and other religious leaders and councilmen.

2 They demanded to know by what right He had done what He did in the Temple.

3 "I'll ask you a question first," He replied.

4 "Was John sent by God, or was he merely preaching his own ideas?"

5 They talked it over among themselves. "If we say his message was from heaven, then we are trapped, because He will ask, 'Then why didn't you believe him?'

6 But if we say John was not sent from God, the people will mob us, for they are convinced that he was a prophet."

7, 8 Finally they replied, "We don't know!" And Jesus responded, "Then I won't answer your question either."

9 Then He turned to the people again and told them this story: "A man planted a vineyard and rented it out to some farmers, and went away to a distant land to live for several years.

10 When harvest time came, he sent one of his men to the farm to collect his share of the crops. But the tenants beat him up and sent him back empty-handed.

11 Then he sent another, but the same thing happened; he was beaten up and insulted and sent away empty-handed.

12 A third man was sent and the same thing happened. He, too, was wounded and chased away.

13 'What shall I do?' the owner asked himself. 'I know! I'll send my cherished son. Surely they will show respect for him.'

14 But when the tenants saw his son, they said, 'This is our chance! This fellow will inherit all the land when his father dies. Come on. Let's kill him, and then it will be ours.'

15 So they dragged him out of the vineyard and killed him. What do you think the owner will do now?

16 I'll tell you—he will come and kill them and rent the vineyard to others."

"God forbid!" replied His listeners.

17 But Jesus looked at them, and said, "Then what does the Scripture mean where it says, 'The Stone rejected by the builders was made the cornerstone'?"

18 And He added, "Whoever stumbles over that Stone shall be broken; and those on whom it falls will be crushed to dust."

19 When the chief priests and religious leaders heard that He had told this story, they wanted Him arrested immediately, for they realized that they were the wicked

tenants in His story. But they were afraid that His arrest would start a riot. So they tried to get Him to say something that could be reported to the Roman governor as reason for His arrest.

20 Watching their opportunity, they sent secret agents pretending to be honest men.

21 They said to Jesus, "Sir, we know what an honest teacher You are. You always tell the truth and don't budge an inch in the face of what others think, but teach the way of God.

22 Now tell us—is it right to pay taxes to the Roman government, or not?"

23 He saw through their trickery and said,

24 "Show Me a coin. Whose portrait is this on it? And whose name?" They replied, "Caesar's—the Roman emperor's."

25 He said, "Then give the emperor all that is his —and give to God all that is His!"

26 Thus their attempt to outwit Him before the people failed; and marveling at His answer, they were silent.

27 Then some Sadducees—men who believed that death is the end of existence, that there is no resurrection—

28 Came to Jesus with this: "The laws of Moses state that if a man dies without children, the man's brother shall marry the widow and their children will legally belong to the dead man, to carry on his name.

29 "We know of a family of seven brothers. The oldest married and then died without any children.

30 His brother married the widow and he, too, died. Still no children.

31 And so it went, one after the other, until each of them had married her and died, leaving no children.

32 Finally the woman died also.

33 Now here is our question: Whose wife will she be in the resurrection? For all of them were married to her!"

34, 35 Jesus replied, "Marriage is for men here on earth, but those who are counted worthy of being raised from the dead and going to heaven do not marry.

36 And they never die again; in these respects they are like angels, and are sons of God, for they have been raised up in new life from the dead.

37, 38 But as to your real question—whether or not

there is a resurrection—why, even the writings of Moses himself prove this. For when he describes God's appearance to him in the burning bush, he speaks of God as 'the God of Abraham, the God of Isaac, and the God of Jacob.' To say the Lord is some person's God means that person is alive, not dead! And from His point of view all men are living."

39 "Well said, sir!" remarked some of the experts in the Jewish law who were standing there.

40 And that ended their questions, for they dared ask no more!

41 Then He presented *them* with a question! "Why is it," He asked, "that Christ, the Messiah, is said to be a descendant of King David?

42, 43 For David himself wrote in the book of Psalms: 'God said to my Lord, the Messiah, "Sit at My right hand until I place Your enemies beneath Your feet."'

44 How can the Messiah be both David's son and David's God at the same time?"

45 Then, with the crowds listening, He turned to His disciples and said,

46 "Beware of these experts in religion, for they love to parade in dignified robes and to be bowed to by the people as they walk along the street. And how they love the seats of honor in the synagogues and at religious festivals!

47 But even while they are praying long prayers with great outward piety, they are planning schemes to cheat widows out of their property. Therefore, God's heaviest sentence awaits these men."

CHAPTER 21

A s He stood in the Temple, He was watching the rich men tossing their gifts into the collection box.

2 Then a poor widow came and dropped in two small copper coins.

3 "Really," He remarked, "this poor widow has given more than all the rest of them combined.

4 For they have given a little of what they didn't

need, but she, poor as she is, has given everything she has."

5 Some of His disciples began talking about the beautiful stonework of the Temple and the memorial decorations on the walls.

6 But Jesus said, "The time is coming when these things you are admiring will be knocked down, and not one stone will be left on top of another; all will become one vast heap of rubble."

7 "Master!" they exclaimed. "When? And will there be any warning ahead of time?"

8 He replied, "Don't let anyone mislead you. For many will come announcing themselves as the Messiah, and saying, 'The time has come.' Don't believe them!

9 And when you hear of wars and insurrections beginning, don't panic. True, wars must come, but the end won't follow immediately—

10 For nation shall rise against nation and kingdom against kingdom,

11 And there will be great earthquakes, and famines in many lands, and epidemics, and terrifying things happening in the heavens.

12 But before all this happens, there will be a time of special persecution for you, and you will be dragged into synagogues and prisons and before kings and governors for My name's sake.

13 But as a result, the Messiah will be widely known and honored.

14 Therefore, don't be concerned about how to answer the charges against you,

15 For I will give you the right words and such logic that none of your opponents will be able to reply!

16 Even those closest to you—your parents, brothers, relatives and friends will betray you and have you arrested; and some of you will be killed.

17 And everyone will hate you because you are Mine and are called by My name.

18 But not a hair of your head will perish!

19 For if you stand firm, you will win your souls.

20 But when you see Jerusalem surrounded by armies, then you will know that the time of its destruction has arrived.

21 Then let the people of Judea flee to the hill. Let

those in Jerusalem try to escape, and those outside the city must not attempt to return.

22 For those will be days of God's judgment, and the words of the ancient Scriptures written by the prophets will be abundantly fulfilled.

23 Woe to expectant mothers in those days, and those with tiny babies. For there will be great distress upon this nation and wrath upon this people.

24 They will be brutally killed by enemy weapons, or sent away as exiles and captives to all the nations of the world; and Jerusalem shall be conquered and trampled down by the Gentiles until the period of Gentile triumph ends in God's good time.

25 Then there will be strange events in the skies— warnings, evil omens and portents in the sun, moon and stars; and down here on earth the nations will be in turmoil, perplexed by the roaring seas and strange tides.

26 The courage of many people will falter because of the fearful fate they see coming upon the earth, for the stability of the very heavens will be broken up.

27 Then the peoples of the earth shall see Me, the Man from Heaven, coming in a cloud with power and great glory.

28 So when all these things begin to happen, stand straight and look up! For your salvation is near."

29 Then He gave them this illustration: "Notice the fig tree, or any other tree.

30 When the leaves come out, you know without being told that summer is near.

31 In the same way, when you see the events taking place that I've described, you can be just as sure that the Kingdom of God is near.

32 I solemnly declare to you that when these things happen, the end of this age has come.

33 And though all heaven and earth shall pass away, yet My words remain forever true.

34 Watch out! Don't let My sudden coming catch you in a trap; don't let Me find you living in careless ease, carousing and drinking, and occupied with the problems of this life.

35 For that day will come on all men everywhere throughout the world.

36 Keep a constant watch. And pray that if possible

you may arrive in My presence without having to experience these horrors.

37, 38 Every day Jesus went to the Temple to teach, and the crowds began gathering early in the morning to hear Him. And each evening He returned to spend the night on the Mount of Olives.

CHAPTER 22

And now the Passover celebration was drawing near— the Jewish festival when only bread made without yeast was used.

2 The chief priests and other religious leaders were actively plotting Jesus' murder, trying to find a way to kill Him without starting a riot—a possibility they greatly feared.

3 When Satan entered into Judas Iscariot, one of the twelve disciples,

4 He went over to the chief priests and captains of the Temple guards to discuss the best ways to betray Jesus to them.

5 They were, of course, delighted to know that he was ready to help them and promised him a reward.

6 So he began to look for an opportunity for them to arrest Jesus quietly when the crowds weren't around.

7 Now the day of the Passover celebration arrived when the Passover lamb was killed and eaten with the unleavened bread.

8 Jesus sent Peter and John ahead to find a place to prepare their Passover meal.

9 "Where do You want us to go?" they asked.

10 And He replied, "As soon as you enter Jerusalem, you will see a man walking along carrying a pitcher of water. Follow him into the house he enters,

11 And say to the man who lives there, 'Our Teacher says for you to show us the guest room where He can eat the Passover meal with His disciples.'

12 He will take you upstairs to a large room all ready for us. That is the place. Go ahead and prepare the meal there."

13 They went off to the city and found everything

just as Jesus had said. And they prepared the Passover supper.

14 Jesus and the others arrived, and at the proper time all sat down together at the table,

15 And He said, "I have looked forward to this hour with deep longing, anxious to eat this Passover meal with you before My suffering begins.

16 For I tell you now that I won't eat it again until all it represents has taken place in the Kingdom of God."

17 Then He took a glass of wine; and when He had given thanks for it, He said, "Take this and share it among yourselves.

18 For I will not drink wine again until the Kingdom of God has come."

19 Then He took a loaf of bread; and when He had thanked God for it, He broke it apart and gave it to them, saying, "This is My body, given for you. Eat it in remembrance of Me."

20 After supper He gave them another glass of wine, saying, "This wine is the token of God's new agreement to save you—an agreement sealed with the blood I shall pour out to purchase back your souls.

21 But here at this table, sitting among us as a friend, is the man who will betray Me.

22 I must die. It is part of God's plan. But, oh, the horror awaiting that man who betrays Me!"

23 Then the disciples wondered among themselves which of them would ever do such a thing.

24 And they began to argue among themselves as to who would have the highest rank (in the coming Kingdom).*

25 Jesus told them, "In this world the kings and great men order about the slaves, who have no choice but to like it!

26 But among you, the one who serves you best will be your leader.

27 Out in the world the master sits at the table and is served by his servants! But not here! For I am your servant!

28 Nevertheless, since you have stood true to Me in these terrible days,

29 And since My Father has granted Me a Kingdom, I, here and now, grant you the right

30 To eat and drink at My table in that Kingdom; and you will sit on thrones judging the twelve tribes of Israel!

31 Simon, Simon, Satan has asked to have you, to sift you like wheat,

32 But I have pleaded in prayer for you that your faith should not completely fail. So when you have repented and turned to Me again, strengthen and build up the faith of your brothers."

33 Simon said, "Lord, I am ready to go to jail with You, and even to die with You."

34 But Jesus said, "Peter, let Me tell you something. Between now and tomorrow morning when the rooster crows, you will deny Me three times, declaring that you don't even know Me."

35 Then Jesus asked them, "When I sent you out to preach the Good News and you were without money, duffle bag, or extra clothes, how did you get along?"

"Fine," they replied.

36 "But now," He said, "take a duffle bag if you have one, and your money. And if you don't have a sword, you had better sell your clothes and buy one!

37 For the time has come for this prophecy about Me to come true: 'He will be condemned as a criminal!' Yes, everything written about Me by the prophets will come true."

38 "Master," they replied, "we have two swords among us!"

"Two are enough!" He said.

39 Then, accompanied by the disciples, He left the upstairs room and went as usual to the Mount of Olives.

40 There He told them, "Pray God that you will not be overcome by temptation."

41, 42 He walked away, perhaps a stone's throw, and knelt down and prayed this prayer: "Father, if You are willing, please take away this cup of horror from Me. But I want Your will, not Mine."

43 Then an angel from heaven appeared and strengthened Him,

44 For He was in such agony of spirit that He broke into a sweat of blood, with great drops falling to the ground as He prayed more and more earnestly.

45 At last He stood up again and returned to the
disciples—only to find them asleep, exhausted from grief.

46 "Asleep!" He said. "Get up! Pray God that you
will not fall when you are tempted."

47 But even as He said this, a mob approached, led
by Judas, one of His twelve disciples. Judas walked over
to Jesus and kissed Him on the cheek in friendly greeting.

48 But Jesus said, "Judas, how can you do this—
betray the Messiah with a kiss?"

49 When the other disciples saw what was about to
happen, they exclaimed, "Master, shall we fight? We
brought along the swords!"

50 And one of them slashed at the High Priest's servant, and cut off his right ear.

51 But Jesus said, "Don't resist anymore." And He
touched the place where the man's ear had been and
restored it.

52 Then Jesus addressed the chief priests and captains of the Temple guards and the religious leaders who
headed the mob. "Am I a robber," He asked, "that you
have come armed with swords and clubs to get Me?

53 Why didn't you arrest Me in the Temple? I was
there every day! But this is your moment—the time when
Satan's power reigns supreme!"

54 So they seized Him and led Him to the High
Priest's residence, and Peter followed at a distance.

55 The soldiers lit a fire in the courtyard and sat
around it for warmth, and Peter joined them.

56 A servant girl noticed him in the firelight and
began staring at him. Finally she spoke: "This man was
with Jesus!"

57 Peter denied it! "Woman," he said, "I don't even
know the man!"

58 After a while someone else looked at him and
said, "You must be one of them !"

"No, sir, I am not!" Peter replied.

59 About an hour later someone else flatly stated,
"I know this fellow is one of Jesus' disciples, for both
are from Galilee."

60 But Peter said, "Man, I don't know what you are
talking about." And as he said the words, a rooster
crowed.

61　At that moment Jesus turned and looked at Peter. Then Peter remembered what He had said—"Before the rooster crows tomorrow morning, you will deny Me three times."

62　And Peter walked out of the courtyard and started crying bitterly.

63, 64　Now the guards in charge of Jesus began mocking Him. They blindfolded Him and hit Him with their fists and asked, "Who hit You that time, prophet?"

65　And they threw all sorts of other insults at Him.

66　Early the next morning at daybreak the Jewish Supreme Court assembled, including the chief priests and all the top religious authorities of the nation. Jesus was led before this council

67, 68　And instructed to state whether or not He claimed to be the Messiah. But He replied, "If I tell you, you won't believe Me or let Me present My case.

69　But the time is soon coming when I, the Man of Glory, shall be enthroned beside Almighty God."

70　They all shouted, "Then You claim You are the Son of God?"

And He replied, "Yes, I am."

71　"What need do we have for other witnesses?" they shouted, "for we ourselves have heard Him say it."

CHAPTER 23

Then the entire Council took Jesus over to Pilate, the governor.*

2　They began at once accusing Him: "This fellow has been leading our people to ruin by telling them not to pay their taxes to the Roman government and by claiming He is our Messiah—a King."

3　So Pilate asked Him, "Are You their Messiah—their King?"

"Yes," Jesus replied, "It is as you say."

4　Then Pilate turned to the chief priests and to the mob and said, "So? That isn't a crime!"

5　Then they became desperate! "But He is causing riots against the government everywhere He goes, all over Judea, from Galilee to Jerusalem!"

6　"Is He then a Galilean?" Pilate asked.

7 When they told him yes, Pilate said to take Him to King Herod, for Galilee was under Herod's jurisdiction; and Herod happened to be in Jerusalem at the time.

8 Herod was delighted at the opportunity to see Jesus, for he had heard a lot about Him and had been hoping to see Him perform a miracle.

9 He asked Jesus question after question, but there was no reply.

10 Meanwhile the chief priests and the other religious leaders stood there shouting their accusations.

11 Now Herod and his soldiers began mocking and ridiculing Jesus; and putting a kingly robe on Him, they sent Him back to Pilate.

12 That day Herod and Pilate—enemies before—became fast friends.

13 Then Pilate called together the chief priests and other Jewish leaders, along with the people,

14 And announced his verdict: "You brought this man to me, accusing Him of leading a revolt against the Roman government. I have examined Him thoroughly on this point and find Him innocent.

15 Herod came to the same conclusion and sent Him back to us—nothing this man has done calls for the death penalty.

16 I will therefore have Him scourged with leaded thongs, and release Him."

17, 18 But now a mighty roar rose from the crowd as with one voice they shouted, "Kill Him, and release Barabbas to us!"

19 (Barabbas was in prison for starting an insurrection in Jerusalem against the government and for murder.)

20 Pilate argued with them, for he wanted to release Jesus.

21 But they shouted, "Crucify Him! Crucify Him!"

22 Once more, for the third time, he demanded, "Why? What crime has He committed? I will therefore scourge Him and let Him go."

23 But they shouted louder and louder for Jesus' death, and their voices prevailed.

24 So Pilate sentenced Jesus to die as they demanded.

25 And he released Barabbas, the man in prison for

insurrection and murder, at their request. But he delivered Jesus over to them to do with as they would.

26 As the crowd led Jesus away to His death, Simon of Cyrene, who was just coming into Jerusalem from the country, was forced to follow, carrying Jesus' cross.

27 Great crowds trailed along behind, and many grief-stricken women.

28 But Jesus turned and said to them, "Daughters of Jerusalem, don't weep for Me, but for yourselves and for your children.

29 For the days are coming when the women who have no children will be counted fortunate indeed.

30 Mankind will beg the mountains to fall on them and crush them and the hills to bury them.

31 For if such things as this are done to Me, the Living Tree, what will they do to you?"

*　　*　　*　　*　　*

32, 33 Two others, criminals, were led out to be executed with Him at a place called "The Skull." There all three were crucified—Jesus on the center cross, and the two criminals, one on either side.

34 "Father, forgive these people," Jesus said, "for they don't know what they are doing."

And the soldiers gambled for His clothing, throwing dice for each piece.

35 The crowd watched.

And the Jewish leaders laughed and scoffed. "He was so good at helping others," they said, "let's see Him save Himself if He is really God's Chosen One, the Messiah."

36 The soldiers mocked Him, too, by offering Him a drink—of sour wine.

37 And they called to Him, "If You are the King of the Jews, save Yourself!"

38 A signboard was nailed to the cross above Him, with these words: "THIS IS THE KING OF THE JEWS."

39 One of the criminals hanging beside Him scoffed, "So You're the Messiah, are You? Prove it by saving Yourself—and us too, while You're at it!"

40, 41 But the other criminal protested. "Don't you even fear God when you are dying? We deserve to die for our evil deeds, but this man hasn't done one thing wrong."

42 Then he said, "Jesus, remember me when You come into Your Kingdom."

43 And Jesus replied, "Today you will be with Me in Paradise. This is a solemn promise."

44 By now it was noon, and darkness fell across the whole land for three hours, until 3 o'clock—

45 The light from the sun was gone—and the thick veil hanging in the Temple was split apart.

46 Then Jesus shouted, "Father, I commit My spirit to You," and with those words He died.

47 When the captain of the Roman military unit handling the executions saw what had happened, he was stricken with awe before God and said, "Surely this man was innocent."

48 And when the crowd that came to see the crucifixion saw that Jesus was dead, they went home in deep sorrow.

49 Meanwhile Jesus' friends, including the women who had followed Him down from Galilee, stood in the distance watching.

50, 51, 52 Then a man named Joseph, a member of the Jewish Supreme Court, from the city of Arimathea in Judea, went to Pilate and asked for the body of Jesus. He was a godly man who had been expecting the Messiah's coming and had not agreed with the decision and actions of the other Jewish leaders.

53 So he took down Jesus' body and wrapped it in a long linen cloth and laid it in a new, unused tomb hewn into the rock (at the side of a hill*).

54 This was done late on Friday afternoon, the day of preparation for the Sabbath.

55 As the body was taken away, the women from Galilee followed and saw it carried into the tomb.

56 Then they went home and prepared spices and ointments to embalm Him; but by the time they were finished it was the Sabbath, so they rested all that day as required by the Jewish law.

CHAPTER 24

B ut very early on Sunday morning they took the ointments to the tomb—

2 And found that the huge stone covering the entrance had been rolled aside.

3 So they went in—but the Lord Jesus' body was gone!

4 They stood there puzzled, trying to think what could have happened to it. Suddenly two men appeared before them, clothed in shining robes so bright their eyes were dazzled.

5 The women were terrified and bowed deeply before them. Then the men asked, "Why are you looking in a tomb for someone who is alive?

6, 7 He isn't here! He has come back to life again! Don't you remember what He told you back in Galilee—that the Messiah must be betrayed into the power of evil men and be crucified and that He would rise again the third day?"

8 Then they remembered

9 And returned to Jerusalem and told His eleven disciples—and everyone else—what had happened.

10 (The women who went to the tomb were Mary Magdalene and Joanna and Mary the mother of James, and several others.)

11 But the story sounded like a fairy tale to the men —they didn't believe it.

12 However, Peter ran to the tomb to look. Stooping, he peered in and saw the empty linen wrappings; and then he went back home again, wondering what had happened.

13 That same day, Sunday, two of Jesus' followers were walking to the village of Emmaus, seven miles out of Jerusalem.

14 As they walked along they were talking of Jesus' death,

15 When suddenly Jesus Himself came along and joined them and began walking beside them!

16 But they didn't recognize Him, for God kept them from doing so.

17 "You seem to be in a deep discussion about some-

thing," He said. "What are you so concerned about?"
They stopped short, sadness written across their faces.

18 And one of them, Cleopas, replied, "You must
be the only person in all Jerusalem who hasn't heard
about the terrible things that happened there last week."

19 "What things?" Jesus asked.

"The things that happened to Jesus, the Man from
Nazareth," they said. "He was a Prophet who did incredible miracles and was a mighty Teacher, highly re-
garded by both God and man.

20 But the chief priests and our religious leaders
arrested Him and handed Him over to the Roman government to be condemned to death, and they crucified Him.

21 But we had thought He was the glorious Messiah
and that He had come to rescue Israel. And now—besides
all this, which happened three days ago—

22 Some women from our group of His followers
were at His tomb early this morning and came back with
an amazing report

23 That His body was missing and that they had
seen some angels there who had told them Jesus is alive!

24 Some of our men ran out to see, and sure enough,
Jesus' body was gone, just as the women had said."

25 Then Jesus said to them, "You are such foolish,
foolish people! You find it so hard to believe all that the
prophets wrote in the Scriptures!

26 Wasn't it clearly predicted by the prophets that
the Messiah would have to suffer these things before
entering His time of glory?"

27 Then Jesus quoted them passage after passage
from the writings of the prophets, beginning with the
book of Genesis and going right on through the Old Testament, explaining what the passages meant and what they
said about Himself.

28 By this time they were nearing Emmaus and the
end of their journey. Jesus would have gone farther,

29 But they begged Him to stay the night with them,
as it was getting late. So He went home with them.

30 When they sat down to eat, He asked God's blessing on the food and then took a small loaf of bread and
broke it and was passing it over to them,

31 When suddenly—it was as though their eyes were

opened—they recognized Him! And at that moment He disappeared!

32 They began telling each other how their hearts had felt strangely warm as He talked with them, explaining the Scriptures during the walk down the road.

33, 34 Within the hour they were on their way back to Jerusalem. The eleven disciples and the other followers of Jesus greeted them with these words, "The Lord has really risen! He appeared to Peter!"

35 Then the two from Emmaus told their story of how Jesus had appeared to them as they were walking along and how they had recognized Him as He was breaking the bread.

36 And just as they were telling about it, Jesus Himself was suddenly standing there among them, and He greeted them!

37 But the whole group was terribly frightened, thinking they were seeing a ghost!

38 "Why are you frightened?" He asked. "Why do you doubt that it is really I?

39 Look at My hands! Look at My feet! You can see that it is I, Myself! Touch Me and make sure that I am not a ghost! For ghosts don't have bodies, as you see that I do!"

40 As He spoke, He held out His hands for them to see (the marks of the nails*), and showed them (the wounds in*) His feet.

41 Still they stood there undecided, filled with joy and doubt. Then He asked them, "Do you have anything here to eat?"

42 They gave Him a piece of broiled fish,

43 And He ate it as they watched!

44 Then He said, "When I was with you before, do you not remember My telling you that everything written about Me by Moses and the prophets and in the Psalms must all come true?"

45 Then He opened their minds to understand at last these many Scriptures!

46 And He said, "Yes, it was written long ago that the Messiah must suffer and die and rise again from the dead on the third day;

47 And that this message of salvation should be taken

to all nations, starting from Jerusalem: *There is forgiveness of sins for all who turn to Me.*

48   You have seen these prophecies come true,

49   And now I will send (the Holy Spirit*) upon you, just as My Father promised. Don't begin telling others yet—stay here in the city until He comes and fills you with power from heaven."

50   Then Jesus led them out along the road* to Bethany, and lifting His hands to heaven, He blessed them,

51   And then began rising into the sky, and went on to heaven.

52   And they worshiped Him, and returned to Jerusalem, filled with mighty joy,

53   And were continually in the Temple, praising God.

THE BOOK OF ACTS

Jesus, the miracle-working teacher who was worshipped by a small group of Jews as their heaven-sent Savior, had demonstrated unprecedented power by rising from the grave three days after his execution, just as he had predicted he would do. But Jesus soon left his ecstatic followers, "rising into the sky, and . . . on to heaven," as Luke describes Jesus' departure at the end of his book. What would the nondescript band of fanatics do now, lacking their leader, a program, and money to promote their cause?

The Book of Acts, written by the same chronicler who narrated the stupendous events of Jesus' life on earth, tells what happened to the rag-tag band of Jesus' followers. Acts describes the coming of the Holy Spirit into the lives of the people who believed in Jesus Christ, transforming them into dedicated, fearless individuals who told others about their Savior and aroused the same fierce loyalty or murderous hostility in their hearers as had their Master. The impassioned message of the Christians and the relentless opposition of established religions struck sparks that blazed across land and sea, kindling fires of faith which eventually conquered the Roman Empire and altered the history of the world.

The most trying—and the most triumphant—years of the Christian Church, from about A.D. 44 to A.D. 60, are here recounted by Luke, the traveling companion and physician of Paul the Apostle, Christendom's first and greatest missionary.

Acts

CHAPTER 1

Dear Theophilus,

In my first letter I told you about Jesus' life and teachings and how He returned to heaven after giving His chosen apostles further instructions from the Holy Spirit.

3 During the 40 days after His crucifixion He appeared to the apostles from time to time in human form and proved to them in many ways that it was actually He Himself they were seeing. And on these occasions He talked to them about the Kingdom of God.

4 In one of these meetings He told them not to leave Jerusalem until the Holy Spirit came upon them in fulfillment of the Father's promise. Jesus had spoken about this before—

5 "John baptized you with water," He had said, "but you shall be baptized with the Holy Spirit in just a few days."

6 Another time when He appeared to them, they asked Him, "Lord, are You going to free Israel (from Rome*) now and restore us as an independent nation?"

7 "The Father sets those dates," He replied. "They are not for you to know.

8 But when the Holy Spirit has come upon you, you will receive power to preach with great effect about my death and resurrection to the people in Jerusalem, throughout Judea, in Samaria and to the ends of the earth."

9 It was not long afterwards that He rose into the sky and disappeared into a cloud, leaving them staring after Him.

10 As they were straining their eyes for another glimpse, suddenly two white-robed men were standing there among them,

11 And they said, "Men of Galilee, why are you standing here staring at the sky? Jesus has gone away to heaven, and some day, just as He went, so He will return!"

12 They were at the Mount of Olives at the time, so now they walked the half mile back to Jerusalem

13, 14 And held a prayer meeting in an upstairs room of the house where they were staying. Here is the list of those who were present:

Peter,
John,
James,
Andrew,
Philip,
Thomas,
Bartholomew,
Matthew,
James (son of Alphaeus),
Simon (also called "The Zealot").
Judas (son of James),
And the brothers of Jesus.

Several women, including Jesus' mother, were also there.

15 This prayer meeting went on for several days. On one of these days, when about 120 people were present, Peter stood up and addressed them as follows:

16 "Brothers, it was necessary for the Scriptures to come true concerning Judas, who betrayed Jesus by guiding the mob to where He was. For what Judas did was predicted long ago by the Holy Spirit speaking through King David.

17 Judas was one of us; he was chosen to be an apostle just as we were.

18 He bought a field with the money he received for his treachery and falling headlong, he burst open, spilling out his insides.

19 The news of his death spread rapidly among all the people of Jerusalem, and they named the place 'The Field of Blood.'

20 King David's prediction of this appears in the Book of Psalms, where he says, 'Let his home become desolate with no one living in it. And again, 'Let his work be given to someone else to do.'

21, 22 So now we must choose someone else to
take Judas' place and to join us as witnesses of Jesus'
resurrection. Let us select someone who has been with
us constantly from our first association with the Lord—
from His baptism by John until the day He was taken
from us into heaven."

23 The assembly nominated two men: Joseph Justus
(also called Barsabbas) and Matthias.

24 Then they all prayed for the right man to be
chosen. "Oh Lord," they said, "You know every heart;
show us which of these men You have chosen as an
apostle to replace Judas the traitor, who has gone on to
his proper place."

25 Then they drew straws,* and in this manner Matthias was chosen and became an apostle with the eleven.

CHAPTER 2

S even weeks* had now gone by since Jesus' death and
resurrection, and the Day of Pentecost arrived. As
the believers met together that day,

2 Suddenly there was a sound like the roaring of a
mighty windstorm in the skies above them and it filled
the house where they were meeting.

3 Then what looked like flames or tongues of fire appeared and settled on their heads.

4 And everyone present was filled with the Holy Spirit
and began speaking in languages they didn't know, for
the Holy Spirit gave them this ability.

5 Many godly Jews were in Jerusalem that day for
the religious celebrations, having arrived from many
nations.

6 And when they heard the roaring in the sky above
the house, crowds came running to see what it was all
about, and were stunned to hear their own languages being spoken by the disciples.

7 "How can this be?" they exclaimed. "For these
men are all from Galilee,

8 And yet we hear them speaking all the native
languages of the lands where we were born!

9 Here we are—Parthians, Medes, Elamites, men from
Mesopotamia, Judea, Cappadocia, Pontus, Ausia,

10 Phrygia, Pamphylia, Egypt, the Cyrene language areas of Libya, visitors from Rome—both Jews and Jewish converts—

11 Cretans, and Arabians. And we all hear these men telling in our own languages about the mighty miracles of God!

12 They stood there amazed and perplexed. "What can this mean?" they asked each other.

13 But others in the crowd were mocking. "They're drunk, that's all!" they said.

14 Then Peter stepped forward with the eleven apostles, and shouted to the crowd, "Listen, all of you, visitors and residents of Jerusalem alike!

15 Some of you are saying these men are drunk! It isn't true! It's much too early for that! People don't get drunk by 9 a.m.!

16 No! What you see this morning was predicted centuries ago by the prophet Joel—

17 'In the last days,' God said, 'I will pour out My Holy Spirit upon all mankind, and your sons and daughters shall prophesy, and your young men shall see visions, and your old men dream dreams.

18 Yes, the Holy Spirit shall come upon all My servants, men and women alike, and they shall prophesy.

19 And I will cause strange demonstrations in the heavens and on the earth—blood and fire and clouds of smoke;

20 The sun shall turn black and the moon blood-red before that awesome Day of the Lord arrives.

21 But anyone who asks for mercy from the Lord shall have it and shall be saved.'

22 Oh men of Israel, listen! God publicly endorsed Jesus of Nazareth by doing tremendous miracles through Him, as you well know.

23 But God, following His prearranged plan, let you use the Roman government to nail Him to the cross and murder Him.

24 Then God released Him from the horrors of death and brought Him back to life again, for death could not keep this man within its grip.

25 King David quoted Jesus as saying, 'I know the Lord is always with Me, He is helping Me. God's mighty power supports Me.

26 No wonder My heart is filled with joy and My
tongue shouts His praises! For I know all will be well
with Me in death—

27 You will not leave My soul in hell or let the body
of Your Holy Son decay.

28 You will give Me back My life, and give Me wonderful joy in Your presence.'

29 Dear brothers, think! (David wasn't referring to
himself when he spoke these words I have quoted*),
for he died and was buried, and his tomb is still here
among us!

30 But he was a prophet, and knew God had promised with an unbreakable oath that one of David's own
descendants (would be the Messiah*) and sit on David's
throne.

31 David was looking far into the future and pre-
dicting the Messiah's resurrection, and saying that the
Messiah's soul would not be left in hell and His body
would not decay.

32 He was speaking of Jesus, and we all are witnesses that Jesus rose from the dead.

33 And now He sits on the throne of highest honor
in heaven, next to God. And just as promised, the Father
has sent the Holy Spirit—with the results you are seeing
and hearing today.

34 (No, David was not speaking of himself in these
words of his I quoted*), for he never ascended into the
skies. Moreover, he further stated, 'God spoke to my
Lord, the Messiah, and said to Him, Sit here in honor
beside Me

35 Until I bring Your enemies into complete subjec-
tion.'

36 Therefore I clearly state to everyone in Israel
that God has made this Jesus you crucified to be the
Lord, the Messiah!"

37 These words of Peter's moved them deeply, and
they said to him and to the other apostles, "Brother,
what should we do?"

38 And Peter said to them, "Each one of you must
turn from sin, return to God, and be baptized in the name
of Jesus Christ for the forgiveness of your sins; then you
also shall receive this gift, the Holy Spirit.

39 For Christ promised Him to each one of you who

has been called by the Lord our God, and to your children and even to those in distant lands!"

40 Then Peter preached a long sermon, telling about Jesus and strongly urging all his listeners to save themselves from the evils of their nation.

41 And those who believed Peter were baptized— about 3,000 in all!

42 They joined with the other believers in regular attendance at the apostles' teaching sessions and at the Communion services and prayer meetings.

43 A deep sense of awe was on them all, and the apostles did many miracles.

44 And all the believers met together constantly and shared everything with each other,

45 Selling their possessions and dividing with those in need.

46 They worshiped regularly together every day at the Temple, met in small groups in homes for Communion and shared their meals with great joy and thankfulness,

47 Praising God. The whole city was favorable to them, and each day God added to them all who were being saved.

CHAPTER 3

Peter and John went to the Temple one afternoon to take part in the three o'clock daily prayer meeting.

2 As they approached the Temple, they saw a man lame from birth carried along the street and laid beside the Temple gate—the one called The Beautiful Gate—as was his custom every day.

3 Seeing Peter and John pass by he asked them for some money.

4 They looked at him intently, and then Peter said, "Look here!"

5 He looked expectantly, waiting for a gift.

6 But Peter said, "We don't have any money for you! But I'll give you something else! I command you in the name of Jesus Christ of Nazareth, *walk*!"

7, 8 Then Peter took the lame man by the hand and pulled him to his feet. And as he did, the man's feet and ankle-bones were healed and strengthened so that he came up with a leap, stood there a moment and began walking! Then walking, leaping and praising God, he went into the Temple with him!

9   When the people inside saw him walking and heard him praising God,

10   And realized he was the lame beggar they had seen so often at The Beautiful Gate, they were inexpressibly surprised!

11   They all rushed out to Solomon's Portico, where he was holding tightly to Peter and John! Everyone stood there awed by the wonderful thing that had happened.

12   Peter saw his opportunity and addressed the crowd! "Men of Israel," he said, "what is so surprising about this? And why look at us as though we by our own power and godliness had made this man walk?

13   For it is the God of Abraham, Isaac, Jacob and of all our ancestors who has brought glory to His servant Jesus by doing this. I refer to the Jesus whom you rejected before Pilate despite Pilate's determination to release Him.

14   You didn't want Him freed—this holy, righteous one. Instead you demanded the release of a murderer.

15   And you killed the Author of Life; but God brought Him back to life again. And John and I are witnesses of this fact, for after you killed Him we saw Him alive!

16   Jesus' name has healed this man—and you know how lame he was before. Faith in Jesus' name—faith given us from God—has caused this perfect healing.

17   Dear brothers, I realize that what you did to Jesus was done in ignorance; and the same can be said for your leaders.

18   But God was fulfilling the prophecies that the Messiah must suffer all these things.

19   Now change your mind and attitude to God and turn to Him, so He can cleanse away your sins and send you wonderful times of refreshment from the presence of the Lord

20   And send Jesus your Messiah back to you again.

21, 22   He must remain in heaven until the final recovery of all things from sin, as prophesied from ancient times. Moses, for instance, said long ago, 'The Lord God will raise up a Prophet among you, who will resemble Me! Listen carefully to everything He tells you.

23 Anyone who will not listen to Him shall be utterly destroyed.'

24 Samuel and every prophet since have all spoken about what is going on today.

25 You are the children of those prophets; and you are included in God's promise to your ancestors to bless the entire world through the Jewish race—that is the promise God gave to Abraham.

26 And as soon as God had brought His servant to life again, He sent Him first of all to you men of Israel, to bless you by turning you back from your sins."

CHAPTER 4

While they were talking to the people, the chief priests, the captain of the Temple police, and some of the Sadducees came over to them,

2 Very disturbed that Peter and John were claiming that Jesus had risen from the dead.

3 They arrested them and since it was already evening, jailed them overnight.

4 But many of the people who heard their message believed it, so that the number of believers now reached a new high of about 5,000 men!

5 The next day it happened that a council of all the Jewish leaders was in session in Jerusalem—

6 Ananias the High Priest was there, and Caiaphas, John, Alexander, and others of the High Priest's relatives.

7 So the two disciples were brought in before them. "By what power, or by whose authority have you done this?" the council demanded.

8 Then Peter, filled with the Holy Spirit, said to them, "Honorable leaders and elders of our nation,

9 If you mean the good deed done to the cripple, and how he was healed,

10 Let me clearly state to you and to all the people of Israel that it was done in the name and power of Jesus from Nazareth, the Messiah, the man you crucified and God raised back to life again. It is by His authority that this man stands here healed!

11 For Jesus the Messiah is the (one referred to in

the Scriptures when they speak of) a 'stone discarded by the builders which became the capstone of the arch.'*

12   There is salvation in no one else! Under all heaven there is no other name for men to call upon to save them."

13   When the council saw the boldness of Peter and John, and could see that they were obviously uneducated non-professionals, they were amazed and realized what being with Jesus had done for them!

14   And the council could hardly discredit the healing of the man when he was standing right there beside them!

15   So they sent them out of the council chamber and conferred among themselves.

16   "What shall we do with these men?" they asked each other. "We can't deny that they have done a tremendous miracle, and everybody in Jerusalem knows about it.

17   But perhaps we can stop them from spreading their propaganda. We will threaten them with dire consequences if they publicly mention Jesus again."

18   So they called them back in, and told them never again to speak about Jesus.

19   But Peter and John replied, "You decide whether God wants us to obey you instead of Him!

20   We cannot stop telling about the wonderful things we saw Jesus do and heard Him say."

21   The council threatened them further, and finally let them go because they didn't know how to punish them without starting a riot. For everyone was praising God for this wonderful miracle—

22   The healing of a man more than forty years old!

23   As soon as they were free, Peter and John found the other disciples and told them what the council had said.

24   Then all the believers united in this prayer: "Oh Lord, Creator of heaven and earth, and of the sea and everything in them—

25, 26   You spoke long ago by the Holy Spirit through our ancestor King David, your servant, saying, 'Why do the heathen rage against the Lord, and the foolish nations plan their little plots against Almighty God?

The kings of the earth unite to fight against *Him*, against the anointed Son of God!'

27 That is what is happening here in this city today! For Herod the king, and Pontius Pilate the governor, and all the Romans—as well as the people of Israel—are united against Jesus, Your anointed Son, Your holy servant.

28 They won't stop at anything that You in Your wise power will let them do.

29 And now, Oh Lord, hear their threats, and grant to Your servants great boldness in their preaching.

30 And send Your healing power, and may miracles and wonders be done by the name of Your holy servant Jesus."

31 After this prayer, the building shook where they were meeting and they were all filled with the Holy Spirit and boldly preached God's message.

32 All the believers were of one heart and mind, and no one felt that what he owned was his own; all shared everything alike.

33 And the apostles preached powerful sermons about the resurrection of the Lord Jesus, and there was warm fellowship among all the believers.

34, 35 And there was no poverty; for all who owned land or houses sold them and brought the money to the apostles to give to others in need.

36 For instance, there was Joseph (the one the apostles nicknamed "Barny the Preacher"! He was of the tribe of Levi, from the island of Cyprus).

37 He was one of those who owned a field and sold it, and brought the money to the apostles for distribution to those in need.

CHAPTER 5

But in another case, a man named Ananias (with his wife Sapphira) sold some property,

2 And brought only part of the money, claiming it was the full price. (Sapphira had agreed to this deception).

3 But Peter said, "Ananias, Satan has filled your

heart! When you claimed this was the full price, you were lying to the Holy Spirit.

4 The property was yours to sell or not, as you wished. And after selling it, it was yours to decide how much to give. How could you do a thing like this? You weren't lying to us, but to God."

5 As soon as Ananias heard these words, he fell to the floor dead! Everyone was terrified,

6 And the younger men covered him with a sheet and took him out and buried him.

7 About three hours later his wife came in, not knowing what had happened.

8 Peter asked her, "Did you people sell your land for such and such a price?"

"Yes," she said, "we did."

9 And Peter said, "How could you and your husband even think of doing a thing like this—conspiring together to test the Spirit of God's ability to know what is going on? Just outside that door are the young men who buried your husband, and they will carry you out too."

10 Instantly she fell to the floor dead, and the young men came in and, seeing that she was dead, carried her out and buried her beside her husband.

11 Terror gripped the entire church and all others who heard what had happened.

12 Meanwhile the apostles were meeting regularly at the Temple in the area known as Solomon's Cloister, and they did many remarkable miracles among the people.

13 The other believers didn't dare join them there, but all had the highest regard for them.

14 And more and more believers were added to the Lord, crowds both of men and women.

15 Sick people were brought out into the streets on beds and mats so that at least Peter's shadow would fall across some of them as he went by!

16 And the crowds came in from the Jerusalem suburbs, bringing their sick folk and those possessed by demons; and every one of them was healed.

17 But the High Priest and his relatives and friends among the Sadducees reacted with violent jealousy

18 And arrested the apostles, and put them in the public jail.

19 But an angel of the Lord came at night, opened the gates of the jail and brought them outside. Then he told them,

20 "Go over to the Temple and preach publicly about this Life!"

21 They arrived at the Temple about daybreak, and immediately began preaching! Later that morning* the High Priest and his courtiers arrived at the Temple and convening the Jewish Council and the entire Senate, they sent for the apostles to be brought for trial.

22 But when the police arrived at the jail, the men weren't there, so they returned to the Council and reported,

23 "The jail doors were locked, and the guards were standing outside, but when we opened the gates, no one was there!"

24 When the police captain and the chief priests heard this, they were frantic, wondering what would happen next and where all this would end!

25 Then someone arrived with the news that the men they had jailed were out in the Temple, preaching to the people!

26, 27 The police captain went with his officers and arrested them (without violence, for they were afraid the people would kill them if they roughed up the disciples) and brought them in before the council.

28 "Didn't we tell you never again to preach about this Jesus?" the High Priest demanded. "And instead you have filled all Jerusalem with your teaching and intend to bring the blame for this man's death on us!"

29 But Peter and the apostles replied, "We must obey God rather than men.

30 The God of our ancestors brought Jesus back to life again after you had killed Him by hanging Him on a cross.

31 Then, with mighty power, God exalted Him to be a Prince and Savior, so that the people of Israel would have an opportunity for repentance, and for their sins to be forgiven.

32 And we are witnesses of these things, and so is the Holy Spirit, who is given by God to all who obey Him."

33 At this, the Council was furious, and decided to kill them.

34 But one of their members, a Pharisee named Gamaliel, (an expert on religious law and very popular with the people), stood up and requested that the apostles be sent outside the Council chambers while he talked.

35 Then he addressed his colleagues as follows: "Men of Israel, take care what you are planning to do to these men!

36 Some time ago there was that fellow Theudas, who pretended to be someone great. About 400 others joined him, but he was killed, and his followers were harmlessly dispersed.

37 After him, at the time of the taxation, there was Judas of Galilee. He drew away some people as disciples, but he also died, and his followers scattered.

38 And so my advice is, leave these men alone. If what they teach and do is merely on their own, it will soon be overthrown.

39 But if it is of God, you will not be able to stop them, lest you find yourselves fighting even against God."

40 The Council accepted his advice, called in the apostles, had them beaten up, and then told them never again to speak in the name of Jesus, and finally let them go.

41 They left the Council Chambers rejoicing that God had counted them worthy to suffer dishonor for His name.

42 And every day, in the Temple and in the city, they continued to teach and preach that Jesus is the Messiah.

CHAPTER 6

But with the believers multiplying rapidly, there were rumblings of discontent. Those who spoke only Greek complained that their widows were being discriminated against, that they were not being given as much food, in the daily distribution, as the widows who spoke Hebrew.

2 So The Twelve called a meeting of all the believers. "We should spend our time preaching, not administering a feeding program," they said.

3 "Now look around among yourselves, dear brothers, and select seven men, wise and full of the Holy Spirit,

who are well thought of by everyone; and we will put them in charge of this business.

4 Then we can spend our time in prayer, preaching and teaching."

5 This sounded reasonable to the whole assembly, and they elected the following:

Stephen (a man unusually full of faith and the Holy Spirit),

Philip,

Prochorus,

Nicanor,

Timon,

Parmenas,

Nicolaus of Antioch (a Gentile convert to the Jewish faith, who had become a Christian).

6 These seven were presented to the apostles, who prayed for them and laid their hands on them in blessing.

* * * * *

7 God's message was preached in ever-widening circles, and the number of the disciples increased vastly in Jerusalem; and many of the Jewish priests were converted too.

8 Stephen, the man so full of faith and the Holy Spirit's power, did spectacular miracles among the people.

9 But one day some of the men from the Jewish cult of "The Freedmen," started an argument with him, and they were soon joined by Jews from Cyrene, Alexandria in Egypt, and the Turkish provinces of Cilicia, and Ausia.

10 But none of them were able to stand up to Stephen's wisdom and spirit.

11 So they brought in some men to lie about him, claiming they had heard Stephen curse Moses, and even God.

12 This accusation roused the crowds to fury against Stephen, and the Jewish leaders arrested him and brought him before the Council.

13 Again the lying witnesses testified that Stephen was constantly speaking against the Temple and against the laws of Moses.

14 They declared, "We have heard him say that this

fellow Jesus of Nazareth will destroy the Temple, and throw out all of Moses' laws."

15   At this point everyone in the Council Chamber saw Stephen's face become as radiant as an angel's!

CHAPTER 7

Then the High Priest asked him, "Are these accusations true?"

2   This was Stephen's lengthy reply:

"The glorious God appeared to our ancestor Abraham in Iraq before he moved to Syria,

3   And told him to leave his native land, to say goodby to his relatives and to start out for a country that God would direct him to.

4   So he left the land of the Chaldeans and lived in Haran, in Syria, until his father died. Then God brought him here to the land of Israel,

5   But gave him no property of his own, not one little tract. However, God promised that eventually the whole country would belong to him and his descendants—though as yet he had no children!

6   But God also told him that these descendants of his would leave the land and live in a foreign country and there become slaves for 400 years.

7   'But I will punish the nation that enslaves them,' God told him, 'and afterwards My people will return to this land of Israel and worship Me here.'

8   God also gave Abraham the ceremony of circumcision at that time, as evidence of the covenant between God and the people of Abraham. And so Isaac, Abraham's son, was circumcised when he was eight days old. Isaac became the father of Jacob, and Jacob was the father of the twelve patriarchs of the Jewish nation.

9   These men were very jealous of Joseph and sold him to be a slave in Egypt. But God was with him,

10   And delivered him out of all of his anguish, and gave him favor before Pharaoh, king of Egypt. God also gave Joseph unusual wisdom, so that Pharaoh appointed him governor over all Egypt, as well as putting him in charge of all the affairs of the palace.

11   But a famine set in over Egypt and Caanan, and

there was great misery for our ancestors. When their food was gone,

12 Jacob heard that there was still grain in Egypt, so he sent his sons to buy some.

13 The second time they went, Joseph revealed his identity to his brothers, and they became known to Pharaoh.

14 Then Joseph sent for his father Jacob and all his brothers' families to come to Egypt, 75 persons in all.

15 So Jacob came to Egypt, where he died, and all his sons.

16 All of them were taken to Shechem and buried in the tomb Abraham bought from the sons of Hamor, Shechem's father.

17 As the time drew near when God would fulfill His promise to Abraham to free his descendants from slavery, the Jewish people greatly multiplied in Egypt,

18 Until a king was crowned who hadn't known Joseph.

19 This king plotted against our race, forcing parents to abandon their children in the fields.

20 About that time Moses was born—a child of divine beauty. His parents hid him at home for three months,

21 And when at last they could no longer keep him hidden, and had to abandon him, Pharaoh's daughter found him and adopted him as her own son,

22 And taught him all the wisdom of the Egyptians, and he became a mighty prince and orator.

23 One day as he was nearing his 40th birthday, it came into his mind to visit his brothers, the people of Israel.

24 During this visit he saw an Egyptian mistreating a man of Israel. So Moses killed the Egyptian.

25 Moses supposed his brothers would realize that God had sent him to help them, but they didn't.

26 The next day he visited them again and saw two men of Israel fighting. He tried to be a peacemaker. 'Gentlemen,' he said, 'you are brothers and shouldn't be fighting like this! It is wrong!'

27 But the man in the wrong told Moses to mind his own business. 'Who made *you* a ruler and judge over us?' he asked.

28 'Are you going to kill me as you killed that Egyptian yesterday?'

29 At this, Moses fled the country, and lived in the land of Midian, where his two sons were born.

30 Forty years later, in the desert near Mount Sinai, an Angel appeared to him in a flame of fire in a bush.

31 Moses saw it and wondered what it was, and as he ran to see, the voice of the Lord called out to him,

32 'I am the God of your ancestors—of Abraham, Isaac and Jacob.' Moses shook with terror and dared not look.

33 And the Lord said to him, 'Take off your shoes, for you are standing on holy ground.

34 I have seen the anguish of My people in Egypt, and heard their cries. I have come down to deliver them. Come, I will send you to Egypt.'

35 And so God sent back the same man His people had previously rejected with the question, 'Who made *you* a ruler and judge over us?' Moses was sent to be their ruler and savior.

36 And by means of many remarkable miracles he led them out of Egypt and through the Red Sea, and back and forth through the wilderness for 40 years.

37 Moses himself told the people of Israel, 'God will raise up a Prophet much like me from among your brothers.

38 How true this proved to be, for in the wilderness, Moses was the go-between—the mediator between the people of Israel and the Angel who gave them the Law of God, the Living Word, on Mount Sinai.

39 But our fathers rejected Moses and wanted to return to Egypt.

40 They told Aaron, 'Make idols for us, so that we will have gods to lead us back; for we don't know what has become of this Moses, who brought us out of Egypt.'

41 So they made a calf-idol and sacrificed to it, and rejoiced in this thing they had made.

42 Then God turned away from them and gave them up, and let them serve the sun, moon and stars as their gods! In the book of Amos' prophecies the Lord God asks, "Was it to Me you were sacrificing during those 40 years in the desert, Israel?

43 No, your real interest was in your heathen gods

—Sakkuth, and the star god Kaiway, and in all the images you made. So I will send you into captivity far away beyond Babylon.'

44 Our ancestors carried along with them a portable Temple, or Tabernacle, through the wilderness. In it they kept the stone tablets with the Ten Commandments written on them. This building was constructed in exact accordance with the plan shown to Moses by the Angel.

45 Years later, when Joshua led the battles against the Gentile nations, this Tabernacle was taken with them into their new territory, and used until the time of King David.

46 God blessed David greatly, and David asked for the privilege of building a permanent Temple for the God of Jacob.

47 But it was Solomon who actually built it.

48, 49 However, God doesn't live in temples made by human hands. 'The heaven is My throne' says the Lord through His prophets, 'And earth is My footstool. What kind of home could you build, asks the Lord! Would I stay in it?

50 Didn't I make both heaven and earth?'

51 You stiff-necked heathen! Must you forever resist the Holy Spirit? But your fathers did, and so do you!

52 Name one prophet your ancestors didn't persecute! They even killed the ones who predicted the coming of the Righteous One—the Messiah whom you betrayed and murdered.

53 Yes, and you deliberately destroyed God's Laws, though you received them from the hands of angels."

54 The Jewish leaders were stung to fury by Stephen's accusation, and ground their teeth in rage.

55 But Stephen, full of the Holy Spirit, gazed steadily upward into heaven and saw the glory of God and Jesus standing at God's right hand.

56 And he told them, "Look, I see the heavens opened and Jesus the Messiah standing beside God, at His right hand!"

57 Then they mobbed him, putting their hands over their ears, and drowning out his voice with their shouts,

58 And dragged him out of the city to stone him. The official witnesses—the executioners—took off their coat and laid them at the feet of a young man named Saul.

59 Then as the murderous stones came hurtling at him, Stephen prayed, "Lord Jesus, receive my spirit,"

60 And he fell to his knees, shouting, "Lord, don't charge them with this sin!" and with that, he died.

CHAPTER 8

Saul was in complete agreement with the killing of Stephen. Beginning that day a great wave of persecution swept over the church in Jerusalem, and everyone except the apostles fled into Judea and Samaria.

2 (Some godly Jews came and with great sorrow buried Stephen.)

3 Saul was like a wild man, going everywhere to devastate the believers, even entering private homes and dragging out men and women alike and jailing them.

4 But the believers who had fled Jerusalem went everywhere preaching the Good News about Jesus!

5 Philip, for instance, went to the city of Samaria and told the people there about Christ.

6 Crowds listened intently to what he had to say, because of the miracles he did.

7 Many evil spirits were cast out, screaming as they left their victims, and many who were paralyzed or lame were healed,

8 So there was much joy in that city!

9, 10, 11 A man named Simon had formerly been a sorcerer there for many years; he was a very influential, proud man because of the amazing things he could do—in fact, the Samaritan people often spoke of him as the Messiah.

12 But now they believed Philip's message that Jesus was the Messiah, and his words concerning the Kingdom of God; and many men and women were baptized.

13 Then Simon himself believed and was baptized; he followed Philip wherever he went and was amazed by the miracles he did.

14 When the apostles back in Jerusalem heard that the people of Samaria had accepted God's message, they sent down Peter and John.

15 As soon as they arrived, they began praying for these new Christians to receive the Holy Spirit,

16 For as yet He had not come upon any of them. For they had only been baptized in the name of the Lord Jesus.

17 Then Peter and John laid their hands upon these believers, and they received the Holy Spirit.

18 When Simon saw this—that the Holy Spirit was given when the apostles placed their hands upon peoples' heads—he offered money to buy this power.

19 "Let me have this power too," he exclaimed, "so that when I lay my hands on people, they will receive the Holy Spirit!"

20 But Peter replied, "Your money perish with you for thinking God's gift can be bought!

21 You can have no part in this, for your heart is not right before God.

22 Turn from this great wickedness and pray. Perhaps God will yet forgive your evil thoughts—

23 For I can see that there is jealousy and sin in your heart."

24 "Pray for me," Simon exclaimed, "that these terrible things won't happen to me."

25 After testifying and preaching in Samaria, Peter and John returned to Jerusalem, stopping at several Samaritan villages along the way to preach the Good News to them too.

26 But as for Philip, an angel of the Lord said to him, "Go over to the road that runs from Jerusalem through the Gaza Desert, arriving around noon.

27 So he did, and who should be coming down the road but the Treasurer of Ethiopia, an eunuch of great authority under Candace the queen. He had gone to Jerusalem to worship at the Temple,

28 And was now returning in his chariot, reading aloud from the book of the prophet Isaiah.

29 The Holy Spirit said to Philip, "Go over and walk along beside the chariot!"

30 Philip ran over and heard what he was reading and asked, "Do you understand it?"

31 "Of course not!" the man replied. "How can I when there is no one to instruct me?" And he begged Philip to come up into the chariot and sit with him!

32 The passage of Scripture he had been reading from was this:

"He was led as a sheep to the slaughter,
And as a lamb is silent before the shearers, so he
opened not his mouth;

33 In His humiliation, justice was denied Him; And
who can express the wickedness of the people of His
generation?* For His life is taken from the earth."

34 The eunuch asked Philip, "Was Isaiah talking
about himself or someone else?"

35 So Philip began with this same Scripture and
then used many others to tell him about Jesus.

36 As they rode along, they came to a small body
of water, and the eunuch said, "Look! Water! Why can't
I be baptized?"

37 "You can," Philip answered, "if you believe with
all your heart."

"And the eunuch replied, "I believe that Jesus Christ
is the Son of God."

38 He stopped the chariot, and they went down into
the water. Philip baptized him,

39 And when they came up out of the water, the
Spirit of the Lord caught away Philip, and the eunuch
never saw him again. But he went on his way rejoicing.

40 Meanwhile, Philip discovered himself at Azotus!
He preached the Good News there and in every city along
the way, until he came to Caesarea.

CHAPTER 9

But Saul, still breathing threats with every breath and
eager to destroy every Christian, went to the High Priest
in Jerusalem.

2 He requested a letter addressed to synagogues in
Damascus, requiring their cooperation in the persecution
of any believers he found there, both men and women,
so that he could bring them in chains to Jerusalem.

3 As he was nearing Damascus on this mission, suddenly a brilliant light from heaven spotted down upon
him!

4 He fell to the ground and heard a voice saying to
him, "Saul! Saul! Why are you persecuting Me?"

5 "Who is speaking, sir?" Paul asked.

And the voice replied, "I am Jesus, the one you are persecuting!

6 Now get up and go into the city and await My further instructions."

7 The men with Paul stood speechless with surprise, for they heard the sound of someone's voice but saw no one!

8 As Saul picked himself up off the ground, he found that he was blind so he had to be led into Damascus. He was there three days, blind, and went without food and water all that time.

10 Now there was in Damascus a believer named Ananias. The Lord spoke to him in a vision, calling, "Ananias!"

"Yes, Lord!" he replied.

11 And the Lord said, "Go over to Straight Street and find the house of a man named Judas and ask there for Saul of Tarsus. He is praying to Me right now,

12 And I have shown him a vision of a man named Ananias coming in and laying his hands on him so that he can see again!"

13 "But Lord," exclaimed Ananias, "I have heard from many the terrible things this man has done to the believers in Jerusalem!

14 And we hear that he has arrest warrants with him from the chief priests, authorizing him to arrest every believer in Damascus!"

15 But the Lord said, "Go and do what I have told you! For Paul is my chosen instrument to take My message to the nations and before kings, as well as to the people of Israel.

16 And I will show him how much he must suffer for Me."

17 So Ananias went over and found Saul and laid his hands on him and said, "Brother Saul, the Lord Jesus, who appeared to you on the road, has sent me here so that you may be filled with the Holy Spirit and to give you back your sight."

18 Instantly (it was as though scales fell from his eyes) Saul could see, and was immediately baptized.

19 Then he ate and was strengthened. He stayed with the believers in Damascus for a few days

20 And went at once to the synagogue to tell everyone

there the Good News about Jesus—that He is indeed the Son of God!

21 All who heard him were amazed. "Isn't this the same man who persecuted Jesus' followers so bitterly in Jerusalem?" they asked. "And we understand that he came here to arrest them all and take them in chains to the chief priests."

22 Saul became more and more fervent in his preaching, and the Damascus Jews couldn't withstand his proofs that Jesus was indeed the Christ.

23 After a while the Jewish leaders determined to kill him.

24 But Saul was told what they were planning and that they were watching the gates of the city day and night, prepared to murder him.

25 So during the night some of his converts let him down in a basket through an opening in the city wall!

26 Upon arrival in Jerusalem he tried to meet with the believers, but they were all afraid of him. They thought he was faking!

27 But Barnabas brought him to the apostles and told them how Saul had seen the Lord on the way to Damascus, what the Lord had said to him, and about his powerful preaching in the name of Jesus.

28 Then they accepted him, and after that he was constantly with the believers

29 And preached boldly in the name of the Lord. But some Greek-speaking Jews, with whom he had argued, plotted to murder him.

30 When the other believers learned of it, they took him to Caesarea and then sent him to his home* in Tarsus.

31 Meanwhile, the church had peace throughout Judea, Galilee and Samaria, and grew in strength and numbers. The believers learned how to walk in the fear of the Lord and in the comfort of the Holy Spirit.

32 Peter traveled from place to place (to visit them), and in his travels came to the believers in the town of Lydda.

33 There he met a man named Aeneas, paralyzed and bedridden for eight years.

34 Peter said to him, "Aeneas! Jesus Christ has healed you! Get up and make your bed!" And he was healed instantly.

35 Then the whole population of Lydda and Sharon turned to the Lord when they saw Aeneas walking around.

36 In the city of Joppa there was a woman named Dorcas ("Gazelle"), a believer who was always doing kind things for others, especially for the poor.

37 About this time she became ill and died. Her friends prepared her for burial and laid her in an upstairs room.

38 But when they learned that Peter was nearby at Lydda, they sent two men to beg him to return with them to Joppa.

39 This he did; as soon as he arrived, they took him upstairs where Dorcas lay. The room was filled with weeping widows who were showing one another the coats and other garments Dorcas had made for them.

40 But Peter asked them all to leave the room; then he knelt and prayed. Turning to the body he said, "Get up, Dorcas," and she opened her eyes! And when she saw Peter, she sat up!

41 He gave her his hand and helped her up and called in the believers and widows, presenting her to them!

42 The news raced through the town, and many believed in the Lord.

43 And Peter stayed a long time in Joppa, living with Simon, the tanner.

CHAPTER 10

In Caesarea there lived a Roman army officer, Cornelius, a captain of an Italian regiment.

2 He was a godly man, deeply reverent (and so was his entire household). He gave generously to charity and was a man of prayer.

3 While wide awake one afternoon he had a vision— it was about three o'clock—and in this vision he saw an angel of God coming toward him. "Cornelius!" the angel said.

4 Cornelius stared at him in terror. "What do you want, sir?" he asked the angel.

And the angel replied, "Your prayers and charities have not gone unnoticed by God!

5, 6 Now send some men to Joppa to find a man named Simon Peter, who is staying with Simon, the tanner, down by the shore, and ask him to come and visit you."

7 As soon as the angel was gone, Cornelius called two of his household servants and a godly soldier, one of his personal bodyguard,

8 And told them what had happened and sent them off to Joppa.

9, 10 The next day, as they were nearing the city, Peter went up on the flat roof of his house to pray. It was noon and he was hungry, but while lunch was being prepared, he fell into a trance.

11 He saw the sky open, and a great canvas sheet,* suspended by its four corners, settle to the ground.

12 In the sheet were all sorts of animals, snakes and birds (forbidden to the Jews for food*).

13 Then a voice said to him, "Go kill and eat any of them you wish."

14 "Never, Lord," Peter declared, "I have never in all my life eaten such creatures, for they are forbidden by our Jewish laws."

15 The voice spoke again, "Don't contradict God! If He says something is *kosher,* then it is!"

16 The same vision was repeated three times! Then the sheet was pulled up again to heaven!

17 Peter was very perplexed. What could the vision mean? What was he supposed to do? Just then the men sent by Cornelius had found the house and were standing outside at the gate,

18 Inquiring whether this was the place where Simon Peter lived!

19 Meanwhile, as Peter was puzzling over the vision, the Holy Spirit said to him, "Three men have come to see you.

20 Go down and meet them and go with them. All is well, I have sent them."

21 So Peter went down. "I'm the man you're looking for," he said. "Now what is it you want?"

22 So they told him about Cornelius the Roman officer, a good and godly man, well thought of by the Jews, and how an angel had instructed him to send for Peter to come and tell him what God wanted him to do.

23 So Peter invited them in and lodged them over-night. The next day he went with them, accompanied by some other believers from Joppa.

24 They arrived in Caesarea the following day, and Cornelius was waiting for him. (Cornelius had called together his relatives and close friends to meet Peter.)

25 As Peter entered his home, Cornelius fell to the floor before him in worship.

26 But Peter said, "Stand up! I'm not a god!"

27 So he stood; they talked together for a while and then went in where the others were assembled.

28 Peter told them, "You know it is against the Jewish laws for me to come into a Gentile home like this. But God has shown me in a vision that I should never think of anyone as inferior.

29 So I came as soon as I was sent for. Now tell me what you want."

30 Cornelius replied, "Four days ago I was praying as usual at this time of the afternoon, when suddenly a man was standing before me clothed in a radiant robe!

31 He told me, 'Cornelius, your prayers are heard and your charities have been noticed by God!

32 Now send some men to Joppa and summon Simon Peter, who is staying in the home of Simon, a tanner, down by the shore.'

33 So I sent for you at once, and you have done well to come so soon. Now here we are, waiting before the Lord, anxious to hear what He has told you to tell us!"

34 Then Peter replied, "I see very clearly that the Jews are not God's only favorites!

35 In every nation He has those who worship Him and do good deeds and are acceptable to Him.

36, 37 I'm sure you have heard about the Good News for the people of Israel—that there is peace with God through Jesus, the Messiah, who is Lord of all creation. This message has spread all through Judea, beginning with John the Baptist in Galilee.

38 And you no doubt know that Jesus of Nazareth was anointed by God with the Holy Spirit and with power, and He went around doing good and healing all who were possessed by demons, for God was with Him.

39 And we apostles are witnesses of all He did through-

out Israel and in Jerusalem, where He was murdered on a cross.

40, 41   But God brought Him back to life again three days later and showed Him to certain witnesses God had selected beforehand—not to the general public, but to us who ate and drank with Him after He rose from the dead.

42   And He sent us to preach the Good News everywhere and to testify that Jesus is ordained of God to be the Judge of all—living and dead.

43   And all the prophets have written about Him, saying that everyone who believes in Him will have their sins forgiven through His name."

44   Even as Peter was saying these things, the Holy Spirit fell upon all those listening!

45   The Jews who came with Peter were amazed that the gift of the Holy Spirit would be given to Gentiles too!

46, 47   But there could be no doubt about it, for they heard them speaking in tongues and praising God. Peter asked, "Can anyone object to my baptizing them, now that they have received the Holy Spirit just as we did?"

48   So he did,* baptizing them in the name of Jesus, the Messiah. Afterwards Cornelius begged him to stay with them for several days.

CHAPTER 11

Soon the news reached the apostles and other brothers in Judea that Gentiles also were being converted!

2   But when Peter arrived back in Jerusalem, the Jewish believers argued with him!

3   "You fellowshiped with Gentiles and even ate with them," they accused.

4   Then Peter told them the whole story.

5   "One day in Joppa," he said, "while I was praying, I saw a vision—a huge sheet, let down by its four corners from the sky.

6   Inside the sheet were all sorts of animals, reptiles and birds (which we are not to eat*).

7   And I heard a voice say, 'Kill and eat whatever you wish.'

8 'Never, Lord,' I replied. 'For I have never yet eaten anything forbidden by our Jewish laws!'

9 But the voice came again, 'Don't say it isn't right when God declares it is!'

10 This happened *three times* before the sheet and all it contained disappeared into heaven.

11 Just then three men who had come to take me with them to Caesarea arrived at the house where I was staying!

12 The Holy Spirit told me to go with them and not to worry about their being Gentiles! These six brothers here accompanied me, and we soon arrived at the home of the man who had sent the messengers.

13 He told us how an angel had appeared to him and told him to send messengers to Joppa to find Simon Peter!

14 'He will tell you how you and all your household can be *saved!*' the angel had told him.

15 Well, I began telling them the Good News, but just as I was getting started with my sermon, the Holy Spirit fell on them, just as He fell on us at the beginning!

16 Then I thought of the Lord's words when He said, 'Yes, John baptized with water, but you shall be baptized with the Holy Spirit.'

17 And since it was *God* who gave these Gentiles the same gift He gave us when we believed on the Lord Jesus Christ, who was I to argue?"

18 When the others heard this, all their objections were answered and they began praising God! "Yes," they said, "God has given to the Gentiles, too, the privilege of turning to Him and receiving eternal life!"

19 Meanwhile, the believers who fled from Jerusalem during the persecution after Stephen's death traveled as far as Phoenicia, Cyprus and Antioch, scattering the Good News, but only to Jews.

20 However, some of the believers who went to Antioch from Cyprus and Cyrene gave their message about the Lord Jesus to some Greeks as well as to the Jews.

21 And the Lord honored this effort so that large numbers of these Gentiles became believers.

22 When the church at Jerusalem heard what had happened, they sent Barnabas to Antioch to help the new converts.

23 When he arrived and saw the wonderful things God was doing, he was filled with excitement and joy, and encouraged the believers to stay close to the Lord whatever the cost.

24 Barnabas was a kindly person, full of the Holy Spirit and strong in faith. As a result large numbers of people were added to the Lord.

25 Then Barnabas went on to Tarsus to hunt for Saul.

26 When he found him, he brought him back to Antioch; and both of them stayed there for a full year teaching the many new converts. (It was there at Antioch that the believers were first called "Christians.")

27 During this time some prophets came down from Jerusalem to Antioch,

28 And one of them, named Agabus, stood up in one of the meetings to predict by the Spirit that a great famine was coming upon the land of Israel. (This was fulfilled during the reign of Claudius.)

29 So the believers decided to send relief to the Christians in Judea, each giving as much as he could.

30 They did this, consigning their gifts to Barnabas and Saul to take to the elders of the church in Jerusalem.

CHAPTER 12

About that time King Herod moved against some of the believers,

2 And killed the apostle* James (John's brother).

3 When Herod saw how much this pleased the Jewish leaders, he arrested Peter during the Passover celebration

4 And imprisoned him, placing him under guard of 16 soldiers. Herod's intention was to deliver Peter to the Jews for execution after the Passover.

5 But earnest prayer was going up to God for his safety all the time he was in prison.

6 The night before he was to be executed, he was asleep, double-chained between two soldiers with others standing guard before the prison gate,

7 When suddenly there was a light in the cell and an angel of the Lord stood beside Peter! The angel slapped

him on the side to awaken him, and said, "Quick! Get up!" And the chains fell off his wrists!

8 Then the angel told him, "Get dressed and put on your shoes." And he did. "Now put on your coat and follow me!" the angel ordered.

9 So Peter left the cell, following the angel. But all the time he thought it was a dream or vision, and didn't believe it was really happening.

10 They passed the first and second cell blocks and came to the iron gate to the street, and this opened to them of its own accord! So they passed through and walked along together for a block, and then the angel left him.

11 Peter finally realized what had happened! "It's really true!" he said to himself. "The Lord has sent His angel and saved me from Herod and from what the Jews were hoping to do to me!"

12 After a little thought he went to the home of Mary, mother of John Mark, where many were gathered for a prayer meeting.

13 He knocked at the door in the gate, and a girl named Rhoda came to open it.

14 When she recognized Peter's voice, she was so overjoyed that she ran back inside to tell everyone that Peter was standing outside in the street!

15 They didn't believe her. "You're out of your head," they said. But when she insisted they decided, "It is his angel. (They must have killed him.*)

16 Meanwhile Peter continued knocking! When they finally went out and opened the door, their surprise knew no bounds.

17 He motioned for them to quiet down and told them what had happened and how the Lord had brought him out of jail.

"Tell James and the other brothers about it," he said —and left for safer quarters.

18 At dawn, the jail was in great commotion. What had happened to Peter?

19 When Herod sent for him and found that he wasn't there, he had the 16 guards arrested, court-martialed and sentenced to death. Afterwards he left to live in Caesarea for a while.

20 While he was in Caesarea, a delegation from Tyre

and Sidon arrived to see him. He was highly displeased
with the people of these two cities, but the delegates made
friends with Blastus, the royal secretary, and asked for
peace, for their cities were economically dependent upon
trade with Herod's country.

21 An appointment with Herod was granted, and
when the day arrived, he put on his royal robes, sat on
his throne and made a speech to them.

22 At its conclusion the people gave him a great ova-
tion, shouting, "It is the voice of a god and not of a man!"

23 Instantly an angel of the Lord struck Herod with
a sickness, so that he was filled with maggots and died—
because he accepted the people's worship instead of
giving the glory to God.

*   *   *   *   *

24 God's Good News spread rapidly and there were
many new believers.

25 Barnabas and Paul now visited Jerusalem and,
as soon as they had finished their business, returned (to
Antioch*), taking John Mark with them.

CHAPTER 13

Among the prophets and teachers of the church at Antioch were Barnabas and Symeon (also called "The Black
Man"), Lucius (from Cyrene), Manaen (the foster-brother
of King Herod) and Saul.

2 One day as these men were worshiping and fasting
the Holy Spirit said, "Dedicate Barnabas and Saul for a
special job I have for them!"

3 So after more fasting and prayer, the men laid
their hands on them—and sent them on their way.

4 Directed by the Holy Spirit, they went to Seleucia
and then sailed for Cyprus.

5 There, in the town of Salamis, they went to the
Jewish synagogue and preached. (John Mark went with
them as their assistant.)

6, 7 Afterwards they preached from town to town
across the entire island until finally they reached Paphos
where they met a Jewish sorcerer, a fake prophet named

Bar-Jesus. He had attached himself to the governor, Sergius Paulus, a man of considerable insight and understanding. The governor invited Barnabas and Saul to visit him, for he wanted to hear their message from God.

8 But the sorcerer, Elymas (his name in Greek), interfered and urged the governor to pay no attention to what Saul and Barnabas said, trying to keep him from trusting the Lord.

9 Then Saul, filled with the Holy Spirit, glared angrily at the sorcerer and said,

10 "You son of the Devil, full of every sort of trickery and villainy, enemy of all that is good, will you never end your opposition to the Lord?

11 And now God has laid His hand of punishment upon you, and you will be stricken awhile with blindness." Instantly mist and darkness fell upon him, and he began wandering around begging for someone to take his hand and lead him.

12 When the governor saw what happened, he believed and was astonished at the power of God's message.

13 Now Paul and those with him left Paphos by ship for Turkey, landing at the port town of Perga. There John deserted them and returned to Jerusalem.

14 But Barnabas and Paul went on to Antioch, a city in the province of Pisidia. On the Sabbath they went into the synagogue for the services.

15 After the usual readings from the Books of Moses and from The Prophets, those in charge of the service sent them this message: "Brothers, if you have any word of instruction for us, come and give it!"

16 So Paul stood, waved a greeting to them and began. "Men of Israel," he said, "and all others here who reverence God, (let me begin my remarks with a bit of history.*)

17 The God of this nation Israel chose our ancestors and honored them in Egypt by gloriously leading them out of their slavery.

18 And He nursed them through 40 years of wandering around in the wilderness.

19, 20 Then He destroyed seven nations in Canaan, and gave Israel their land as an inheritance. Judges ruled for about 450 years, and were followed by Samuel the prophet.

21 Then the people begged for a king, and God gave them Saul (son of Kish), a man of the tribe of Benjamin, who reigned for 40 years.

22 But God removed him and replaced him with David as king, a man about whom God said, 'David (son of Jesse) is a man after My own heart, for he will obey Me.'

23 One of this man's descendants, Jesus, is God's promised Savior of Israel!

24 But before He came, John the Baptist preached the need for everyone in Israel to turn from their sins to God.

25 As John was finishing his work, he asked, 'Who do you think I am? I am not the Messiah! But He is coming soon—and in comparison with Him, I am utterly worthless.'

26 Brothers, you sons of Abraham and also all you Gentiles here who reverence God, this salvation is for all of us!

27 The Jews in Jerusalem and their leaders fulfilled prophecy by killing Jesus; for they didn't recognize Him, or realize that He is the One the prophets had written about, though they heard the prophets' words read every Sabbath.

28 They found no just cause to execute Him, but asked Pilate to have Him killed anyway.

29 When they had fulfilled all the prophecies concerning His death, He was taken from the cross and placed in a tomb.

30 But God brought Him back to life again!

31 And He was seen many times during the next few days by the men who had accompanied Him to Jerusalem from Galilee—these men have constantly testified to this in public witness.

32, 33 And now Barnabas and I are here to bring you this Good News—that God's promise to our ancestors has come true in our own time, in that God brought Jesus back to life again. This is what the second Psalm is talking about when it says concerning Jesus, 'Today I have honored You as My Son.'

34 For God had promised to bring Him back to life again, no more to die. This is stated in the scripture that

says, 'I will do for You the wonderful thing I promised David.'

35 In another Psalm He explained more fully, saying, 'God will not let His Holy One decay.'

36 This was not a reference to David, for after David had served his generation according to the will of God, he died and was buried, and his body decayed.

37 (No, it was a reference to another*)—someone God brought back to life, whose body was not touched at all by the ravages of death.

38 Brothers! Listen! In this man Jesus, there is forgiveness for your sins!

39 Everyone who trusts in Him is freed from all guilt and declared righteous—something the Jewish law could never do.

40 Oh, be careful! Don't let the prophets' words apply to you! For they said,

41 'Look and perish, you despisers (of the truth), For I am doing something in your day—something that you won't believe when you hear it announced.' "

42, 43 As the people left the synagogue that day, they asked Paul to return and speak to them again the next week.

43 And many Jews and godly Gentiles who worshiped at the synagogue followed Paul and Barnabas down the street as the two men urged them to accept the mercies God was offering.

44 The following week almost the entire city turned out to hear them preach the Word of God.

45 But when the Jewish leaders saw the crowds, they were jealous and cursed and argued against whatever Paul said.

46 Then Paul and Barnabas spoke out boldly and declared, "It was necessary that this Good News from God should be given first to you Jews. But since you have rejected it, and shown yourselves unworthy of eternal life —well, we will offer it to Gentiles.

47 For this is as the Lord commanded when He said, 'I have made you a light to the Gentiles, to lead them to salvation from the farthest corners of the earth.' "

48 When the Gentiles heard this, they were very glad and rejoiced in Paul's message; and as many as wanted eternal life, believed.

49 So God's message spread all through the region.

50 Then the Jewish leaders stirred up both the godly women and the civic leaders of the city and incited a mob against Paul and Barnabas, and ran them out of town.

51 But they shook off the dust of their feet against the town and went on to the city of Iconium.

52 And their converts were filled with joy and with the Holy Spirit.

CHAPTER 14

At Iconium, Paul and Barnabas went together to the synagogue and preached with such power that many— both Jews and Gentiles—believed.

2 But the Jews who spurned God's message stirred up distrust among the Gentiles against Paul and Barnabas, saying all sorts of evil things about them.

3 Nevertheless they stayed there a long time, preaching boldly, and the Lord proved their message was from Him by giving them power to do great miracles.

4 But the people of the city were divided in their opinion about them. Some agreed with the Jewish leaders, and some backed the apostles.

5, 6 When Paul and Barnabas learned of a plot to incite a mob of Gentiles, Jews and Jewish leaders to attack and stone them, they fled for their lives, going to the cities of Lycaonia, Lystra, Derbe, and the surrounding area,

7 And preaching the Good News.

8 While they were at Lystra, they came upon a man with crippled feet. He had been that way from birth, so he had never walked.

9 He was listening as Paul preached, and Paul noticed him and realized he had faith to be healed!

10 So Paul yelled at him, "Stand up!" and the man leaped to his feet and started walking!

11 When the listening crowd saw what Paul had done, they shouted (in their local dialect, of course), "These men are gods in human bodies!"

12 They decided that Barnabas was the Greek god Jupiter, and that Paul, because he was the chief speaker, was Mercury!

13   The local priest of the Temple of Jupiter, which
was located on the outskirts of the city, brought them
cartloads of flowers and sacrificed oxen to them at the city
gates before the crowds.

14   But when Barnabas and Paul saw what was happening, they ripped at their clothing in dismay and ran
out among the people, shouting,

15   "Men! What are you doing? We are merely human beings like yourselves! We have come to bring you
the Good News that you are invited to turn from the
worship of these foolish things and to pray instead to the
living God who made heaven and earth and sea and everything in them.

16   In bygone days He permitted the nations to go
their own ways,

17   But He never left Himself without a witness; there
were always His reminders—the kind things He did such as
sending you rain and good crops and giving you food and
gladness."

18   But even so, Paul and Barnabas could scarcely
restrain the people from sacrificing to them!

19   Yet only a few days later, some Jews arrived
from Antioch and Iconium and turned the crowds into a
murderous mob that stoned Paul and dragged him out
of the city, apparently dead!

20   But as the believers stood around him, he got up
and went back into the city! The next day he left with
Barnabas for Derbe.

21   After preaching the Good News there and making
many disciples, they returned again to Lystra, Iconium
and Antioch,

22   Where they helped the believers to grow in love
for God and each other. They encouraged them to continue in the faith in spite of all the persecution, reminding them that they must enter into the Kingdom of God
through many tribulations.

23   Paul and Barnabas also appointed elders in every
church and prayed for them with fasting, turning them
over to the care of the Lord in whom they trusted.

24   Then they traveled back through Pisidia to Pamphylia,

25   Preached again in Perga, and went on to Attalia.

26   Finally they returned by ship to Antioch, where

their journey had begun, and where they had been committed to God for the work now completed.

27 Upon arrival they called together the believers and reported on their trip, telling how God had opened the door of faith to the Gentiles too!

28 And they stayed there with the believers at Antioch for a long while.

CHAPTER 15

While Paul and Barnabas were at Antioch, some men from Judea arrived and began to teach the believers that unless they adhered to the ancient Jewish custom of circumcision, they could not be saved.

2 Paul and Barnabas argued and discussed this with them at length, and finally the believers sent them to Jerusalem, accompanied by some local men, to talk to the apostles and elders there about this question.

3 After the entire congregation had escorted them out of the city the party of delegates went on to Jerusalem, stopping along the way in the cities of Phoenicia and Samaria to visit the believers, telling them—much to everyone's joy—that the Gentiles, too, were being converted.

4 Arriving in Jerusalem, they met with the church leaders—all the apostles and elders were present—and Paul and Barnabas reported on what God had been doing through their ministry.

5 Then some of the men who had been Pharisees before their conversion stood to their feet and declared that all Gentile converts must be circumcised and required to follow all the Jewish customs and ceremonies.

6 So the apostles and church elders set a further meeting to decide this question.

7 At that meeting after long discussion, Peter stood and addressed them as follows:

"Brothers, you all know that God chose me from among you long ago to preach the Good News to the Gentiles, so that they also could believe.

8 God, who knows men's hearts, confirmed the fact that He accepts Gentiles by giving them the Holy Spirit, just as He gave Him to us.

9 He made no distinction between them and us, for He cleansed their lives through faith, just as He did ours.

10 And now are you going to correct God by burdening them with a yoke that neither we nor our fathers were able to bear?

11 Don't we believe that all are saved the same way, by the free gift of the Lord Jesus?"

12 There was no further discussion, and everyone now listened as Barnabas and Paul told about the miracles God had done through them among the Gentiles.

13 When they had finished, James took the floor. "Brothers," he said, "listen to me.

14 Peter has told you about the time God first visited the Gentiles to take from them a people to bring honor to His name.

15 And this fact of Gentile conversion agrees with what the prophets predicted. For instance, listen to this passage (from the prophet Amos*):

16 'Afterwards,' (says the Lord), 'I will return and renew the broken contract with David,

17 So that Gentiles, too, will find the Lord—all those marked with My name.'

18 That is what the Lord says, who reveals His plans made from the beginning.

19 And so my judgment is that we should not insist that the Gentiles who turn to God must obey our Jewish laws.

20 Except that we should write to them to refrain from eating meat sacrificed to idols, from all fornication, and also from eating unbled meat of strangled animals.

21 For in every city on every Sabbath for many generations, these things have been preached against in Jewish synagoges."

22 Then the apostles and elders and the whole congregation voted to send delegates to Antioch with Paul and Barnabas to report on this decision. The men chosen were two of the church leaders—Judas (also called Barsabbas) and Silas.

23 This is the letter they took along with them:

"From: The apostles, elders and brothers at Jerusalem.

To: The Gentile brothers in Antioch, Syria and Cilicia. Greetings!

24 We understand that some believers from here

have upset you and questioned your salvation, but they had no such instructions from us.

25 So it seemed wise to us, having unanimously agreed on our decision, to send to you these two official representatives, along with our beloved Barnabas and Paul.

26 These men—Judas and Silas, who have risked their lives for the sake of our Lord Jesus Christ—will confirm orally what we have decided concerning your question.

27, 28, 29 For it seemed good to the Holy Spirit and to us to lay no greater burden of Jewish laws on you than to abstain from eating food offered to idols and from unbled meat of strangled animals, and of course from fornication. If you do this, it is enough. Farewell."

30 The four men went at once to Antioch, where they called a general meeting of the Christians and gave them the letter.

31 There was great joy throughout the church that day as they read it.

32 Then Judas and Silas, both being gifted speakers, preached long sermons to the believers, strengthening their faith.

33 They stayed several days, and then Judas and Silas returned to Jerusalem taking greetings and appreciation to those who had sent them.

34, 35 Paul and Barnabas stayed on at Antioch to assist several others who were preaching and teaching there.

36 Several days later Paul suggested to Barnabas that they return again to Turkey, and visit each city where they had preached before,* to see how the new converts were getting along.

37 Barnabas agreed, and wanted to take along John Mark.

38 But Paul didn't like that idea at all, since John had deserted them in Pamphylia.

39 Their disagreement over this was so sharp that they separated. Barnabas took Mark with him and sailed for Cyprus,

40, 41 While Paul chose Silas and, with the blessing of the believers, left for Syria and Cilicia, to encourage the churches there.

CHAPTER 16

Paul and Silas went first to Derbe, and then on to Lystra where they met Timothy, a believer whose mother was a Christian Jewess but his father a Greek.

2   Timothy was well thought of by the brothers in Lystra and Iconium,

3   So Paul asked him to join them on their journey. In deference to the Jews of the area, he circumcised Timothy before they left, for everyone knew that his father was a Greek (and hadn't permitted this before*).

4   Then they went from city to city, making known the decision concerning the Gentiles, as decided by the apostles and elders in Jerusalem.

5   So the church grew daily in faith and numbers.

6   Next they traveled through Phrygia and Galatia, because the Holy Spirit had told them not to go into the Turkish province of Ausia at that time.

7   Then going along the borders of Mysia they headed north for the province of Bithynia, but again the Spirit of Jesus said no.

8   So instead they went on through Mysia province to the city of Troas.

9   That night Paul had a vision. In his dream he saw a man over in Macedonia, Greece, pleading with him, "Come over here and help us."

10   Well, that settled it. We would go to Macedonia, for we could only conclude that God was sending us to preach the Good News there.

11   We went aboard a boat at Troas and sailed straight across to Samothrace, and the next day on to Neapolis,

12   And finally reached Philippi, a Roman* colony just inside the Macedonian border, and stayed there several days.

13   On the Sabbath, we went a little ways outside the city to a river bank where we understood some people met for prayer; and we taught the Scriptures to some women who came.

14   One of them was Lydia, a saleswoman from Thyatira, a merchant of purple cloth. She was already a worshiper of God and, as she listened to us, the Lord

opened her heart and she accepted all that Paul was saying.

15 She was baptized along with all her household and asked us to be her guests. "If you agree that I am faithful to the Lord," she said, "come and stay at my home." And she urged us until we did.

16 One day as we were going down to the place of prayer beside the river, we met a demon-possessed slave girl who was a fortuneteller, and earned much money for her masters.

17 She followed along behind us shouting, "These men are servants of God and they have come to tell you how to have your sins forgiven."

18 This went on day after day until Paul, in great distress, turned and spoke to the demon within her. "I command you in the name of Jesus Christ to come out of her," he said. And instantly it left her.

19 Her masters' hopes of wealth were now shattered; they grabbed Paul and Silas and dragged them before the judges at the marketplace.

20, 21 "These Jews are corrupting our city," they shouted. "They are teaching the people to do things that are against the Roman laws."

22 A mob was quickly formed against Paul and Silas, and the judges ordered them stripped and beaten with wooden whips.

23 Again and again the rods slashed down across their bared backs, causing the blood to flow; and afterwards they were thrown into prison. The jailer was threatened with death if they escaped.*

24 So he took no chances, but put them into the inner dungeon and clamped their feet into the stocks.

25 Around midnight, as Paul and Silas were praying and singing hymns to the Lord—and the other prisoners were listening—

26 Suddenly there was a great earthquake; the prison was shaken to its foundations, all the doors flew open— and the chains of every prisoner fell off!

27 The jailer wakened to see the prison doors wide open, and assuming the prisoners had escaped, he drew his sword to kill himself.

28 But Paul yelled to him, "Don't do it! We are all here!"

29 The jailer, trembling with fear, called for lights

and ran to the dungeon and fell down before Paul and Silas.

30 He brought them out and said, "Sirs, what must I do to be saved?"

31 They replied, "Believe on the Lord Jesus and you will be saved, and your entire household."

32 Then they told him and all his household the Good News from the Lord.

33 That same hour he washed their stripes and he and all his family were baptized.

34 Then he brought them up into his house and set a meal before them. How he and his household rejoiced because all were now believers!

35 The next morning the judges sent police officers over to tell the jailer, "Let those men go!"

36 So the jailer told Paul they were free to leave!

37 But Paul replied, "Oh no they don't! They have publicly beaten us without trial and jailed us—and we are Roman citizens! So now they want us to leave secretly? Never! Let them come themselves and release us!"

38 The police officers reported to the judges, who feared for their lives when they heard Paul and Silas were Roman citizens.

39 So they came to the jail and begged them to go, and brought them out and pled with them to leave the city.

40 Paul and Silas then returned to the home of Lydia where they met with the believers and preached to them once more before leaving town.

CHAPTER 17

Now they traveled through the cities of Amphipolis and Apollonia and came to Thessalonica, where there was a Jewish synagogue.

2 As was Paul's custom, he went there to preach, and for three Sabbaths in a row he opened the Scriptures to the people,

3 Explaining the prophecies about the sufferings of the Messiah and His coming back to life, and proving that Jesus is the Messiah.

4 Some who listened were persuaded and became con-

verts—including a large number of godly Greek men, and also many important women of the city.

5 But the Jewish leaders were jealous and incited some worthless fellows from the streets to form a mob and start a riot. They attacked the home of Jason, planning to take Paul and Silas to the City Council for punishment.

6 Not finding them there, they dragged out Jason and some of the other believers, and took them before the Council. "Paul and Silas have turned the rest of the world upside down, and now they are here disturbing our city," they shouted,

7 "And Jason has let them into his home. They are all guilty of treason, for they claim another king, Jesus instead of Caesar."

8, 9 The people of the city, as well as the judges, were concerned at these reports and only let them go after they had posted bail.

10 That night the Christians hurried Paul and Silas to Beroea, and, as usual,* they went to the synagogue to preach.

11 But the people of Beroea were more open-minded than those in Thessalonica, and gladly listened to the message. They searched the scriptures day by day to check up on Paul and Silas' statements to see if they were really so.

12 As a result, many of them believed, including several prominent Greek women and many men also.

13 But when the Jews in Thessalonica learned that Paul was preaching in Beroea, they went over and stirred up trouble.

14 The believers acted at once, sending Paul on to the coast, while Silas and Timothy remained behind.

15 Those accompanying Paul went on with him to Athens, and then returned to Beroea with a message for Silas and Timothy to hurry and join him.

16 While Paul was waiting for them in Athens, he was deeply troubled by all the idols he saw everywhere throughout the city.

17 He went to the synagogue for discussions with the Jews and the devout Gentiles, and spoke daily in the public square to all who happened to be there.

18 He also had an encounter with some of the Epi-

curean and Stoic philosophers. Their reaction, when he told them about Jesus and His resurrection, was, "He's a dreamer," or, "He's pushing some foreign religion."

19 But they invited him to the forum at Mars Hill. "Come and tell us more about this new religion," they said,

20 "For you are saying some rather startling things and we want to hear more."

21 (I should explain that all the Athenians as well as the foreigners in Athens seemed to spend all their time discussing the latest new ideas!)

22 So Paul, standing before them at the Mars Hill forum, addressed them as follows:

"Men of Athens, I notice that you are very religious,

23 For as I was out walking I saw your many altars, and one of them had this inscription on it—'To the Unknown God.' You have been worshiping Him without knowing who He is, and now I wish to tell you about Him.

24 He made the world and everything in it, and since He is Lord of heaven and earth, He doesn't live in manmade temples;

25 And human hands can't minister to His needs—for He has no needs! He Himself gives life and breath to everything, and satisfies every need there is.

26 He created all the people of the world from one man, Adam,* and scattered the nations across the face of the earth. He decided beforehand which should rise and fall, and when. He determined their boundaries.

27 His purpose in all of this is that they should seek after God, and perhaps feel their way toward Him and find Him—though He is not far from any one of us.

28 For in Him we live and move and are! As one of your own poets says it, 'We are the sons of God.'

29 If this is true, we shouldn't think of God as an idol made by men from gold or silver or chipped from stone.

30 God tolerated man's past ignorance about these things, but now He commands everyone to put away idols and worship only Him.

31 For He has set a day for justly judging the world by the man He has appointed, and has pointed Him out by bringing Him back to life again."

32 When they heard Paul speak of the resurrection

of a person who had been dead, some laughed, but others said, "We want to hear more about this later."

33   That ended Paul's discussion with them,

34   But a few joined him and became believers. Among them was Dionysius, a member of the City Council, and a woman named Damaris, and others.

CHAPTER 18

Then Paul left Athens and went to Corinth.

2, 3   There he became acquainted with a Jew named Aquila, born in Pontus, who had recently arrived from Italy with his wife, Priscilla. They had been expelled from Italy as a result of Claudius Caesar's order to deport all Jews from Rome. Paul lived and worked with them, for they were tentmakers just as he was.

4   Each Sabbath found him at the synagogue, trying to convince the Jews and Greeks alike.

5   After the arrival of Silas and Timothy from Macedonia, Paul spent his full time preaching and testifying to the Jews that Jesus is the Messiah.

6   But when the Jews opposed him and blasphemed, hurling abuse at Jesus, Paul shook off the dust from his robe and said, "Your blood be upon your own heads—I am innocent—from now on I will preach to the Gentiles."

7   After that he stayed with Titus Justus, a Gentile* who worshiped God and lived next door to the synagogue.

8   Crispus, the leader of the synagogue, and all his household believed in the Lord and were baptized—as were many others in Corinth.

9   One night the Lord spoke to Paul in a vision and told him, "Don't be afraid! Speak out! Don't quit!

10   For I am with you and no one can harm you. Many people here in this city belong to Me."

11   So Paul stayed there the next year and a half, teaching the truths of God.

12   But when Gallio became governor of Achaia, the Jews rose in concerted action against Paul and brought him before the governor for judgment.

13   They accused Paul of "persuading men to worship God in ways that are contrary to Roman law."

14   But just as Paul started to make his defense,

Gallio turned to his accusers and said, "Listen, you Jews, if this were a case involving some crime, I would be obliged to listen to you,

15 But since it is merely a bunch of questions of semantics and personalities and your silly Jewish laws, you take care of it. I'm not interested and I'm not touching it."

16 And he drove them out of the courtroom.

17 Then the mob* grabbed Sosthenes, the new leader of the synagogue, and beat him outside the courtroom! But Gallio couldn't have cared less.

18 Paul stayed in the city several days after that and then said good-bye to the Christians and sailed for the coast of Syria, taking Priscilla and Aquila with him. (At Cenchrea, Paul had his head shaved according to Jewish custom, for he had taken a vow.)

19 Arriving at the port of Ephesus, he left us aboard ship while he went over to the synagogue for a discussion with the Jews.

20 They asked him to stay for a few days, but he felt that he had no time to lose.

21 "I must by all means be at Jerusalem for the holiday," he said. But he promised to return to Ephesus later if God permitted; and so we set sail again.

22 The next stop was at the port of Caesarea from where he visited the church (at Jerusalem*) and then sailed on to Antioch.

23 After spending some time there, he left for Turkey again, going through Galatia and Phrygia visiting all the believers, encouraging them and helping them grow in the Lord.

24 As it happened, a Jew named Apollos, a wonderful Bible teacher and preacher, had just arrived in Ephesus from Alexandria in Egypt.

25, 26 While he was in Egypt, someone had told him about John the Baptist and all that John had said about Jesus, but that is all he knew! He had never heard the rest of the story! So he was preaching boldly and enthusiastically in the synagogue, "The Messiah is coming! Get ready to receive Him!" Priscilla and Aquila were there and heard him—and it was a powerful sermon. Afterwards they met with him and explained what had happened to Jesus since the time of John, and all that it meant!

27 Apollos had been thinking about going to Greece, and the believers encouraged him in this. They wrote to their fellow-believers there, telling them to welcome him. And upon his arrival in Greece, he was greatly used of God to strengthen the church,

28 For he powerfully refuted all the Jewish arguments in public debate, showing by the Scriptures that Jesus is indeed the Messiah.

CHAPTER 19

While Apollos was in Corinth, Paul traveled through Turkey and arrived in Ephesus, where he found several disciples.

2 He asked them, "Did you receive the Holy Spirit when you believed?"

"No," they replied, "we don't know what you mean. What is the Holy Spirit?"

3 "Then what beliefs did you acknowledge at your baptism?" he asked.

And they replied, "What John the Baptist taught."

4 Then Paul pointed out to them that John's baptism was to demonstrate a desire to turn from sin to God and that those receiving his baptism must then go on to believe in Jesus, the one John said would come later.

5 As soon as they heard this, they were baptized in the name of the Lord Jesus.

6 Then, when Paul laid his hands upon their heads, the Holy Spirit came on them, and they spoke in other languages and prophesied.

7 (The men involved were about 12 in number).

8 Then Paul went to the synagogue and preached boldly each Sabbath day* for three months, telling what he believed and why, and persuading many to believe in Jesus.

9 But some rejected his message and publicly spoke against Christ, so he left, refusing to preach to them again. Pulling out the believers he began a separate meeting at the lecture hall of Tryannus and preached there daily.

10 This went on for the next two years, so that everyone in the Turkish province of Ausia—both Jews and Greeks—heard the Lord's message.

11 And God gave Paul the power to do unusual miracles,

12 So that even when his handkerchiefs or parts of his clothing were placed upon sick people, they were healed and any demons within them came out.

13 A team of itinerant Jews who were traveling from town to town casting out demons planned to experiment by using the name of the Lord Jesus. The incantation they decided on was this: "I adjure you by Jesus, whom Paul preaches, to come out!"

14 Seven sons of Sceva, a Jewish chief priest, were doing this.

15 But when they tried it on a man possessed by a demon, the demon replied, "I know Jesus and I know Paul, but who are you?"

16 And the man leaped on two of them and beat them up, so that they fled from his home naked and badly injured.

17 The story of what happened spread quickly all through Ephesus, to Jews and Greeks alike; and a solemn fear descended on the city, and the name of the Lord Jesus was greatly honored.

18 Many of the believers who had been practicing black magic confessed their deeds.

19 Many of them brought their incantation books and charms and burned them at a public bonfire. (Someone estimated the value of the books at $10,000).

20 This indicates how deeply the whole area was stirred by God's message.

21 Afterwards, Paul felt impelled by the Holy Spirit to go across to Greece before returning to Jerusalem. "And after that," he said, "I must go to Rome!"

22 He sent his two assistants, Timothy and Erastus, on ahead to Greece while he stayed awhile longer in Turkey.

23 But about that time, a big blowup developed in Ephesus concerning the Christians.

24 It began with Demetrius, a silversmith who employed many craftsmen to manufacture silver shrines of the Greek goddess Diana.

25 He called a meeting of his men, together with others employed in related trades, and addressed them as follows:

"Gentlemen, this business is our income.

26 As you know so well from what you've seen and heard, this man Paul has persuaded many, many people that handmade gods aren't gods at all. As a result, our sales volume is going down! And this trend is evident not only here in Ephesus, but throughout the entire province!

27 Of course, I am not only talking about the business aspects of this situation and our loss of income, but also of the possibility that the temple of the great goddess Diana will lose its influence, and that Diana—this magnificent goddess worshiped not only throughout this part of Turkey but all around the world—will be forgotten!"

28 At this their anger boiled and they began shouting, "Great is Diana of the Ephesians."

29 Crowds began to gather and soon the city was filled with confusion. Everyone rushed to the amphitheater, dragging along Gaius and Aristarchus, Paul's traveling companions for trial.

30 Paul wanted to go in, but the disciples wouldn't let him.

31 Some of the Roman officers of the province, friends of Paul, also sent a message to him, begging him not to risk his life by entering.

32 Inside, the people were all shouting, some one thing and some another—everything was in confusion. In fact, most of them didn't even know why they were there.

33 Alexander was spotted among the crowd by some of the Jews and dragged forward. He motioned for silence and tried to speak.

34 But when the crowd realized he was a Jew, they started shouting again and kept it up for two hours: "Great is Diana of the Ephesians! Great is Diana of the Ephesians!"

35 At last the mayor was able to quiet them down enough to speak. "Men of Ephesus," he said, "everyone knows that Ephesus is the center of the religion of the great Diana, whose image fell down to us from heaven.

36 Since this is an indisputable fact, you shouldn't be

disturbed no matter what is said, and should do nothing rash.

37 You have brought these men here who have stolen nothing from her temple and not defamed her.

38 If Demetrius and the craftsmen have a case against these men, the courts are currently in session and the judges can take the case at once. Let them go through legal channels.

39 If you have complaints about other matters, they can be settled at the regular City Council meetings,

40 For we are in danger of being called to account by the Roman government for today's riot, since there is no cause for it. And if Rome demands an explanation, I won't know what to say."

41 Then he dismissed them, and they dispersed.

CHAPTER 20

W hen it was all over, Paul sent for the disciples, preached a farewell message to them, said good-by and left for Greece,

2 Preaching to the believers along the way, in all the cities he passed through.

3 He was in Greece three months and was preparing to sail for Syria when he discovered a plot by the Jews against his life, so he decided to go north to Macedonia first.

4 Several men were traveling with him, going as far as Turkey, they were Sopater of Berea, the son of Pyrrhus; Aristarchus and Secundus, from Thessalonica; Gaius, from Derbe; and Timothy. Two of his own group, Tychicus and Trophimus, were returning to their homes in Turkey,

5 And had gone on ahead and were waiting for us at Troas.

6 As soon as the Passover ceremonies ended, we boarded ship at Philippi in northern Greece and five days later arrived in Troas, Turkey, where we stayed a week.

7 On Sunday, we gathered for a communion service, with Paul preaching. And since he was leaving the next day, he talked until midnight!

8 The upstairs room where we met was lighted with many flickering lamps;

9 And as Paul spoke on and on, a young man named

Eutychus, sitting on the window sill, went fast asleep and fell three stories to his death below.

10, 11, 12 Paul went down and gathered him into his arms. "Don't worry," he said, "he's all right!" And he was! What a wave of awesome joy swept through the crowd! They all went back upstairs and ate the Lord's Supper together; then Paul preached another long sermon—so it was dawn when he finally left them!

13 Paul was going by land to Assos, and we went on ahead by ship.

14 Paul joined us there and we sailed together to Mitylene;

15 The next day we passed Chios; the next, we touched at Samos; and a day later we arrived at Miletus.

16 Paul had decided against stopping at Ephesus this time, as he was hurrying to get to Jerusalem, if possible, for the celebration of Pentecost.

17 But when we landed at Miletus, he sent a message to the elders of the church at Ephesus asking them to come down to the boat to meet him.

18 When they arrived he told them, "You men know that from the day I set foot in Turkey until now

19 I have done the Lord's work humbly—yes, and with tears—and have faced grave danger from the plots of the Jews against my life.

20 Yet I never shrank from telling you the truth, both publicly and in your homes.

21 I have had one message for Jews and Gentiles alike—the necessity of turning from sin to God through faith in our Lord Jesus Christ.

22 And now I am going to Jerusalem, drawn there irresistibly by the Holy Spirit, not knowing what awaits me,

23 Except that the Holy Spirit has told me in city after city that jail and suffering lie ahead.

24 But life is worth nothing unless I use it for doing the work assigned me by the Lord Jesus—the work of telling others the Good News about God's mighty kindness and love.

25 And now I know that none of you among whom I went about teaching the Kingdom will ever see me again.

26 Let me now say clearly that no man's blood can be laid at my door,

27 For I didn't shrink from declaring all God's message to you.

28 And now beware! Be sure that you feed and shepherd God's flock—His church, purchased with His blood —for the Holy Spirit is holding you responsible as overseers.

29 I know full well that after I leave you, false teachers, like vicious wolves, will appear among you, not sparing the flock.

30 Some of you yourselves will distort the truth in order to draw a following.

31 Watch out! Remember the three years I was with you—my constant watchcare over you, night and day—my many tears for you.

32 And now I entrust you to God and His care and to His wonderful words, which are able to build your faith and give you all the inheritance of those who are set apart for Himself.

33 I have never been hungry for money or fine clothing—

34 You know that these hands of mine worked to pay my own way and even to supply the needs of those who were with me.

35 And I was a constant example to you in helping the poor; for I remembered the words of the Lord Jesus, 'It is more blessed to give than to receive.' "

36 When he had finished speaking, he knelt and prayed with them,

37 And they wept aloud as they embraced him in farewell,

38 Sorrowing most of all because he said that he would never see them again. Then they accompanied him down to the ship.

CHAPTER 21

After parting from the Ephesian elders, we sailed straight to Cos; the next day we reached Rhodes and then went to Patara.

2 There we boarded a ship sailing for the Syrian province of Phoenicia.

3 We sighted the island of Cyprus, passed it on our

left and landed at the harbor of Tyre, in Syria, where the ship unloaded.

4 We went ashore and found the local believers and stayed with them a week. These disciples warned Paul —the Holy Spirit prophesying through them—not to go to Jerusalem.

5 At the end of the week when we were to return to the ship, the entire congregation, including wives and children, walked down to the beach with us where we prayed and said our farewells.

6 Then we went aboard and they returned home.

7 The next stop after leaving Tyre was Ptolemais. We greeted the believers, but stayed only one day.

8 The next day we went on to Caesarea and stayed at the home of Philip the Evangelist, one of the first seven deacons.

9 (He had four unmarried daughters who had the gift of prophecy).

10 During our stay of several days, a man named Agabus, who also had the gift of prophecy, arrived from Judea

11 And visited us. He took Paul's belt, bound his own feet and hands with it and said, "The Holy Spirit declares, 'So shall the owner of this belt be bound by the Jews in Jerusalem and turned over to the Romans.'"

12 Hearing this, all of us—the local believers and his traveling companions—begged Paul not to go on to Jerusalem.

13 But he said, "Why all this weeping? You are breaking my heart! For I am ready not only to be jailed at Jerusalem, but also to die for the sake of the Lord Jesus."

14 When it was clear that he wouldn't be dissuaded, we gave up and said, "The will of the Lord be done."

15 So shortly afterwards, we packed our things and left for Jerusalem.

16 Some disciples from Caesarea accompanied us, and on arrival we were guests at the home of Mnason, originally from Cyprus, one of the early believers;

17 And all the believers at Jerusalem welcomed us cordially.

18 The second day Paul took us with him to meet with James and the elders of the Jerusalem church.

19 After greetings were exchanged, Paul recounted the many things God had accomplished among the Gentiles through his work.

20 They praised God but then said, "You know, dear brother, how many thousands of Jews have also believed, and they are all very insistent that Jewish believers must continue to follow the Jewish traditions and customs.

21 Our Jewish Christians here at Jerusalem have been told that you are against the laws of Moses, against our Jewish customs, and that you forbid the circumcision of their children.

22 Now what can be done? For they will certainly hear that you have come.

23 We suggest this: We have four men here who are preparing to shave their heads and take some vows.

24 We suggest that you go with them to the Temple and have your head shaved too—and pay for theirs to be shaved. Then everyone will know that you approve of this custom for the Hebrew Christians and that you yourself obey the Jewish laws and are in line with our thinking in these matters.

25 As for the Gentile Christians, we aren't asking them to follow these Jewish customs at all—except for the ones we wrote to them about; not to eat food offered to idols, not to eat unbled meat from strangled animals, and not to commit fornication."

26, 27 So Paul agreed to their request and the next day went with the men to the Temple for the ceremony, thus publicizing his vow to offer a sacrifice (seven days later*) with the others. The seven days were almost ended when some Jews from Turkey saw him in the Temple and roused a mob against him. They grabbed him,

28 Yelling, "Men of Israel! Help! Help! This is the man who preaches against our people and tells everybody to disobey the Jewish laws. He even talks against the Temple and defiles it by bringing Gentiles in!"

29 (For down in the city earlier that day, they had seen him with Trophimus, a Gentile* from Ephesus in Turkey, and assumed that Paul had taken him into the Temple.)

30 The whole population of the city was electrified

by these accusations and a great riot followed. Paul was dragged out of the Temple, and immediately the gates were closed behind him.

31 As they were killing him, word reached the commander of the Roman garrison that all Jerusalem was in an uproar.

32 He quickly ordered out his soldiers and officers and ran down among the crowd. When the mob saw the troops coming, they quit beating Paul.

33 The commander arrested him and ordered him bound with double chains. Then he asked the crowd who he was and what he had done.

34 Some shouted one thing and some another. When he couldn't find out anything in all the uproar and confusion, he ordered Paul to be taken to the armory.

35 As they reached the stairs, the mob grew so violent that the soldiers lifted Paul to their shoulders to protect him,

36 And the crowd surged behind shouting, "Away with him, away with him!"

37, 38 As Paul was about to be taken inside, he said to the commander, "May I have a word with you?"

"Do you know Greek?" the commander asked, surprised. "Aren't you that Egyptian who led a rebellion a few years ago and took 4,000 members of the Assassins with him into the deserts?"

39 "No," Paul replied, "I am a Jew from Tarsus in Cilicia, a Roman citizen,* and from no small town either! I request permission to talk to these people."

40 The commander agreed, so Paul stood on the stairs and motioned to the people to be quiet; soon a deep silence enveloped the crowd, and he addressed them in Hebrew as follows:

CHAPTER 22

Brothers and fathers, listen to me as I offer my defense."

2 (When they heard him speak in Hebrew, the silence was even greater.)

3 "I am a Jew," he said, "born in Tarsus, a city in Cilicia, but educated here in Jerusalem under Gamaliel, at whose feet I learned to follow our Jewish laws and

customs very carefully. I became very anxious to honor
God in everything I did, just the same as you have tried
to do today.

4   And I persecuted the Christians, hounding them to
death, binding and delivering both men and women to
prison.

5   The High Priest can testify that this is so, or any
member of the Council. For I asked them for letters to
the Jewish leaders in Damascus, with instructions to
let me bring any Christian I found to Jerusalem in chains
to be punished.

6   As I was on the road, nearing Damascus, suddenly
about noon, a very bright light from heaven shone around
me,

7   And I fell to the ground and heard a voice saying to
me, 'Saul, Saul, why are you persecuting me?'

8   'Who is it speaking to me, sir?' I asked. And He
replied, 'I am Jesus of Nazareth, the One you are persecuting.'

9   The men with me saw the light but didn't understand what was said.

10   And I said, 'What shall I do, Lord?' And the Lord
told me, 'Get up and go into Damascus, and there you
will be told what awaits you in the years ahead.'

11   I was blinded by the intense light, and had to be
led into Damascus by my companions.

12   There a man named Ananias, as godly a man as
you could find for obeying the law, and well thought of
by all the Jews of Damascus,

13   Came to me, and standing beside me said,
'Brother Saul, receive your sight!' And that very hour I
could see him!

14   Then he told me, 'The God of our fathers has
chosen you to know His will and to see the Messiah and
hear Him speak.

15   You are to take His message everywhere, telling
what you have seen and heard.

16   And now, why delay? Go and be baptized, and be
cleansed from your sins, calling on the name of the
Lord.'

17, 18   One day while I was praying in the Temple
after my return to Jerusalem, I fell into a trance and saw
a vision of God saying to me, 'Hurry! Leave Jerusalem,

for the people here won't believe you when you give them My message.'

19   'But Lord,' I argued, 'they certainly know that I imprisoned and beat those in every synagogue who believed on You.

20   And when Your witness Stephen was killed, I was standing there agreeing—keeping the robes they laid aside as they stoned him.'

21   But God said to me, 'Leave Jerusalem, for I will send you far away to the *Gentiles*!' "

22   The crowd listened until Paul came to that word, then with one voice they shouted, "Away with such a fellow! Kill him! He isn't fit to live!"

23   They yelled and threw their coats in the air and tossed up handfuls of dust.

24   So the commander brought him inside and ordered him lashed with whips to make him confess his crime. He wanted to find out why the crowd had become so furious!

25   As they tied Paul down to lash him, Paul said to an officer standing there, "Is it legal for you to whip a Roman citizen who hasn't even been tried?"

26   The officer went to the commander and asked, "What are you doing? This man is a Roman citizen!"

27   So the commander went over and asked Paul, "Tell me, are you a Roman citizen?"

"Yes, I certainly am."

28   "I am too," the commander muttered, "and it cost me plenty!"

"But I am a citizen by birth!"

29   The soldiers standing ready to lash him, quickly disappeared when they heard Paul was a Roman citizen, and the commander was frightened because he had ordered him bound and whipped.

30   The next day the commander freed him from his chains and ordered the chief priests into session with the Jewish Council. He had Paul brought in before them to try to find out what the trouble was all about.

CHAPTER 23

Gazing intently at the Council, Paul began: "Brothers, I have always lived before God in all good conscience!"

2 Instantly Ananias the High Priest commanded those close to Paul to slap him on the mouth.

3 Paul said to him, "God shall slap you, you painted pigpen. What kind of judge are you to break the law yourself by ordering me struck like that?"

4 Those standing near Paul said to him, "Is that the way to talk to God's High Priest?"

5 "I didn't realize he was the High Priest, brothers," Paul replied, "for the Scriptures say, 'Never speak evil of any of your rulers.' "

6 Then Paul thought of something! Part of the Council were Sadducees, and part were Pharisees! So he shouted, "Brothers, I am a Pharisee, as were all my ancestors! And I am being tried here today because I believe in the resurrection of the dead!"

7 This divided the Council right down the middle—the Pharisees against the Sadducees—

8 For the Sadducees say there is no resurrection or angels or even eternal spirit within us, but the Pharisees believe in all of these.

9 So a great clamor arose. Some of the Jewish leaders jumped up to argue that Paul was all right. "We see nothing wrong with him," they shouted. "Perhaps a spirit or angel spoke to him (there on the Damascus road*)."

10 The shouting grew louder and louder, and the men were tugging at Paul from both sides, pulling him this way and that. Finally the commander, fearing they would tear him apart, ordered his soldiers to take him away from them by force and bring him back to the armory.

11 That night the Lord stood beside Paul and said, "Don't worry, Paul; just as you have told the people about Me here in Jerusalem, so you must in Rome."

12, 13 The next morning some 40 or more of the Jews got together and bound themselves by a curse neither to eat nor drink until they had killed Paul!

14 Then they went to the chief priests and elders and told them what they had done.

15 "Ask the commander to bring Paul back to the Council," they requested. Pretend you want to ask a few more questions. We will kill him on the way."

16 But Paul's nephew got wind of their plan and came to the armory and told Paul.

17 Paul called one of the officers and said, "Take this boy to the commander. He has something important to tell him."

18 So the officer did, explaining, "Paul, the prisoner, called me over and asked me to bring this young man to you to tell you something."

19 The commander took the boy by the hand, and leading him aside asked, "What is it you want to tell me, lad?"

20 "The Jews," he told him, "are going to ask you to bring Paul before the Council again tomorrow, pretending they want to get some more information.

21 But don't do it! There are more than 40 men hiding along the road ready to jump him and kill him. They have bound themselves under a curse to neither eat nor drink till he is dead. They are out there now, expecting you to agree to their request."

22 "Don't let a soul know you told me this," the commander warned the boy as he left.

23, 24 Then the commander called two of his officers and ordered, "Get 200 soldiers ready to leave for Caesarea by nine o'clock tonight! Also take 200 spearmen and 70 mounted cavalry and get Paul safely to Felix, the governor!" He also ordered them to give Paul a horse to ride on.

25 Then he wrote this letter to the governor:

26 *"From:* Claudius Lysias
To: His Excellency, Governor Felix.
Greetings!

27 This man was seized by the Jews and they were killing him when I sent the soldiers to rescue him, for I learned that he was a Roman citizen.

28 Then I took him to their Council to try to find out what he had done.

29 I soon discovered it was something about their

Jewish beliefs, certainly nothing worthy of imprisonment or death.

30 But when I was informed of a plot to kill him, I decided to send him on to you and will tell his accusers to bring their charges before you."

31 So that night, as ordered, the soldiers took Paul to Antipatris.

32 They returned to the armory the next morning, leaving him with the horsemen to take him to Caesarea.

33 When they arrived in Caesarea, they presented Paul and the letter to the governor.

34 He read it and then asked Paul where he was from.

"Cilicia," Paul answered.

35 "I will hear your case fully when your accusers arrive, the governor told him," and ordered him kept in the prison in King Herod's palace.

CHAPTER 24

Five days later Ananias the High Priest arrived with some of the Jewish leaders and the lawyer Tertullus, to make their accusations against Paul.

2 When Tertullus was called forward, he laid their charges against Paul in the following address to the governor:

"Your Excellency, you have given quietness and peace to us Jews and have reduced the discrimination against us.

3 We are very, very grateful to you.

4 But lest I be tedious, please listen to me in your kindness as I briefly outline our case against this man.

5 For we have found him to be a troublemaker, a man who is constantly inciting the Jews throughout the entire world to riots and rebellions against the Roman government. He is a ringleader of the sect known as the Nazarenes.

6 Moreover, he was trying to defile the Temple when we arrested him. We would have given him what he justly deserves,

7 But Lysias, the commander of the garrison, came and took him violently away from us, .

8 Demanding that he be tried by Roman law. You can find out the truth of our accusations by examining him yourself."

9 Then all the other Jews chimed in, declaring that everything Tertullus said was true.

10 Now it was Paul's turn. The governor motioned for him to rise and speak. Paul began: "I know, sir, that you have been a judge of Jewish affairs for many years, and this gives me confidence as I make my defense.

11 You can quickly discover that it was no more than twelve days ago that I arrived in Jerusalem to worship at the Temple,

12 And you will discover that I have never incited a riot in any synagogue or on the streets of any city;

13 And these men certainly cannot prove the things they accuse me of doing.

14 But one thing I do confess, that I believe in the way of salvation, which they refer to as a sect; I follow that system of serving the God of our ancestors; I firmly believe in the Jewish law and everything written in the books of prophecy;

15 And I believe, just as these men do, that there will be a resurrection of both the righteous and ungodly.

16 Bcause of this I try with all my strength to always maintain a clear conscience before God and man.

17 After several years away, I returned to Jerusalem with money to aid the Jews, and to offer a sacrifice to God.

18 My accusers saw me in the Temple as I was presenting my thank offering.* I had shaved my head as their laws required, and there was no crowd around me, and no rioting! But some Jews from Turkey were there

19 (Who ought to be here if they have anything against me)—

20 But look! Ask these men right here what wrongdoing their Council found in me,

21 Except that I said one thing I shouldn't when I shouted out, 'I am here before the Council to defend myself for believing that the dead will rise again!' "

22 Felix, who knew Christians didn't go around starting riots, told the Jews to wait for the arrival of Lysias, the garrison commander, and then he would decide the case.

23 He ordered Paul to prison but instructed the

guards to treat him gently and not to forbid any of his friends from visiting him or bringing him gifts to make his stay more comfortable.

24 A few days later Felix came with Drusilla, his legal wife, a Jewess. Sending for Paul, they listened as he told them about faith in Christ Jesus.

25 And as he reasoned with them about righteousness and self-control and the judgment to come, Felix was terrified. "Go away for now," he replied, "and when I have a more convenient time, I'll call for you again."

26 He also hoped that Paul would bribe him, so he sent for him from time to time and talked with him.

27 Two years went by in this way; then Felix was succeeded by Porcius Festus. And because Felix wanted to gain favor with the Jews, he left Paul in chains.

CHAPTER 25

Three days after Festus arrived in Caesarea to take over his new responsibilities, he left for Jerusalem,

2 Where the chief priests and other Jewish leaders got hold of him and gave him their story about Paul.

3 They begged him to bring Paul to Jerusalem at once. (Their plan was to waylay and kill him.)

4 But Festus replied that since Paul was at Caesarea and he himself was returning there soon,

5 Those with authority in this affair should return with him for the trial.

6 Eight or ten days later he returned to Caesarea and the following day opened Paul's trial.

7 On Paul's arrival in court the Jews from Jerusalem gathered around, hurling many serious accusations which they couldn't prove.

8 Paul denied the charges: "I am not guilty," he said. "I have not opposed the Jewish laws or desecrated the Temple or rebelled against the Roman government."

9 Then Festus, anxious to please the Jews, asked him, "Are you willing to go to Jerusalem and stand trial before me?"

10, 11 But Paul replied, "No! I demand my privilege of a hearing before the Emperor himself. You know very well I am not guilty. If I have done something worthy of death, I don't refuse to die! But if I am innocent, neither you nor anyone else has a right to turn me over to these men to kill me. *I appeal to Caesar.*"

12   Festus conferred with his advisors and then replied, "Very well! You have appealed to Caesar, and to Caesar you shall go!"

13   A few days later King Agrippa arrived with Bernice for a visit with Festus.

14   During their stay of several days Festus discussed Paul's case with the king. "There is a prisoner here," he told him, "whose case was left for me by Felix.

15   When I was in Jerusalem, the chief priests and other Jewish leaders gave me their side of the story and asked me to have him killed.

16   Of course I quickly pointed out to them that Roman law does not convict a man before he is tried. He is given an opportunity to defend himself face to face with his accusers.

17   When they came here for the trial, I called the case the very next day and ordered Paul brought in.

18   But the accusations made against him weren't at all what I supposed they would be.

19   It was something about their religion, and about Someone called Jesus who died, but Paul insists is alive!

20   I was perplexed as to how to decide a case of this kind and asked him whether he would be willing to stand trial on these charges in Jerusalem.

21   But Paul appealed to Caesar! So I ordered him back to jail until I could arrange to get him to the Emperor."

22   "I'd like to hear the man myself," Agrippa said. And Festus replied, "You shall—tomorrow!"

23   So the next day, after the king and Bernice had arrived at the courtroom with great pomp, accompanied by military officers and prominent men of the city, Festus ordered Paul brought in.

24   Then Festus addressed the audience: "King Agrippa and all present," he said, "this is the man whose death is demanded both by the local Jews and those in Jerusalem!

25   But in my opinion he has done nothing worthy of death. However, he appealed his case to Caesar, and I have no alternative but to send him.

26 But what shall I write the Emperor? For there is no real charge against him! So I have brought him before you all, and especially you, King Agrippa, to examine him and then tell me what to write.

27 For it doesn't seem reasonable to send a prisoner to the Emperor without any charges against him!"

CHAPTER 26

Then Agrippa said to Paul, "Go ahead. Tell us your story." So Paul, with many gestures, presented his defense:

2 "I am fortunate, King Agrippa," he began, "to be able to present my answers before you,

3 For I know you are an expert on Jewish laws and customs. Now please listen patiently!

4 As the Jews are well aware, I was given a thorough Jewish training from my earliest childhood in Tarsus and later at Jerusalem, and I lived accordingly.

5 If they would admit it, they know that I have always been the strictest of Pharisees when it comes to obedience to Jewish laws and customs.

6 But the real reason behind their accusations is something else—it is because I am looking forward to the fulfillment of God's promise made to our ancestors.

7 The 12 tribes of Israel strive night and day to attain this same hope I have! Yet, O King, for me it is a crime, they say!

8 But is it a crime to believe in the resurrection of the dead? Does it seem incredible to you that God can bring men back to life again?

9 I used to believe that I ought to do many horrible things to the followers of Jesus of Nazareth.

10 I imprisoned many of the saints in Jerusalem, as authorized by the High Priests; and when they were condemned to death, I cast my vote against them.

11 I used torture to try to make Christians everywhere curse Christ. I was so violently opposed to them that I even hounded them in distant cities in foreign lands.

12 I was on such a mission to Damascus, armed with the authority and commission of the chief priests,

13 When one day about noon, sir, a light from

heaven brighter than the sun shone down on me and my companions.

14 We all fell down, and I heard a voice speaking to me in Hebrew, 'Saul, Saul, why are you persecuting Me? You are only hurting yourself.'

15 'Who are you, Sir?' I asked. And the Lord replied, 'I am Jesus, the One you are persecuting.

16 Now stand up! For I have appeared to you to appoint you as My servant and My witness. You are to tell the world about this experience and about the many other occasions when I shall appear to you.

17 And I will protect you from both your own people and the Gentiles. Yes, I am going to send you to the Gentiles

18 To open their eyes to their true condition so that they may repent and live in the light of God instead of in Satan's darkness, so that they may receive forgiveness for their sins and God's inheritance along with all people everywhere whose sins are cleansed away, who are set apart by faith in Me.'

19 And so, O King Agrippa, I was not disobedient to that vision from heaven!

20 I preached first to those in Damascus, then in Jerusalem and through Judea, and also to the Gentiles that all must forsake their sins and turn to God—and prove their repentance by doing good deeds.

21 The Jews arrested me in the Temple for preaching this and tried to kill me,

22 But God protected me so that I am still alive today to tell these facts to everyone, both great and small. I teach nothing except what the prophets and Moses said—

23 That the Messiah would suffer, and be the First to rise from the dead, to bring light to Jews and Gentiles alike."

24 Suddenly Festus shouted, "Paul, you are insane. Your long studying has broken your mind!"

25 But Paul replied, "I am not insane, Most Excellent Festus. I speak words of sober truth,

26 And King Agrippa knows about these things. I speak frankly for I am sure these events are all familiar to him, for they were not done in a corner!

27 King Agrippa, do you believe the prophets? But I know you do—"

28 Agrippa interrupted him. "With trivial proofs like these, you expect me to become a Christian?"

29 And Paul replied, "Would to God that whether my arguments are trivial or strong, both you and everyone here in this audience might become the same as I am, except for these chains."

30 Then the king and the governor, Bernice and all the others stood and left.

31 As they talked it over afterwards they agreed, "This man hasn't done anything worthy of death or imprisonment."

32 And Agrippa said to Festus, "He could be set free if he hadn't appealed to Caesar!"

CHAPTER 27

A rrangements were finally made to start us on our way to Rome by ship; so Paul and several other prisoners were placed in the custody of an officer named Julius, a member of the imperial guard.

2 We left on a boat bound for Greece, which was scheduled to make several stops along the Turkish coast. I should add that Aristarchus, a Greek from Thessalonica, was with us.

3 The next day when we docked at Sidon, Julius was very kind to Paul and let him go ashore to visit with friends and receive their hospitality.

4 Putting to sea from there, we encountered headwinds that made it difficult to keep the ship on course, so we sailed north of Cyprus between the island and the mainland,*

5 And passed along the coast of the provinces of Cilicia and Pamphylia, landing at Myra, in the province of Lycia.

6 There our officer found an Egyptian ship from Alexandria, bound for Italy, and put us aboard.

7, 8 We had several days of rough sailing, and finally neared Cnidus; but the winds had become too strong, so we ran across to Crete, passing the port of Salmone. Beating into the wind with great difficulty and moving slowly along the southern coast, we arrived at Fair Havens, near the city of Lasea.

9　There we stayed for several days. The weather was becoming dangerous for long voyages by then, because it was late in the year, and Paul spoke to the ship's officers about it.

10　"Sirs," he said, "I believe there is trouble ahead if we go on—perhaps shipwreck, loss of cargo, injuries, and death."

11　But the officers in charge of the prisoners listened more to the ship's captain and the owner than to Paul.

12　And since Fair Havens was an exposed harbor*—a poor place to spend the winter—most of the crew advised trying to go further up the coast to Phoenix, in order to winter there. (Phoenix was a good harbor with only a northwest and southwest exposure.)

13　Just then a light wind began blowing from the south, and it looked like a perfect day for the trip; so they pulled up anchor and sailed along close to shore.

14, 15　But shortly afterwards, the weather changed abruptly and a heavy wind of typhoon strength (a "northeaster," they called it) caught the ship and blew it out to sea. They tried at first to face back to shore but couldn't, so they gave up and let the ship run before the gale.

16　We finally sailed behind a small island named Clauda, where with great difficulty, we hoisted aboard the lifeboat that was being towed behind us,

17　And then banded the ship with ropes to strengthen the hull. The sailors were afraid of being driven across to the quicksands of the African coast, so they lowered the topsails and were thus driven before the wind.

18　The next day as the seas grew higher, the crew began throwing the cargo overboard.

19　The following day they threw out the tackle and anything else they could lay their hands on.

20　The terrible storm raged unabated many days, until at last all hope was gone.

21　No one had eaten for a long time, but finally Paul called the crew together and said, "Men, you should have listened to me in the first place and not left Fair Havens—you would have avoided all this injury and loss!

22   But cheer up! Not one of us will lose our lives, even though the ship will go down.

23   For last night an angel of the God (to whom I belong and whom I serve) stood beside me,

24   And said, 'Don't be afraid, Paul—for you will surely stand trial before Caesar! What's more, God has granted your request and will save the lives of all those sailing with you.'

25   So cheer up! For I believe God! It will be just as He said!

26   But we will be shipwrecked on an island."

27   About midnight on the 14th night of the storm, as we were being driven to and fro on the Adriatic Sea, the sailors suspected land was near.

28   They sounded, and found 120 feet of water below them. A little later they sounded again, and found only 90 feet.

29   At this rate they knew they would soon be driven ashore; and fearing rocks along the coast, they threw out four anchors from the stern and prayed for daylight.

30   Some of the sailors planned to abandon the ship, and lowered the emergency boat as though they were going to put out anchors from the prow.

31   But Paul said to the soldiers and commanding officer, "You will all die unless everyone stays aboard."

32   So the soldiers cut the ropes and let the boat fall off.

33   As the darkness gave way to the early morning light, Paul begged everyone to eat: "You haven't touched food for two weeks," he said.

34   "Please eat something now for your own good. For not a hair of your heads shall perish!"

35   Then he took some hardtack and gave thanks to God before them all, and broke off a piece and ate it.

36   Suddenly everyone felt better and began eating—

37   All two hundred seventy-six of us—for that is the number we had aboard.

38   After eating, the crew lightened the ship again by throwing all the wheat overboard.

39   When it was day, they didn't recognize the coastline, but noticed a bay with a beach and wondered whether they could get between the rocks and be driven up onto the beach.

40   They finally decided to try. Cutting off the anchors and leaving them in the sea, they lowered the rudders, raised the foresail and headed ashore.

41   But the ship hit a sandbar and ran aground. The bow of the ship stuck fast, while the stern was exposed to the violence of the waves and began to break apart.

42   The soldiers advised their commanding officer to let them kill the prisoners lest any of them swim ashore and escape.

43   But Julius* wanted to spare Paul, so he told them no. Then he ordered all who could swim to jump overboard and make for land

44   And the rest to try for it on planks and debris from the broken ship. So everyone escaped safely ashore!

CHAPTER 28

We soon learned that we were on the island of Malta. The people of the island were very kind to us, building a bonfire on the beach to welcome and warm us in the rain and cold.

3   As Paul gathered an armful of sticks to lay on the fire, a poisonous snake, driven out by the heat, fastened itself onto his hand!

4   The people of the island saw it hanging there and said to each other, "A murderer, no doubt! Though he escaped the sea, justice will not permit him to live!"

5   But Paul shook off the snake into the fire and was unharmed.

6   The people waited for him to begin swelling or suddenly fall dead; but when they had waited a long time and no harm came to him, they changed their minds and decided he was a god.

7   Near the shore where we landed was an estate belonging to Publius, the governor of the island. He welcomed us courteously and fed us for three days.

8   As it happened, Publius' father was ill with fever and dysentery. Paul went in and prayed for him, and laying his hands on him, healed him!

9   Then all the other sick people in the island came and were cured.

10   As a result we were showered with gifts, and

when the time came to sail, people put on board all sorts of things we would need for the trip.

11 It was three months after the shipwreck before we set sail again, and this time it was in "The Twin Brothers" of Alexandria, a ship that had wintered at the island.

12 Our first stop was Syracuse, where we stayed three days.

13 From there we circled around to Rhegium; a day later a south wind began blowing, so the following day we arrived at Puteoli,

14 Where we found some believers! They begged us to stay with them seven days. Then, we sailed on to Rome.

15 The brothers in Rome had heard we were coming and came to meet us at the Forum on the Appian Way. Others joined us at The Three Taverns. When Paul saw them, he thanked God and took courage.

16 When we arrived in Rome, Paul was permitted to live wherever he wanted to, though guarded by a soldier.

17 Three days after his arrival, he called together the local Jewish leaders and spoke to them as follows:

"Brothers, I was arrested by the Jews in Jerusalem and handed over to the Roman government for prosecution, even though I had harmed no one nor violated the customs of our ancestors.

18 The Romans gave me a trial and wanted to release me, for they found no cause for the death sentence demanded by the Jewish leaders.

19 But when the Jews protested the decision, I felt it necessary, with no malice against them, to appeal to Caesar.

20 I asked you to come here today so we could get acquainted and I could tell you that it is because I believe the Messiah has come that I am bound with this chain."

21 They replied, "We have heard nothing against you! We have had no letters from Judea or reports from those arriving from Jerusalem.*

22 But we want to hear what you believe, for the only thing we know about these Christians is that they are denounced everywhere!"

23 So a time was set and on that day large numbers

came to his house. He told them about the Kingdom of God and taught them about Jesus from the Scriptures— from the five books of Moses and the books of prophecy. He began lecturing in the morning and went on into the evening!

24   Some believed, and some didn't.

25   But after they had argued back and forth among themselves, they left with this final word from Paul ringing in their ears: "The Holy Spirit was right when He said through Isaiah the prophet,

26   'Say to the Jews, "You will hear and see but not understand,

27   For your hearts are too fat and your ears don't listen and you have closed your eyes against understanding, for you don't want to see and hear and understand and turn to Me to heal you.'

28, 29   So I want you to realize that this salvation from God is available to the Gentiles too, and they will accept it."

30   Paul lived for the next two years in his rented house and welcomed all who visited him,

31   Telling them with all boldness about the Kingdom of God and about the Lord Jesus Christ; and no one tried to stop him.

THE LETTER TO THE ROMANS

Rome, the home of the Caesars and capital of their Eurasion empire, was a goal of the Apostle Paul for several years. He had carried the good news of Christ from Antioch in Syria westward across Asia Minor and into the declining country of Greece. Churches had been established and leaders trained, and the pioneering missionary gazed farther westward, longing to visit the center of the Roman empire and then continue to Spain, the empire's western boundary. When various obstacles delayed the trip that is described at the end of the Book of Acts, Paul wrote this letter to the small Christian Church in Rome.

Paul, ever friendly and full of affection in his letter writing, yet gives his most comprehensive and profound teaching in this letter, tracing man's deepest problems to his alienation from God, and pointing the way to a reconciliation in which "nothing will ever be able to separate us from the love of God which is in Christ Jesus, our Lord." (Romans 8:39)

Romans

CHAPTER 1

Dear Friends in Rome,

1 This letter is from Paul, Jesus Christ's slave, chosen to be a missionary, and sent out to preach God's Good News.

2 This Good News was promised long ago by God's prophets in the Old Testament;

3 It is the Good News about His Son, Jesus Christ our Lord, Who came as a human baby, for He was born into King David's royal family line;

4 And by rising from the dead He proved Himself to be the mighty Son of God, with the holy nature of God Himself.

5 And now, through Christ, all the kindness of God has been poured out upon us undeserving sinners, and now He is sending us out around the world to tell all people everywhere the great things God has done for them, so that they too will believe and obey Him.

6, 7 And you, dear friends in Rome, are among those He dearly loves; you, too, are invited to be His very own—yes, His holy people. May all God's mercies and peace be yours from God our Father and from Jesus Christ our Lord.

8 Let me say first of all that wherever I go I hear you being talked about! For your faith in God is becoming known around the world. How I thank God through Jesus Christ for this good report, and for each one of you.

9 God knows how often I pray for you. Day and night I bring you and your needs in prayer to the One I serve with all my might, telling others the Good News about His Son.

10 And one of the things I keep on praying for is the

opportunity, God willing, to come at last to see you and if possible that I will have a safe trip.

11 For I long to see you so that I can bring you some spiritual food that will help you grow strong in the Lord.

12 Then, too, I need your help, for I not only want to share my faith with you but be encouraged by yours. In that way each of us will be a blessing to the other.

13 I want you to know, dear brothers, that I planned to come many times before (but God did not let me) to work among you and see good results, as I have among the other Gentile churches.

14 For I owe a great debt to you and to everyone else, both to civilized peoples and heathen nations; yes, to the educated and uneducated alike.

15 So, to the fullest extent of my ability, I am ready to come to you in Rome also to preach God's Good News.

16 For I am not ashamed of this Good News about Christ. It is God's powerful method of bringing all who believe it to heaven. This message was preached first to the Jews alone, but now everyone is invited to come to God in this same way.

17 This Good News tells us that God makes us ready for heaven—good in His eyes—when we put our faith and trust in Christ to save us. And the more we trust Him the more clearly we can see that He has taken away our sins and filled us with His goodness. As the Old Testament says it, the man who finds life will find it through trusting God.

18 But God shows His anger from heaven against all sinful, evil men who push away the truth.

19 For the truth about God is known to them by instinct; God has put this knowledge in their hearts.

20 Since earliest times men have seen the earth and sky and all God made, and have known of His existence and great eternal power. So they have no excuse for saying they don't know whether or not there is a God.

21 Yes, they knew about Him all right, but they wouldn't admit it or worship Him or even thank Him for all His daily care. And after a while they began to think up silly ideas of what God was like and what He wanted them to do. The result was that their foolish minds became dark and confused.

22 Claiming themselves to be wise without God, they became utter fools instead.

23 And then instead of worshiping the glorious, ever-living God, they took wood and stone and made idols for themselves, carving them to look like birds and animals and snakes and puny men, and said that these were the great, eternal God, and worshiped them.

24 And so God let them go ahead into every sort of sex sin, and do whatever they wanted to; yes, vile and sinful things with each other's bodies.

25 Instead of believing what they knew was the truth about God, they deliberately chose to believe lies. So they prayed to the things God made, but wouldn't obey the blessed God who made these things.

26 That is why God let go of them and let them do all these evil things, so that even their women turned against God's natural plan for them and indulged in sex sin with each other.

27 And the men, instead of having a normal sex relationship with women, burned with lust for each other, men doing shameful things with other men and, as a result, getting paid within their own souls with the wages they so richly deserved.

28 So it was that when they gave God up and would not even acknowledge Him, God gave them up to doing everything their evil minds could think of.

29 Their lives became full of every kind of wickedness and sin, of greed and hate, envy, murder, fighting, lying, bitterness, and gossip.

30 They were backbiters, haters of God, insolent, proud braggarts, always thinking of new ways of sinning and continually disobedient to their parents.

31 They tried to misunderstand, broke their promises, and were heartless—without pity.

32 They were fully aware of God's death penalty for these crimes, yet they went right ahead and did them anyway, and encouraged others to do them, too.

CHAPTER 2

Well," you may be saying, "what terrible people you have been talking about!" But wait a minute! You are just as bad. When you say they are wicked and should be punished, you are talking about yourself, for you do these very same things.

2 And we know that God, in justice, will punish anyone who does such things as these.

3 Do you think that God will judge and condemn others for doing them and overlook you when you do them, too?

4 Don't you realize how patient He is being with you? Or don't you care? Can't you see that He has been waiting all this time without punishing you to give you time to turn from your sin? His kindness is meant to lead you to repentance.

5 But no, you won't listen; and so you are saving up terrible punishment for yourselves because of your stubborn hardness of heart, for there is going to come a day of wrath when God will be the honest Judge of all.

6 He will give each one whatever payment he deserves.

7 He will give eternal life to those who patiently do the will of God, seeking for glory and honor and for eternal life.

8 But He will terribly punish those who fight against the truth of God and walk in evil ways, for God's anger will be poured out upon them.

9 There will be sorrow and suffering for Jews and Gentiles alike who keep on sinning.

10 But there will be glory and honor and peace from God for all who obey Him, whether they are Jews or Gentiles.

11 For God treats everyone the same.

12-15 He will punish sin, wherever it is found. He will punish the heathen when they sin, even though they never had God's written laws, for down in their heart they know right from wrong. God's laws are written within them; their own conscience accuses them, or sometimes excuses them. And God will punish the Jews for sinning because they have His written laws but don't obey them. They know what is right but don't do it. After all, salvation is not given to those who know what to do, unless they do it.

16 The day will surely come when at God's command Jesus Christ will judge the secret lives of everyone, their

inmost thoughts and motives; this is all part of God's great plan which I have already told you about.

17 You Jews think all is well between yourselves and God because He gave His laws to you; you brag that you are His special friends.

18 Yes, you know what He wants; you know right from wrong and favor the right because you have been taught His laws from earliest youth.

19 You are so sure of the way to God that you could point it out to a blind man. You think of yourselves as beacon lights, directing men to God.

20 You think that you can guide the simple and teach even children the affairs of God, for you really know His laws, which are full of all knowledge and truth.

21 Yes, you teach others—then why don't you teach yourselves? You tell others not to steal—do *you* steal?

22 You say it is wrong to commit adultery—do *you* do it? You say, "Don't pray to idols," but you rob idol temples, which is just as bad.

23 You are so proud of knowing God's laws, *but you dishonor Him by breaking them.*

24 No wonder, as the Scriptures say, the world hates God because of you.

25 Being a Jew is worth something if you obey God's laws, but if you don't, then you are no better off than the heathen.

26 And if the heathen obey God's laws, won't God give them all the rights and honors He planned to give the Jews?

27 In fact, those heathen will be much better off than you Jews who know so much about God and have His promises but don't obey His laws.

28 For you are not real Jews just because you were born of Jewish parents or because you have gone through the Jewish initiation ceremony of circumcision.

29 No, a real Jew is anyone whose heart is right with God. For God is not looking for those who cut their bodies in actual body circumcision, but He is looking for those with changed hearts and minds. Whoever has that kind of change in his life will get his praise from God, even if not from you.

CHAPTER 3

Then what's the use of being a Jew? Are there any special benefits for them from God? Is there any value in the Jewish circumcision ceremony?

2 Yes, being a Jew has many advantages. First of all, God trusted them with His laws (so that they could know and do His will).

3 True, some of them were unfaithful, but just because they broke their promises to God, does that mean God will break His promises to those who love Him?

4 Of course not! Though everyone else in the world is a liar, God is not. Do you remember what the book of Psalms says about this? That God's words will always prove true and right, no matter who questions them.

5 "But," some say, "our breaking faith with God is good, our sins serve a good purpose, for people will notice how good God is when they see how bad we are. Is it fair, then, for Him to punish us when our sins are helping Him?" (That is the way some people talk.)

6 God forbid! Then what kind of God would He be, to overlook sin? How could He ever condemn anyone?

7 For He could not judge and condemn me as a sinner if my dishonesty brought Him glory by pointing up His honesty in contrast to my lies.

8 If you follow through with that idea you come to this: the worse we are, the better God likes it! But the damnation of those who say such things is just. Yet some claim that this is what I preach!

9 Well, then, are we Jews *better* than others? No, not at all, for we have already shown that all men alike are sinners, whether Jews or Gentiles.

10 As the Scriptures say, No one is good—no one in all the world.

11 No one has ever really known God's way, or even truly wanted to.

12 Every one has sinned; all are worthless to God. No one anywhere has kept on doing what is right; not one.

13 Their talk is foul and filthy like the stench from an open grave. Their tongues are loaded with lies. Every-

thing they say has in it the sting and poison of deadly snakes.

14 Their mouths are full of cursing and bitterness.

15 They are quick to kill, hating anyone who disagrees with them.

16 Wherever they go they leave misery and trouble behind them,

17 And they have never known what it is to try to be kind and good.

18 They care nothing about God nor what He thinks of them.

19 So the curse of God lies very heavily upon the Jews, for they are responsible to keep God's laws instead of doing all these evil things; not one of them has any excuse; in fact, all the world stands hushed and guilty before Almighty God.

20 So you can see that no one can ever find God's favor by being good enough. For the more we know of God's laws, the clearer it becomes that we don't obey them, for His laws make us see that we are sinners.

21, 22 But now God has shown us a different way to heaven—not by being "good enough" and trying to keep His laws, but by a new way (though not new, really, for the Old Testament told about it long ago). Now God says He will accept us and make us good and bring us to heaven if we trust Jesus Christ to take away our sins. And we all can be saved in this same way, by coming to Christ, no matter who we are or what we have been like.

23 Yes, all have sinned; all fall short of God's glorious ideal;

24 Yet now God declares that we are good in His eyes if we trust in Jesus Christ, Who freely takes away our sins.

25 For God sent Christ Jesus to take the punishment for our sins and end all God's anger against us. He used Christ's blood and our faith to satisfy God's wrath. In this way He was being entirely fair, even though He did not punish those who sinned in olden times. For He was looking forward to the time when Christ would come and take away those sins.

26 And now in these days also He can receive sinners in this same way, because Jesus took away their sins. But isn't this unfair for God to let criminals go free, and say

that they are good? No, for He does it on the basis of their trust in Jesus Who took away their sins.

27　Then what can we boast about doing to earn our salvation? Nothing at all. Why? Because our salvation is not based on our good deeds; it is based on what Christ has done and our faith in Him.

28　So it is that we are saved by faith in Christ and not by the good things we do.

29　And does God save only the Jews in this way? No, the Gentiles, too, may come to Him in this same manner.

30　God treats us all the same; all, whether Jews or Gentiles, are approved if they have faith.

31　Well then, if we are saved by faith, does this mean that we no longer need obey God's laws? That's what it does NOT mean. In fact, only when we trust Jesus can we truly obey Him.

CHAPTER 4

Abraham was, humanly speaking, the founder of our Jewish nation. What were his experiences concerning this question of being saved by faith? Was it because of his good deeds that God accepted him? If so, then he would have something to boast about. But from God's point of view Abraham had no basis at all for pride.

3　For the Scriptures tell us Abraham *believed God,* and that is why God canceled his sins and declared him just and righteous.

4, 5　But didn't he earn his right to heaven by all the good things he did? No, for being saved is a gift; if a person could earn it by being good, then it wouldn't be free—but it is! It is *given* to those who do *not* work for it. For God declares sinners to be good in His sight if they have faith in Christ to save them from God's wrath.

6　King David spoke of this, describing the happiness of an undeserving sinner who is declared good by God.

7　"Blessed, and to be envied," he said, "are those whose sins are forgiven and put out of sight.

8　"Yes, what joy there is for anyone whose sins are no longer counted against him."

9　Now then, the question: Is this blessing given only to those who have faith in Christ but also keep the Jewish laws, or is the blessing also given to those who do not keep the Jewish rules, but only trust in Christ? Well, what about Abraham? We say that he received these blessings through his faith. Was it by faith alone? Or because he also kept the Jewish rules?

10   For the answer to that question, answer this one: *When* did God give this blessing to Abraham? It was *before he became a Jew*—before he went through the Jewish initiation ceremony of circumcision.

11   It wasn't until later on, *after* God had promised to bless him *because of his faith,* that he was circumcised. The circumcision ceremony was a sign that Abraham already had faith and that God had already accepted him and declared him just and good in His sight—before the ceremony took place. So Abraham is an example of those who believe and are saved without obeying Jewish laws. We see, then, that those who do not keep these rules are justified by God through faith.

12   And those who follow these rules and customs and have been circumcised can see that it is not this ceremony that saves them, for Abraham found favor with God by faith alone, before he was circumcised.

13   So it is clear that God's promise to give the whole earth to Abraham and his descendants was not because Abraham obeyed God's laws but because he trusted God to keep His promise.

14   But if you still claim that God's blessings go to those who are "good enough," then you are saying that God's promises to those who have faith are meaningless, and faith is foolish.

15   But the fact of the matter is this: when we try to gain God's blessing and salvation by keeping His laws, we always end up under His anger, for we always fail to keep them. The only way we can keep from breaking laws is not to have any to break!

16   So God's blessings are given to us by faith, as a free gift; we are certain to get them whether or not we follow Jewish customs, if we have faith like Abraham's, for Abraham is the father of us all when it comes to these matters of faith.

17   That is what the Scriptures mean when they say that God made Abraham the father of many nations. God will accept all people in every nation who trust God as

Abraham did. And this promise is from God Himself, Who makes the dead live again and speaks of future events with as much certainty as though they were already past!

18 So, when God told Abraham that He would give him a son who would have many children and become a great nation, Abraham believed God even though such a promise just couldn't come to pass!

19 And because his faith was strong, he didn't worry about the fact that he was far too old to be a father, at the age of one hundred, and that Sarah his wife, at ninety, was also much too old to have a baby.

20 But Abraham never doubted. He believed God, for his faith and trust were strong, and he praised God for this blessing before it even happened.

21 He was completely sure that God was well able to do anything He promised.

22 And because of Abraham's faith God forgave his sins and called him just and good.

23 Now this wonderful promise—that he was accepted and approved through his faith—wasn't just for Abraham's benefit.

24 It was for us, too, assuring us that God will accept us in the same way He accepted Abraham—when we believe the promises of God Who brought back Jesus our Lord from the dead.

25 He died for our sins and rose again to make us right with God, filling us with God's goodness.

CHAPTER 5

So, now, since we have been made right in God's sight by faith in His promises, we can have real peace with Him because of what Jesus Christ our Lord has done for us.

2 For because of our faith, He has brought us into this place of highest privilege where we now stand, and we confidently and joyfully look forward to actually becoming all that God has had in mind for us to be.

3 We can rejoice, too, when we run into problems and trials for we know that they are good for us—they help us learn to be patient.

4   And patience develops strength of character in us and helps us trust God more each time until finally our hope and faith are strong and steady.

5   Then, when that happens, we will be able to hold our heads high no matter what happens and know that all is well, for we will know how dearly God loves us, and we will feel this warm love everywhere within us because God has given us the Holy Spirit to fill our hearts with His love.

6   When we were utterly helpless with no way of escape, Christ came at just the right time and died for us sinners who had no use for Him.

7   Even if we were good, we really wouldn't expect anyone to die for us, though of course that might be barely possible.

8   But God showed His great love for us by sending Christ to die for us while we were still sinners.

9   And since by His blood He did all this for us as sinners, how much more will He do for us now that He has declared us just and good? Now He will save us from all of God's wrath to come.

10   And since, when we were His enemies we were brought back to God by the death of His Son, what blessings He must have for us now that we are His friends, and He is living within us!

11   Now we have the wonderful joy of the Lord in our lives because of what our Lord Jesus Christ has done in dying for our sins and making us His friends.

12   When Adam sinned the entire human race was declared guilty. His sin brought death into the world, and so everything began to grow old and die.

13   (We know that it was Adam's sin that caused this—and not each person dying because of his own sins—because although of course people were sinning from the time of Adam until Moses, God did not in those days judge them guilty of death for breaking His laws—because He had not yet given His laws to them, nor told them what He wanted them to do.

14   So when they died it was not for these sins of their own; and since they themselves had never disobeyed God's special law against eating the forbidden fruit, as Adam had, their dying was not because of that. It was because, when Adam sinned, all of us were declared guilty with

him and began to die because of his sin.) What a contrast between Adam and Christ Who was yet to come.

15 And what a difference between man's sin and God's forgiveness. For this one man, Adam, brought death to many through his *sin*. But this one man, Jesus Christ, brought forgiveness to many through God's *mercy*.

16 Adam's *one* sin brought the penalty of death to many, while Christ freely takes away *many* sins and gives glorious life instead.

17 The sin of this one man, Adam, caused *death to be king over all,* but all who will take God's gift of forgiveness and approval are *kings of life* because of this one man, Jesus Christ.

18 Yes, Adam's *sin* brought *punishment* to all, but Christ's act of *goodness* makes men *right with God,* so that they can live.

19 Adam caused many to be sinners because he *disobeyed* God, and Christ caused many to be made acceptable to God because He *obeyed.*

20 The Ten Commandments were given so that all could see the extent of their failure to obey God's laws. But the more we see our sinfulness, the more we see God's abounding grace forgiving us.

21 And so sin ruled over all men and brought them to death, but now God's kindness rules instead, giving us right standing with God and resulting in eternal life through Jesus Christ our Lord.

CHAPTER 6

Well then, shall we keep on sinning so that God can keep on showing us more and more kindness and forgiveness?

2, 3 Of course not! Should we keep on sinning when we don't have to? For sin's power over us was broken when we became Christians and were baptized to become a part of Jesus Christ: through His death the power of your sinful nature was shattered.

4 Your old sin-loving nature was buried with Him by baptism when He died, and when God the Father, with glorious power, brought Him back to life again, you were given His wonderful new life to enjoy.

5 For you have become a part of Him, and so you died with Him, so to speak, when He died; and now you share His new life, for you have risen with Him when He rose.

6 Your old evil desires were nailed to the cross with Him; that part of you that loves to sin was crushed and fatally wounded, so that your sin-loving body is no longer under sin's control, no longer needs to be a slave to sin;

7 For when you are deadened to sin you are freed from all its allure and its power over you.

8 And since your old sin-loving nature "died" with Christ, we believe that you are now sharing His new life.

9 Christ rose from the dead and will never die again. Death no longer has any power over Him.

10 He died once for all to end sin's power, but now He lives forever in unbroken fellowship with God.

11 So look upon your old sin nature as dead and unresponsive to sin and be alive instead to God, alert to Him, through Jesus Christ our Lord.

12 Do not let sin control you any longer; do not obey it; do not submit to it by giving in to its desires.

13 Do not let any part of your bodies become tools of wickedness, to be used for sinning; but give yourselves completely to God—every part of you—for you are back from death and you want to be tools in the hands of God, to be used for His good purposes.

14 Sin need never again be your master, for now you are no longer tied to the law where sin enslaves you, but you are free under God's favor and mercy.

15 So now shall we sin and not worry about it? (For our salvation does not depend on keeping the law, but on receiving God's grace!) Of course not!

16 Don't you realize that you can choose your own master? You can choose sin (with death) or else obedience (with goodness). The one to whom you offer yourself, he will take you and be your master and you will be his slave.

17 Thank God that though you once chose to be slaves of sin, now you are obeying with all your heart the teaching to which God has committed you.

18 And now you are free from your old master, sin; and you have become slaves to your new master, goodness and righteousness.

19 I speak this way, using the illustration about slaves, because it makes it easy to understand: just as you used to be slaves to all kinds of sin, so now you must let your-selves be slaves to all that is right and holy.

20 In those days when you were slaves of sin you didn't bother much with goodness.

21 And what was the result? Evidently not good, since you are ashamed now even to think about those things you used to do, for they ruined you.

22 But now you are free from the power of sin and are slaves of God, and His benefits to you include holiness and everlasting life.

23 For the wages of sin is death, but the free gift of God is eternal life through Jesus Christ our Lord.

CHAPTER 7

Don't you understand yet, dear Jewish brothers in Christ, that when a person dies the law no longer holds him in its power?

2 Let me illustrate: when a woman marries, the law binds her to her husband as long as he is alive. But if he dies, she is no longer bound to him. The laws of marriage no longer apply to her.

3 Then she can marry someone else if she wants to. That would be wrong while he was alive, but it is perfectly all right after he dies.

4 Your "husband," your master, used to be the Jewish law; but you "died," as it were, with Christ on the cross; and since you are "dead," you are no longer "married to the law," and it has no more power over you. Then you came back to life again when Christ did, and are a new person. And now you are "married," so to speak, to the One who rose from the dead, so that you can produce good fruit, that is, good deeds for God.

5 When your old nature was still active, sinful desires were at work within you, making you want to do whatever God said not to, and producing sinful deeds, the rotting fruit that comes with death.

6 But now you need no longer worry about the Jewish laws and customs because you "died" while in their cap-tivity, and now you can really serve God; not in the old

way, mechanically obeying a set of rules, but in the new way, with all of your hearts and minds.

7   Well then, am I suggesting that these laws of God are evil? Of course not! No, the law is not sinful but it was the law that showed me my sin. I would never have known the sin in my heart—the evil desires that are hidden there—except the law said, "You must not have evil desires in your heart."

8   But sin used this law against evil desires by reminding me that such desires are wrong and arousing all kinds of forbidden desires within me! Only if there were no laws to break would there be no sinning.

9   That is why I felt fine so long as I did not understand what the law really demanded. But when I found out then I realized that I had broken the law and was a sinner, doomed to die.

10   So as far as I was concerned, the good law which was supposed to show me the way of life resulted instead in my being given the death penalty.

11   Sin fooled me by taking the good laws of God and using them to make me guilty of death.

12   So you see the law itself is wholly right and good.

13   But didn't the law cause my doom? How then can it be good? No, it was sin, devilish stuff that it is, that used what was good to bring about my condemnation. So you can see from the way sin uses God's good laws for its own evil purposes, how cunning and deadly and damnable it is.

14   The law is good. The trouble is not there, but with *me,* because I am too sinful to obey it.

15   I don't understand myself at all, for I really want to do what is right, but I can't. I do what I don't want to— what I hate.

16   I know perfectly well that what I am doing is wrong and that the laws I am breaking are good ones.

17   But I can't help myself because I'm not doing it. It is sin inside me that is stronger than I am that makes me do these evil things.

18   I know I am rotten through and through so far as my old sinful nature is concerned. No matter which way I turn I can't make myself do right. I want to but I can't.

19 When I want to do good, I don't; and when I try not to do wrong, I do it anyway.

20 Now if I am doing what I don't want to, it is plain where the trouble is: sin still has me in its evil grasp.

21 It seems to be a fact of life that when I want to do what is right, I inevitably do what is wrong.

22 I love to do God's will so far as my new nature is concerned;

23 But there is something else deep within me, in my lower nature, that is at war with my mind and wins the fight and makes me a slave to the sin and death that are still within me. In my mind I want to be God's willing servant but instead I find myself still enslaved to sin.

24, 25 So you see how it is: my new life tells me to do right, but the old nature that is still inside me loves to sin. Oh, what a terrible thing this is! Who will free me from my slavery to this deadly lower nature? Thank God! It has been done through Jesus Christ our Lord. He has set me free.

CHAPTER 8

So there is no condemnation awaiting those who belong to Christ Jesus.

2 For the power of the life-giving Spirit—and this power is mine through Christ Jesus—has freed me from the vicious circle of sin and death.

3 We aren't saved from sin's grasp by knowing the commandments of God, because we can't and don't keep them, but God put into effect a different plan to save us. He sent His own Son, in a human body like ours—except that ours are sinful—and destroyed sin's control over us by giving Himself as a sacrifice for our sins.

4 So now we can obey God's laws if we follow after the Holy Spirit and no longer obey the old evil nature within us.

5 Those who let themselves be controlled by their lower natures live only to please themselves; but those who follow after the Holy Spirit find themselves doing those things that please God.

6 Following after the Holy Spirit leads to life and peace, but following after the old nature leads to death,

7   Because the old sinful nature within us is against God. It never did obey God's laws and it never will.

8   That's why those who are still under the control of their old sinful selves, bent on following their old evil desires, can never please God.

9   But you are not like that. You are controlled by your new nature if you have the Spirit of God living in you. (And remember that if anyone doesn't have the Spirit of Christ living in him, he is not a Christian at all.)

10   Yet, even though Christ lives within you, your body will die because of sin; but your spirit will live, for Christ has made it just and good.

11   And if the Spirit of God, Who raised up Jesus from the dead, lives in you, He will make your dying bodies live again after you die, by means of this same Holy Spirit living within you.

12   So, dear brothers, you have no obligations whatever to your old sinful nature to do what it begs you to do.

13   For if you keep on following it you are lost and will perish, but if through the power of the Holy Spirit you crush it and its evil deeds, you will live.

14   For all who are led by the Spirit of God are sons of God.

15   And so we should not be like cringing, fearful slaves, but we should behave like God's very own children, adopted into the bosom of His family, and calling to Him, "Father, Father."

16   For His Holy Spirit speaks to us deep in our hearts, and tells us that we really are God's children.

17   And since we are His children, then we will share His treasures—for all God gives His Son Jesus is ours now too. But we must also share His suffering if we are to share His glory.

18   Yet what we suffer now is nothing compared to the glory He will give us later.

19   For all creation is waiting patiently and hopefully for that future day when God will glorify His children.

20, 21   For on that day thorns and thistles, sin, death, and decay that overcame the world against its will at God's command will all disappear, and the world around us will share in the glorious freedom from sin which God's children enjoy.

22   For we know that even the things of nature, like

animals and plants, groan in sickness and death as they await this great event.

23 And even we Christians, although we have the witness of the Holy Spirit within us, aren't free from trouble; we too wait anxiously for that day when God will give us our full rights as His children, including the new bodies He has promised us—bodies that will not be sick again and that will never die.

24 We are saved by trusting. And trusting means looking forward to getting something we don't have now; (for a man who already has something doesn't need to hope and trust that he will get it.)

25 But if we must keep trusting God for something that hasn't happened yet, it teaches us to wait patiently and confidently.

26 And in the same way—by faith—the Holy Spirit helps us with our daily problems and in our praying. For we don't even know what we should pray for, nor how to pray as we should; but the Holy Spirit prays for us with such feeling that it cannot be expressed in words.

27 And the Father Who knows all hearts knows of course what the Spirit is saying as He pleads for us in harmony with God's own will.

28 And we know that all that happens to us is working for our good if we love God, and if we are fitting into His plans.

29 For from the very beginning God decided that those who came to Him—and all along He knew who would—should become like His Son, so that His Son would be the first, with many brothers.

30 And having chosen us, He called us to come to Him; and when we came, He declared us "not guilty," filled us with Christ's goodness, gave us right standing with Himself, and promised us His glory.

31 What can we ever say to such wonderful things as these? If God is on our side, who can ever be against us?

32 Since He did not even spare His own Son for us but gave Him for us all, won't He also surely give us everything else?

33 Who dares accuse us whom God has chosen for His own? Will God? No! He is the One Who has forgiven us and given us right standing with Himself.

34 Who then will condemn us? Will Christ? NO! For

He is the One Who died for us and came back to life again for us and is sitting at the place of highest honor next to God, pleading for us there in heaven.

35 Who then can ever keep away Christ's love from us? When we have trouble or calamity, when we are hunted down or destroyed, is it because He doesn't love us anymore? And if we are hungry, or penniless, or in danger, or threatened with death, has God deserted us?

36 No, for the Scriptures tell us that for His sake we must be ready to face death at every moment of the day— we are like sheep awaiting slaughter;

37 But despite all this, overwhelming victory is ours through Christ Who loves us.

38 For I am convinced that nothing can ever separate us from His love. Death can't, and life can't. The angels won't, and all the powers of hell itself cannot keep God's love away. Our fears for today, our worries about tomorrow.

39 Or where we are—high above the sky, or in the deepest ocean—nothing will ever be able to separate us from the love of God that is in Christ Jesus, our Lord.

CHAPTER 9

Oh, Israel, my people! Oh, my Jewish brothers! How I long for you to come to Christ. My heart is heavy within me and I grieve bitterly day and night because of you. Christ knows and the Holy Spirit knows that it is no mere pretense when I say that I would be willing to be forever damned if that would save you.

4 God has given you so much, but still you will not listen to Him. He took you as His own special, chosen people and led you along with a bright cloud of glory and told you how very much He wanted to bless you. He gave you His rules for daily life so you would know what He wanted you to do. He let you work for Him in the temple. He gave you mighty promises.

5 Great men of God were your fathers, and Christ Himself was One of you, a Jew so far as His human nature is concerned, He Who now rules over all things and is blessed of God forever.

6 Well then, did God's promise to His Jewish people

become worthless when they refused to come to be saved? Of course not. For His promises are only to those who come. Only they are truly His people. They alone are true Jews. So you see, not everyone born into a Jewish family is truly a Jew.

7 Just because they come from Abraham doesn't make them truly Abraham's children. For the Scriptures say that the promises apply only to Abraham's son Isaac and Isaac's descendants, though Abraham had other children too.

8 This means that not all of Abraham's children are children of God, but only the ones born as a result of God's special promise to Abraham.

9 For God had promised, "Next year I will give you and Sarah a son (Isaac)."

10-13 And years later, when Isaac was grown up and married, and Rebecca his wife was about to bear him twin children, God told her that Esau, the child born first, would be a servant to Jacob, his twin brother. In the words of the Scripture, "I chose to bless Jacob, but not Esau." And God said this before the children were even born, before they had done anything either good or bad. This proves that God was doing what He had decided from the beginning; it was not because of what the children did but because of what God wanted and chose.

14 Was God being unfair? Of course not.

15 For God had said to Moses, "If I want to be kind to someone, I will. And I will take pity on anyone I want to."

16 And so God's blessings are not given just because someone decides to have them or works hard to get them. They are given to those God wants to give them to.

17 Pharaoh King of Egypt was an example of this fact. For God told him He had given him the kingdom of Egypt for the very purpose of displaying the awesome power of God against him: so that all the world would hear about God's glorious name.

18 So you see, God is kind to some just because He wonts to be, and He makes some refuse to listen.

19 Well then, why does God blame them for not listening? Haven't they done what He made them do?

20 No, don't say that. Who are you to criticize God?

Should the thing made say to the One who made it "Why have you made me like this?"

21   When a man makes a jar out of clay, doesn't he have a right to use the same lump of clay to make one jar beautiful, to be used for holding flowers, and another to throw garbage into?

22   And so God has a perfect right to be patient with whomever He wants to, even with those who are fit only for destruction; later on He will show His fury and power against them.

24   And He has a right to take others such as ourselves, who have been made for pouring His glory into, whether we are Jews or Gentiles, and to be kind to us so that everyone can see how very great His glory is.

25   Remember what it says in the book of Hosea? There God says that He will find other children for Himself (who are not from His Jewish family) and will love them, though no one had ever loved them before.

26   And the heathen of whom it once was said, "You are not my people" shall be called "sons of the Living God."

27   Isaiah the prophet cried out concerning the Jews that though there would be millions of them, only a small number would ever be saved.

28   For the Lord will execute His sentence upon the earth, quickly ending His dealings, justly cutting them short.

29   And Isaiah says in another place that except for God's mercy all the Jews would be destroyed—all of them —just as everyone in the cities of Sodom and Gommorrah perished.

30   Well then, what shall we say about these things? Just this, that God has given the Gentiles the opportunity to be saved by faith, even though they really were not seeking God.

31   But the Jews, who tried so hard to be right with God by keeping His laws, did not find His salvation.

32   Why not? Because they were trying to be saved by keeping the law and being good instead of by depending on faith. They have stumbled over the great stumbling-stone.

33   God warned them of this in the Scriptures when He said, "I have put a Rock in the path of the Jews, and

many will stumble over Him (Jesus). But those who believe in Him will never be disappointed."

CHAPTER 10

Dear brothers, the longing of my heart and my prayer is that the Jewish people might be saved.

2 I know what enthusiasm you have for the honor of God, but it is misdirected zeal.

3 For you don't understand that Christ has died to make you right with God. Instead you are trying to make yourselves good enough to gain God's favor by keeping the Jewish laws and customs. But that is not God's way of salvation.

4 You don't understand that Christ gives to those who trust in Him everything you are trying to get by keeping His laws.

5 For as Moses said, if a person could be perfectly good and hold out against temptation all his life and never sin once, only then could he be saved.

6 But the salvation that comes through faith says, "You don't need to search the heavens to find Christ and bring Him down to help you," and,

7 "You don't need to go among the dead to bring Christ back to life again,"

8 For salvation that comes from trusting Christ— which is what we preach—is already within easy reach of each of us; in fact, it is as near as our own hearts and mouths.

9 For if you tell others with your own mouth that Jesus Christ is your Lord, and believe in your own heart that God raised Him from the dead, you will be saved.

10 For it is by believing in his heart that a man becomes right with God; and with his mouth he tells others of his faith, confirming his salvation.

11 For the Scriptures tell us that no one who believes in Christ will ever be disappointed.

12 Jew and Gentile are the same in this respect: they all have the same Lord Who generously gives His riches to all those who ask Him for them.

13 Anyone who calls upon the name of the Lord will be saved.

14 But how shall they ask Him to save them unless they believe in Him? And how can they believe in Him if they have never heard about Him? And how can they hear about Him unless someone tells them?

15 And how will anyone go and tell them unless someone sends him? That is what the Scriptures are talking about when they say, "How beautiful are the feet of those who preach the Gospel of peace, and bring glad tidings of good things." In other words, how welcome are those who come preaching God's Good News!

16 But not everyone who hears the Good News has welcomed it, for Isaiah the prophet said, "Lord, who has believed me when I told them?"

17 Yet faith comes from listening to this Good News —the Good News about Christ, Who is the Word of God.

18 But what about the Jews? Have they heard God's word? Yes, for it has gone wherever they are. The Good News has been told to the ends of the earth.

19 And did they know that God would give His salvation to others if they refused to take it? Yes, for even back in the time of Moses, God had said that He would make His people jealous and try to wake them up by giving His salvation to the foolish heathen nations.

20 And later on Isaiah said boldly that God would be found by people who weren't even looking for Him, and they would be saved.

21 In the meantime, He keeps on reaching out His hands to the Jews but they keep arguing and refusing to come.

CHAPTER 11

I ask then, has God rejected and deserted His people the Jews? Oh, no, not at all. Remember that I myself am a Jew, a descendant of Abraham and a member of Benjamin's family;

2, 3 No, God has not discarded His own people whom He chose from the very beginning. Do you remember what the Scriptures say about this? Elijah the prophet was complaining to God about the Jews, telling God how they had killed the prophets and torn down God's altars; Elijah claimed that he was the only one left in all the land who still loved God, and now they were trying to kill him too.

4 And do you remember how God replied? God said, "No, you are not the only one left. I have seven thousand others besides you who still love Me and have not bowed down to idols!"

5 It is the same today. Not all the Jews have turned away from God. There are a few being saved as a result of God's kindness in choosing them.

6 And if it is by God's kindness, then it is not by their being good enough. For in that case the free gift would no longer be free—it isn't free when it is earned.

7 So this is the situation: most of the Jews have not found the favor of God they are looking for. A few have, the ones God has picked out, but the eyes of the others have been blinded.

8 This is what our Scriptures refer to when they say that God has put them to sleep, shutting their eyes and ears so that they do not understand what we are talking about when we tell them of Christ. And so it is to this very day.

9 King David spoke of this same thing when he said, "Let their good food and other blessings trap them into thinking all is well between themselves and God. Let these good things boomerang upon them and fall back upon their heads to justly crush them."

10 "Let their eyes be dim," he said, "so that they cannot see, and let them walk bent-backed forever with a heavy load."

11 Did God make His Jewish people stumble like this for the purpose of bringing disaster to them? Oh no, His purpose was to make His salvation available to the Gentiles, and then the Jews would be jealous and begin to want God's salvation for themselves.

12 Now if the whole world became rich as a result of God's offer of salvation, when the Jews stumbled over it and turned it down, think how much greater a blessing the world will share in later on when the Jews too come to Christ.

13 As you know, God has appointed me as a special messenger to you Gentiles. I lay great stress on this and remind the Jews about it as often as I can,

14 So that if possible I can make them want what you Gentiles have and in that way save some of them.

15   And how wonderful it is when they become Christians. When God turned away from them it meant that He turned to the rest of the world to offer His salvation; and now it is even more wonderful when some of the Jews come to Christ. It is like dead people coming back to life again.

16   And since Abraham and the prophets are God's people, their children will be too. For if the roots of the tree are holy, the branches will be too.

17   But some of these branches from Abraham's tree, some of the Jews, have been broken off. And you Gentiles who were branches from, we might say, a wild olive tree, were grafted in. So now you too receive the blessing God has promised Abraham and his children, sharing in God's rich nourishment of His own special olive tree.

18   But you must be careful not to brag about being put in to replace the branches that were broken off. Remember that you are important only because you are now a part of God's tree; you are just a branch, not a root.

19   "Well," you may be saying, "those branches were broken off to make room for me so I must be pretty good."

20   Watch out! Remember that those branches, the Jews, were broken off because they didn't believe God, and you are there only because you do. Do not be proud; be humble and grateful—and careful.

21   For if God did not spare the branches He put there in the first place, He won't spare you either.

22   See how God is both so kind and so severe. He is very hard on those who disobey, but very good to you if you continue to love and trust Him. But if you don't, you too will be cut off.

23   On the other hand, if the Jews leave their unbelief behind them and come back to God, God will graft them back into the tree again. He has the power to do it.

24   For if God was willing to take you who were so far away from Him—being part of a wild olive tree—and graft you into His own good tree—a very unusual thing to do—don't you see that He will be far more ready to put the Jews back again, who were there in the first place?

25   I want you to know about this mystery, dear brothers, so that you will not feel proud and start bragging. Yes, it is true that most of the Jews have set themselves against

the Gospel now, but this will last only until all of you Gentiles have come to Christ—those of you who will.

26 And then all Israel will be saved. Do you remember what the prophets said about this? "There shall come out of Zion a Deliverer, and He shall turn the Jews from all ungodliness.

27 "At that time I will take away their sins, just as I promised."

28 Now most of the Jews are enemies of the Gospel. They hate it. But this has been a benefit to you, for it has resulted in God giving His gifts to you Gentiles. But the Jews are still beloved of God because of His promises to Abraham, Isaac, and Jacob.

29 For God's gifts and His call can never be withdrawn; He will never go back on His promises.

30 Once you were rebels against God, but when the Jews refused His gifts God was merciful to you instead.

31 And now the Jews are the rebels, but some day they will share in God's mercy upon you.

32 For God arranged that all be sinners so that He could have mercy upon all alike.

33 Oh what a wonderful God we have! How great are His wisdom and knowledge and riches. How impossible it is for us to understand His decisions and His methods.

34 For who among us can know the mind of the Lord? Who knows enough to be His counselor and guide?

35 And who has ever given anything to the Lord first as payment for something in return?

36 For everything comes from God alone. Everything lives by His power, and everything is for His glory. To him be glory evermore.

CHAPTER 12

And so, dear brothers, I plead with you to give your bodies to God. Let them be a living sacrifice, holy—the kind He can accept. When you think of what He has done for you, is this too much to ask?

2 Don't copy the fashions and customs of this world, but be a new and different person with a fresh newness in all you do and think. Then you will see from your own experience how His ways will really satisfy you.

3 As God's messenger I give each of you God's warning: be honest in your estimate of yourselves, measuring your value by how much faith God has given you.

4, 5 For just as there are many parts to our bodies, so it is with Christ's body. We are all parts of it, and it takes every one of us to make it complete, for we each have different work to do. So we belong to each other, and each needs all the others.

6 God has given each of us the ability to do certain things well. So if God has given you the ability to prophesy, then prophesy whenever you can—as often as your faith is strong enough to produce a message from God.

7 If your gift is that of serving others, serve them well. Teachers should do a good job of teaching.

8 The preacher should see to it that his sermons are strong and helpful. If God has given you money, be generous in helping others with it. If God has given you administrative ability and put you in charge of the work of others, take the responsibility seriously. And if yours is the gift of kindness to others, do it cheerfully.

9 Don't just pretend that you love others: really love them. Hate what is wrong. Stand on the side of the good.

10 Love each other with brotherly affection and delight to honor each other.

11 Never be lazy in your work but serve the Lord enthusiastically.

12 Be glad for all God is planning for you. Be patient in trouble, and prayerful always.

13 When God's children are in need, you be the one to help them out. And get into the habit of inviting guests home for dinner; or, if they need lodging, for the night.

14 If someone harms you, don't curse him; pray that God will bless him.

15 When others are happy, be happy with them. If they are sad, share their sorrow.

16 Work happily together. Don't try to act big. Don't try to get into the good graces of important people, but enjoy the company of ordinary folks. And don't think you know it all!

17 Never pay back evil for evil. Do things in such a way that everyone can see you are honest clear through.

18 Don't quarrel with anyone. Be at peace with everyone, just as much as you possibly can.

19 Dear friends, never avenge yourselves. Let anger cool, for God has said that He will pay back those deserving it.

20 So feed your enemy if he is hungry. If he is thirsty give him something to drink and you will be "heaping coals of fire on his head." In other words, he will feel ashamed of himself for what he has done to you.

21 Don't let evil get the upper hand but conquer evil by doing good.

CHAPTER 13

Obey the government, for God is the One Who has put it there. There is no government anywhere that God has not placed in power.

2 So those who refuse to obey the laws of the land are refusing to obey God, and punishment will follow.

3 For the policeman is not there to frighten people doing right; but those doing evil will always fear him. So if you don't want to be afraid, keep the laws and you will get along well.

4 The policeman is sent by God to help you. But if you are doing something wrong, of course you should be afraid, for he will have you punished. He is sent by God for that very purpose.

5 So you must obey the laws for two reasons: to keep from being punished and because you know you should.

6 Pay your taxes too, for these same two reasons. For government workers need to be paid so that they can keep on doing God's work, serving you.

7 Pay everyone what he ought to have: pay your taxes and import duties gladly, obey those over you and give honor and respect to all those to whom it is due.

8 Pay all your debts except the debt of love for others; never finish paying that! For if you love them, you will be obeying all of God's laws, fulfilling all His requirements.

9 If you love your neighbor as much as you love yourself you will not want to harm or cheat him, or kill him or steal from him. And you won't sin with his wife or want what is his, or do anything else the Ten Commandments say are wrong. All ten are wrapped up in this one, to love your neighbor as you love yourself.

10   Love does no wrong to anyone. That's why it fully satisfies all of God's requirements. It is the only law you need.

11   Another reason for right living is this: you know how late it is; time is running out. Wake up, for the coming of the Lord is nearer now than when we first believed.

12   The night is far gone, the day of His return will soon be here. So we must quit the evil deeds of darkness and put on the armor of upright living.

13   We must be honest and true so that all can see that everything we do is good. We are not to spend our time in wild parties and drunkenness, or in adultery and lust, or in fighting, or wishing for things that don't belong to us.

14   But ask the Lord Jesus Christ to help you live as you should and don't make plans to enjoy evil.

CHAPTER 14

Give a warm welcome to any brother who wants to join you as a member of the church, even if he scarce believes that Christ alone can save him. Don't criticize him for having different ideas from yours about what is right and wrong.

2   For instance, don't argue with him about whether or not to eat meat that has been offered to idols. You may believe there is no harm in this, but the faith of others is weaker; they think it is wrong, and will go without meat at all and eat vegetables rather than eat that kind of meat.

3   Those who think it is all right to eat such meat must not look down on those who won't. And if you are one of those who won't, don't find fault with those who do. For God has accepted them to be His children.

4   They are God's servants, not yours. Let Him tell them what to do. They are responsible to God, not you, and God will help them do what is right.

5   Some think that Christians should observe the Jewish holidays as special days to worship God, but others say it is wrong and foolish to go to all that trouble for every day alike belongs to God. On questions of this kind everyone must decide for himself.

6   If you have special days for worshiping the Lord, you are trying to honor Him; you are doing a good thing.

So is the person who eats meat that has been offered to idols; he is thankful to the Lord for it; he is doing right. And the person who won't touch such meat, he too is anxious to please the Lord, and is thankful.

7 We are not our own bosses to live or die as we ourselves might choose.

8 Living or dying we follow the Lord. Living or dying we are His.

9 That is why Christ died and rose again, so that He can be our Lord both while we live and when we die.

10 You have no right to criticize your brother or look down on him. Remember, each of us will stand personally before the Judgment Seat of Christ.

11 For it is written, "As I live," says the Lord, "every knee shall bow to me and every tongue confess to God."

12 Yes, each of us will give an account of himself to God.

13 So don't criticize each other any more. Try instead to live in such a way that you will never make your brother stumble by letting him see you doing something he thinks is wrong.

14 As a matter of fact, I am perfectly sure on the authority of the Lord Jesus Christ that there is nothing really wrong with eating meat that has been offered to idols. But if someone feels it is wrong, then he shouldn't do it for it is wrong for him.

15 If your brother is bothered by what you eat, you are not acting in love if you go ahead and eat it. Don't let your eating ruin someone for whom Christ died.

16 Don't do that which will cause criticism against yourself even though you know that what you do is right.

17 For after all the important thing for us as Christians is not what we eat or drink but stirring up goodness and peace and joy from the Holy Spirit.

18 If you follow Christ's example in these affairs, God will be glad; and so will your friends.

19 So aim for harmony in the church and to build each other up.

20 Don't undo the work of God for a chunk of meat. Remember, there is nothing wrong with the meat but it is wrong to eat it if it makes another stumble.

21 The right thing to do is to quit eating meat or drinking wine or doing anything else that offends your

brother or makes him sin by causing resentment or influencing him to do what he feels is wrong.

22 You may know that there is nothing wrong with what you plan, even from God's point of view, but keep it to yourself; don't flaunt your faith in front of others who might be hurt by it. In this situation, happy is the man who does not sin by doing what he knows is right.

23 But anyone who feels it is wrong shouldn't do it. He sins if he does, for he thinks it is wrong; and so for him it is wrong. Anything that's done apart from what he feels is right is sin.

CHAPTER 15

Even if we believe that it makes no difference to the Lord that we do these things, still we cannot just go ahead and do them to please ourselves; for we must bear the "burden" of being considerate of the doubts and fears of others—of those who feel these things are wrong. Let's please the other fellow, not ourselves, if it is for his good and builds him up in the Lord.

3 Christ didn't please Himself. As the prophets said, He came for the very purpose of suffering under the insults of those who were against the Lord.

4 And these things that were written by God so long ago are to teach us patience and to encourage us, so that we will look expectantly to God for help.

5 May God Who gives patience, steadiness, and encouragement help you to live in full harmony with each other—each with the attitude of Chirst toward the other.

6 And then all of us can praise the Lord together with one voice, giving glory to God, the Father of our Lord Jesus Christ.

7 So, warmly welcome each other into the church, just as Christ has warmly welcomed you; then God will be glorified.

8 Remember that Jesus Christ came to help the Jews, so that He could fulfill the promises God made to their ancestors.

9 And remember that the Gentiles give glory to God for His mercies to them. That is what the Psalmist meant

when he wrote: "I shall praise You among the Gentiles, and sing to Your name."

10 And in another place, "Be glad, O you Gentiles, along with His people the Jews."

11 And yet again, "Praise the Lord, O you Gentiles, let everyone praise Him."

12 And the prophet Isaiah said, "There shall be an Heir in the house of Jesse, and He will be King over the Gentiles; they will pin their hopes on Him alone."

13 So I pray for you Gentiles that God Who gives you hope will keep you happy and full of peace as you believe in Him. I pray that God will help you overflow with hope in Him through the Holy Spirit's power within you.

14 I know you are wise and good, my brothers, and that you know these things so well that you are able to each others all about them.

15, 16 But even so I have been bold enough to emphasize some of these points, knowing that all you need is this reminder from me; for I am, by God's grace, a special messenger from Jesus Christ to you Gentiles bringing you the Gospel and offering you up as a fragrant sacrifice to God; for you have been made pure and pleasing to Him by the Holy Spirit.

17 So it is right for me to be a little proud of all Christ Jesus has done for you through me.

18 I dare not judge how effectively He has used others, but I know this: He has used me to win the Gentiles to God.

19 I have won them by my message and by the good way I have lived before them, and by miracles done through me as signs from God—all by the Holy Spirit's power. In this way I have preached the full Gospel of Christ all the way from Jerusalem clear over into Illyricum.

20 But my ambition is to go and preach where the name of Christ has never yet been heard, rather than where a church has already been started by someone else.

21 I want to follow the plan spoken of in the Scriptures where Isaiah says that those who have never heard the name of Christ before will see and understand.

22 That is why I have been so long in coming to visit you.

23 But now at last I am through with my work here,

and I am ready to come after these long years of waiting.

24   So when I take the trip to Spain I am planning, I will stop off there in Rome; and after we have had a good time together for a little while, you can start me on my way again.

25   First, though, I must go down to Jerusalem to carry a gift to the Christians there.

26   For you see, the Christians in Macedonia and Achaia have taken up an offering for those in Jerusalem who are going through some hard times.

27   They were very glad to do this, for they feel that they owe a real debt to the Jerusalem Christians. Why? Because the news about Christ came to them from the church in Jerusalem. And since they received this wonderful spiritual gift of the Gospel from them, they feel that the least they can do in return is to give them some food!

28   As soon as I have delivered this money and completed this good deed of theirs, I will come to see you on my way to Spain.

29   And I am sure that when I come the Lord will give me a great blessing for you.

30   Will you be my prayer partners? For the Lord Jesus Christ's sake, and because of your love for me— given to you by the Holy Spirit—pray much with me for my work.

31   Pray that I will be protected from those who are not Christians in Jerusalem. Pray also that the Christians there will be willing to accept the money I am bringing them.

32   Then I will be able to come to you with a happy heart by the will of God, and we can refresh each other.

33   And now may our God, Who gives peace, be with you all. Amen.

CHAPTER 16

Phoebe, a dear Christian woman from the town of Cenchrea, will be coming to see you soon. She has worked hard in the church there. Receive her as your sister in the Lord, giving her a warm Christian welcome. Help her in every way you can, for she has helped many in their needs, including me.

3   Tell Priscilla and Aquila "hello." They have been my fellow workers in the affairs of Christ Jesus.

4   In fact, they risked their lives for me; and I am not the only one who is thankful to them: so are all the Gentile churches.

5   Please give my greetings to all those who meet to worship in their home. Greet my good friend Epaenetus. He was the very first person to become a Christian in Asia.

6   Remember me to Mary, too, who has worked so hard to help us.

7   Then there are Andronicus and Junias, my relatives who were in prison with me. They are respected by the apostles, and became Christians before I did. Please give them my greetings.

8   Say "hello" to Amplias, whom I love as one of God's own children,

9   And Urbanus, our fellow worker, and beloved Stachys.

10   Then there is Apelles, a good man whom the Lord approves, greet him for me. And give my best regards to those working at the house of Aristobulus.

11   Remember me to Herodion my relative. Remember me to the Christian slaves over at Narcissus House.

12   Say "hello" to Tryphena and Tryphosa, the Lord's workers; and to dear Persis, who has worked so hard for the Lord.

13   Greet Rufus for me, whom the Lord picked out to be His very own; and also his dear mother who has been such a mother to me.

14   And please give my greetings to Asyncritus, Phlegon, Hermes, Patrobas, Hermas, and the other brothers who are with them.

15   Give my love to Philologus, Julia, Nereus and his sister, and to Olympas, and all the Christians who are with them.

16   Shake hands warmly with each other. All the churches here send you their greetings.

17   And now there is one more thing to say before I end this letter. Stay away from those who cause divisions and scandals, teaching things about Christ that are against what you have been taught.

18   Such teachers are not working for our Lord Jesus, but only want gain for themselves. They are good speakers and simple-minded people are often fooled by them.

19   But everyone knows that you stand loyal and true. This makes me happy indeed. I want you to remain always very clear about what is right, and to stay innocent of any wrong.

20   The God of peace will soon crush Satan under your feet. The blessings from our Lord Jesus Christ be upon you.

21   Timothy my fellow-worker, and Lucius and Jason and Sosipater, my relatives, send you their good wishes.

22   I, Tertius, the one who is writing this letter for Paul, send my greetings too, as a Christian brother.

23   Gaius says to say "hello" to you for him. I am his guest, and the church meets here in his home. Erastus, the city treasurer, sends you his greetings and so does Quartus, a Christian brother.

24   Goodbye. May the grace of our Lord Jesus Christ be with you all.

25-27   I commit you to God, Who is able to make you strong and steady in the Lord, just as the Gospel says, and just as I have told you. This is God's plan of salvation for you Gentiles, kept secret from the beginning of time. But now as the prophets foretold and as God commands, this message is being preached everywhere, so that people all around the world will have faith in Christ and obey Him. To God, Who alone is wise, be the glory forever through Jesus Christ our Lord. Amen.

                                        Sincerely,
                                        Paul

THE LETTER OF JAMES

This letter leads from Paul's class in theology in Romans out into the community and homes where we live what we believe. It tells us, as well as the Jewish Christians to whom it was specifically addressed, that preaching without performance is false faith. If a person has genuine faith in God, says James, his deeds and attitudes will prove his godliness.

The writer, James, was one of the leaders of the Christian Church in Jerusalem. As the center of Jewish faith, Jerusalem was a forbidding place to demonstrate the "new religion," yet tradition says the Christians lived and died showing a quality of love that astonished onlookers.

James

CHAPTER 1

From: James: a servant of God and of the Lord Jesus Christ.

To: Jewish Christians scattered everywhere. Greetings!

2 Dear brothers, is your life full of difficulties and temptations? Then be happy,

3 For when the way is rough, your patience has a chance to grow.

4 So let it grow, and don't try to squirm out of your problems. For when your patience is finally in full bloom, then you will be ready for anything, strong in character, full and complete.

5 If you want to know what God wants you to do, ask Him, and He will gladly tell you, for He is always ready to give a bountiful supply of wisdom to all who ask Him; He will not resent it.

6 But when you ask Him, be sure that you really expect Him to tell you, for a doubtful mind will be as unsettled as a wave of the sea that is driven and tossed by the wind,

7, 8 And every decision you then make will be uncertain, as you turn first this way, and then that. So if you don't ask with faith, don't expect the Lord to give you any solid answers.

9 A Christian who doesn't amount to much in this world should be glad, for he is great in the Lord's sight.

10, 11 But a rich man should be glad that his riches mean nothing to the Lord, for he will soon be gone, like a flower that has lost its beauty and fades away, withered—killed by the scorching summer sun. So it is with rich men. They will soon die and leave behind all their busy activities.

12　Happy is the man who doesn't give in and do wrong when he is tempted, for afterwards he will get as his reward the crown of life that God has promised those who love Him.

13　And remember, when someone wants to do wrong it is never God who is tempting him, for God never wants to do wrong and never tempts anyone else to do it.

14　But temptation is the pull of man's own evil thoughts and wishes.

15　Then the evil thoughts lead to evil actions and afterwards to the death penalty from God.

16　So don't be misled dear brothers.

17　But whatever is good and perfect comes to us from God, the Creator of all light, and He shines forever without change or shadow.

18　And it was a happy day for Him when He gave us our new lives, through the truth of His Word, and we became, as it were, the first children in His new family.

19　Dear brothers, don't ever forget that it is best to listen much, speak little, and not become angry;

20　For anger doesn't make us good, as God demands that we must be.

21　So get rid of all that is wrong in your life, both inside and outside, and humbly be glad for the wonderful message we have received, for it is able to save our souls as it grows in our hearts.

22　And remember, it is a message to obey, not just to listen to. So don't fool yourselves:

23　For if a person just listens and doesn't obey, he is like a man looking at his face in a mirror;

24　As soon as he walks away, he can't see himself anymore or remember what he looks like.

25　But if he keeps looking steadily into God's law for free men he will not only remember it, but do what it says, and God will greatly bless that man in everything he does.

26　If anyone says he is a Christian but doesn't control his sharp tongue, he is just fooling himself and his religion isn't worth much.

27　The Christian who is pure and without fault, from God the Father's point of view, is the one who takes care of orphans and widows, and whose soul remains true to the Lord—not soiled and dirtied by its contacts with the world.

CHAPTER 2

Dear brothers, how can you claim that you belong to the Lord Jesus Christ, the Lord of glory, if you show favoritism to rich people and look down on poor people?

2 If a man comes into your church dressed in expensive clothes and with valuable gold rings on his fingers, and at the same moment another man comes in who is poor and dressed in threadbare clothes,

3 And you make a lot of fuss over the rich man and give him the best seat in the house and say to the poor man, "You can stand over there if you like, or else sit on the floor"—well,

4 This kind of action casts a question mark across your faith—are you really a Christian at all?—and shows that you are guided by evil motives.

5 Listen to me, dear brothers: God has chosen poor people to be rich in faith, and the kingdom of heaven is theirs, for that is the gift God has promised to those who love Him.

6 And yet, of the two strangers, you have despised the poor man. Don't you realize that it is usually the rich men who pick on you and drag you into court?

7 And all too often they are the ones who laugh at Jesus Christ, whose noble name you bear.

8 Yes indeed, it is good when you truly obey our Lord's command, "You must love and help your neighbors just as much as you love and take care of yourself."

9 But you are breaking this law of our Lord's when you favor the rich and fawn over them, it is sin.

10 And the person who keeps every law of God, but makes one little slip, is just as guilty as the person who has broken every law there is.

11 For the God Who said you must not marry a woman who already has a husband, also said you must not murder, so even though you have not broken the marriage laws by committing adultery, but have mur-

dered someone, you have entirely broken God's laws and
stand utterly guilty before Him.

12 You will be judged on whether or not you are
doing what Christ wants you to. So watch what you do
and what you think;

13 For there will be no mercy to those who have
shown no mercy. But if you have been merciful, then
God's mercy towards you will win out over His judgment against you.

14 Dear brothers, what's the use of saying that you
have faith and are Christians if you aren't proving it by
helping others? Will *that* kind of faith save anyone?

15 If you have a friend who is in need of food and
clothing

16 And you say to him, "Well, goodbye and God bless
you, stay warm and eat hearty," and then don't give him
clothes or food, what good does that do?

17 So you see, it isn't enough just to have faith. You
must also do good to prove that you have faith. Faith
without good deeds is dead and useless.

18 But someone may say, "You think the way to
God is by faith alone, plus nothing; well, I say that good
deeds are important too, for without good deeds you
cannot show me whether you have faith or not; but anyone can see that I believe by the way I act."

19 You think "believing" is enough, do you? Believing
in one God? Well, remember that the devils believe this
too, and believe it so strongly that they tremble in terror!

20 Dear foolish man! When will you ever learn that
"believing" is useless without *doing* what God wants you
to? Faith that does not result in good deeds is not real
faith.

21 Don't you remember that even father Abraham
was declared good because of what he *did*, when he was
willing to obey God, even if it meant offering his son
Isaac to die on the altar?

22 You see, he was trusting God so much that he
was willing to do whatever God told him to; his faith
was made complete by what he did, by his actions, his
good deeds.

23 And so it happened just as the Scriptures say, that
Abraham trusted God, and the Lord declared him good

in God's sight, and he was even called "The Friend of God."

24   So you see, a man is saved by what he does, as well as by what he believes.

25   Rahab, the wicked woman, is another example of this. She was saved because of what she did when she hid those messengers and sent them safely away by a different road.

26   Just as the body is dead when there is no spirit in it, so faith is dead if it is not the kind that results in good deeds.

CHAPTER 3

Dear brothers, don't be too eager to tell others their faults, for we all make many mistakes, and when we teachers, who should know better, do wrong, our punishment will be greater than it would be for others;

2   If anyone can control his tongue, it proves that he has perfect control over himself in every other way.

3   We can make a large horse turn around and go wherever we want by means of a small bit in his mouth.

4   And a tiny rudder makes a huge ship turn wherever the pilot wants it to go, even though the wind is strong.

5   So also the tongue is a small thing, but what terrible results it can cause. A great forest can be set on fire by one tiny spark.

6   And the tongue is a flame of fire. It is full of wickedness and poisons every part of the body. And the tongue is set on fire by hell itself, and can turn our whole lives into a blazing flame of destruction and disaster.

7   Men have trained, or can train, every kind of animal or bird that lives and every kind of snake and fish,

8   But no human being can tame the tongue. It is always ready to pour out its deadly poison.

9   Sometimes it praises our heavenly Father, and sometimes it breaks out into curses against men who are made like God.

10   And so blessing and cursing come pouring out of the same mouth. Dear brothers, surely this is not right!

11   Does a spring of water bubble out first with fresh water and then with bitter water?

12   Can you pick olives from a fig tree, or figs from a grape vine? No, and you can't draw fresh water from a salty pool.

13   If you are wise, live a life of steady goodness, so that only good deeds will pour forth. And if you don't brag about them, then you will be truly wise!

14   And by all means don't brag about being wise and good if you are bitter and jealous and selfish; that is the worst sort of lie.

15   For jealousy and selfishness are not God's kind of wisdom. Such things are earthly, unspiritual, inspired by the devil, and come from hell itself.

16   For wherever there is jealousy or selfish ambition, there will be disorder and every other kind of evil.

17   But the wisdom that comes from heaven is first of all pure and full of quiet gentleness. Then it is peace-loving and courteous. It allows discussion and is willing to yield to others; it is full of mercy and good deeds. It is wholehearted and straightforward and sincere.

18   And those who are peacemakers will plant seeds of peace and reap a harvest of goodness.

CHAPTER 4

What is causing the quarrels and fights among you? Isn't it because there is a whole army of evil desires within you?

2   You want what you don't have so you kill to get it. You long for what others have, and can't afford it, so you start a fight to take it away from them. And yet the reason you don't have what you want is because you don't ask God for it.

3   And when you do ask you don't get it because your whole aim is wrong—you want only what will give *you* pleasure.

4   You are like an unfaithful wife who loves her husband's enemies. Don't you realize that making friends with God's enemies—the evil pleasure of this world—makes God your enemy? I say it again, that if your aim is to enjoy the evil pleasure of the unsaved world, you cannot also be a friend of God.

5   Or what do you think the Scriptures mean when

they say that the Holy Spirit, Whom God has placed within us, watches over us with tender jealousy?

6 But He gives us strength to stand against all such evil longings. As the Scriptures say, God gives strength to the humble but sets Himself against the proud and haughty.

7 So give yourselves humbly to God. Resist the devil and he will flee from you.

8 And when you draw close to God, God will draw close to you. Wash your hands, oh sinners, and fill your hearts with God alone to make them pure and true to Him.

9 Let there be tears for the wrong things you have done. Let there be sorrow and sincere grief. Let there be sadness instead of laughter and gloom instead of joy.

10 Then when you feel your worthlessness before the Lord, He will lift you up, encourage and help you.

11 Don't criticize and speak evil about each other, dear brothers. If you do, you will be fighting against God's law of loving one another, declaring it is wrong. But your job is to obey the law, not to decide whether it is right or wrong.

12 And He alone, Who made the law, can rightly judge among us. He alone decides to save us or destroy. So what right do you have to judge or criticize others?

13 Look here, you people who say "Today or tomorrow we are going to such and such a town, stay there a year, and open up a profitable business."

14 How do you know what is going to happen tomorrow? For the length of your lives is as uncertain as the morning fog; now you see it, soon it is gone.

15 What you ought to say is "If the Lord wants us to, we shall live and do this or that."

16 Otherwise you will be bragging about your own plans, and such self-confidence never pleases God.

17 Remember too that knowing what is right to do and then not doing it is sin.

CHAPTER 5

Look here, you rich men, now is the time to cry and groan with violent grief in view of all the terrible troubles ahead of you.

2 For your wealth is rotting away, and your fine clothes are becoming moth-eaten rags.

3 The value of your gold and silver is dropping fast, yet it will stand as evidence against you, and eat your flesh like fire. That is what you have stored up for yourselves in that coming day of judgment.

4 For listen! Hear the cries of the field workers whom you have cheated of their pay. Their cries have reached the ears of the Lord of Hosts.

5 You have spent your years here on earth having fun, satisfying your every whim, and now your fat hearts are ready for the slaughter.

6 You have condemned and killed good men who had no power to defend themselves against you.

7 But on the other hand, you, dear brothers, be patient until the Lord returns. Be like a patient farmer who expects to wait until the autumn for his precious harvest to ripen.

8 Yes, be patient. And take courage, for the coming of the Lord is near.

9 Don't grumble about each other, brothers. Are you yourselves above criticism? For see! the great Judge is coming. He is almost here, (let Him do whatever criticizing must be done).

10 For examples of patience in suffering, look at the Lord's prophets.

11 We know how happy they are now because they stayed true to Him then, even though they suffered greatly for it. Job is an example of a man who continued to trust the Lord in sorrow, and from his experiences we can see how the Lord's plan finally ended in good, and that the Lord is full of tenderness and mercy.

12 But most of all, dear brothers, do not swear either by heaven or earth or anything else; just say a simple "yes," or "no," so that you will not sin and receive God's curse.

13 Is anyone among you suffering? He should keep on praying about it; and those who have reason to be thankful should continually be singing praises to the Lord.

14 Is anyone sick? He should call for the elders of the church and they should pray over him and pour a little oil upon him, calling on the Lord to heal him.

15 And their prayer, if offered in faith, will heal him, for the Lord will make him well; and if his sickness was caused by some sin, the Lord will forgive him.

16 Admit your faults to one another and pray for each other so that you may be healed. The earnest prayer of a righteous man has great power and wonderful results.

17 Elijah was as perfectly human as we are, and yet when he prayed earnestly that no rain would fall, none fell for the next three and one half years!

18 Then he prayed again, this time that it *would* rain, and down it poured and the grass turned green and the gardens began to grow again.

19 Dear brothers, if anyone has slipped way from God and no longer trusts the Lord, and someone helps him understand the Truth again,

20 That person who brings him back to God will save a wandering soul from death and bring about the forgiveness of his many sins.

THE BOOK OF THE REVELATION

Many people have tried to predict the future, with varying degrees of success. This book foretells the future of the world and the coming kingdom of Jesus Christ as it was revealed to the Apostle John. Symbolic and figurative speech fill the book, making interpretation very difficult. Yet the awesome consequences of the events, the vivid imagery of the symbols, and the tantalizing meanings of the language have endlessly intrigued scholars and schoolboys. And capping the peaks of John's visions are the momentous words: "If you read this prophecy . . . you will receive a special blessing from the Lord," and "If anyone adds anything to what is written here, God shall add to him the plagues described in this book." (Revelation 1:3; 22:18)

The Revelation

CHAPTER 1

This book unveils some of the future activities soon to occur in the life of Jesus Christ. God permitted Him to reveal these things to His servant John in a vision; and then an angel was sent from heaven to explain the vision's meaning.

2 John wrote it all down—the words of God and Jesus Christ and everything he heard and saw.

3 If you read this prophecy aloud to the church, you will receive a special blessing from the Lord. Those who listen to it being read and do what it says will also be blessed. For the time is near when these things will all come true.

*   *   *   *

4 *From:* John
To: The seven churches in Turkey.
Dear Friends:

May you have grace and peace from God who is, and was, and is to come! and from the seven-fold Spirit before His throne;

5 And from Jesus Christ who faithfully reveals all truth to us. He was the first to rise again from death, to die no more. He is far greater than any king in all the earth. All praise to Him who always loves us and who set us free from our sins by pouring out His life blood for us.

6 He has gathered us into His kingdom and made us priests of God His Father. Give to Him everlasting glory! He rules forever! Amen!

7 See! He is arriving surrounded by clouds; and

every eye shall see Him—yes, and those who pierced Him. And the nations will weep in sorrow and in terror when He comes. Yes! Amen! Let it be so!

8 "I am the A and Z, the Beginning and the Ending of all things," says God, who is the Lord, the All Powerful One who is, and was, and is coming again!

9 It is I, your brother John, a fellow sufferer for the Lord's sake who is writing this letter to you. I too have shared the patience Jesus gives, and we will share His kingdom!

I was on the island of Patmos, exiled there for preaching the Word of God, and for telling what I knew about Jesus Christ.

10 It was Sunday and I was worshiping, when suddenly I heard a loud voice behind me, a voice that sounded like a trumpet blast,

11 Saying, "I am A and Z, the First and Last!" And then I heard Him say, "Write down everything you see, and send your letter to the seven churches in Turkey: to the church in Ephesus, the one in Smyrna, and those in Pergamos, Thyatira, Sardis, Philadelphia, and Laodicea."

12 When I turned to see who was speaking, there behind me were seven candlesticks of gold.

13 And standing among them was One who looked like Jesus who called himself the Son of Man, wearing a long robe circled with a golden band across His chest.

14 His hair was white, as wool or snow, and His eyes penetrated like flames of fire.

15 His feet gleamed like burnished bronze, and His voice thundered like the waves against the shore.

16 He held seven stars in His right hand and a sharp, double-bladed sword in His mouth, and His face shone like the power of the sun in unclouded brilliance.

17, 18 When I saw Him, I fell at His feet as dead; but He laid His right hand on me and said, "Don't be afraid! Though I am the First and Last, the Living One who died, who is now alive forevermore, who has the keys of hell and death—don't be afraid!

19 Write down what you have just seen, and what will soon be shown to you.

20 This is the meaning of the seven stars you saw in My right hand, and the seven golden candlesticks: The

seven stars are the leaders of the seven churches, and the seven candlesticks are the churches themselves.

CHAPTER 2

Write a letter to the leader of the church at Ephesus and tell him this:

I write to inform you of a message from Him who walks among the churches and holds their leaders in His right hand. He says to you:

2   I know how many good things you are doing. I have watched your hard work and your patience; I know you don't tolerate sin among your members, and you have carefully examined the claims of those who say they are apostles but aren't. You have found out how they lie.

3   You have patiently suffered for Me without quitting.

4   Yet there is one thing wrong: you don't love Me as at first!

5   Think about those times of your first love (how different now!) and turn back to Me again and work as you did before; or else I will come and remove your candlestick from its place among the churches.

6   But there is this about you that is good: you hate the deeds of the licentious Nicolaitanes, just as I do.

7   Let this message sink into the ears of anyone who listens to what the Spirit is saying to the churches: To everyone who is victorious, I will give fruit from the Tree of Life in the Paradise of God.

*   *   *   *

8   *To the leader of the church in Smyrna write this letter:*

This message is from Him who is the First and Last, who was dead and then came back to life.

9   I know how much you suffer for the Lord, and I know all about your poverty (but you have heavenly riches!). I know the slander of those opposing you, who say that they are Jews—the children of God—but they aren't, for they support the cause of Satan.

10   Stop being afraid of what you are about to suffer

—for the devil will soon throw some of you into prison to test you. You will be persecuted for "ten days." Become faithful even when facing death and I will give you the crown of life—an unending, glorious future.*

11 Let everyone who can hear, listen to what the Spirit is saying to the churches: he who is victorious shall not be hurt by the Second Death.

12 *Write this letter to the leader of the church in Pergamos:*

This message is from Him who wields the sharp and double-bladed sword.

13 I am fully aware that you live in the city where Satan's throne is, at the center of Satanic worship; and yet you have remained loyal to Me, and refused to deny Me, even when Antipas, My faithful witness, was martyred among you by Satan's devotees.

14 And yet I have a few things against you. You tolerate some among you who do as Balaam did when he taught Balak how to ruin the people of Israel by involving them in sexual sin, and encouraging them to go to idol feasts.

15 Yes, you have some of these very same followers of Balaam among you!

16 Change your mind and attitude, or else I will come to you suddenly and fight against them with the sword of My mouth.

17 Let everyone who can hear, listen to what the Spirit is saying to the churches: Every one who is victorious shall eat of the hidden manna, the secret nourishment from heaven; and I will give to each a white stone, and on the stone will be engraved a new name that no one else knows except the one receiving it.

* * * *

18 *Write this letter to the leader of the church in Thyatira:*

This is a message from the Son of God, whose eyes penetrate like flames of fire, whose feet are like glowing brass.

19 I am aware of all your good deeds—your kindness to the poor, your gifts and service to them; also I know

your love and faith and patience, and I can see your constant improvement in all these things.

20   Yet I have this against you: You are permitting that woman Jezebel, who calls herself a prophetess, to teach My servants that sex sin is not a serious matter; she urges them to practice immorality and to eat meat that has been sacrificed to idols.

21   I gave her time to change her mind and attitude, but she refused.

22   Pay attention now to what I am saying: I will lay her upon a sickbed of intense affliction, along with all her immoral followers, unless they turn again to Me, repenting of their sin with her;

23   And I will strike her children dead. And all the churches shall know that I am He who searches deep within men's hearts and minds; I will give to each of you whatever you deserve.

24, 25   As for the rest of you in Thyatira who have not followed this false teaching ("deeper truths," as they call them—depths of Satan, really), I will ask nothing further of you; only hold tightly to what you have until I come.

26   To every one who overcomes—who to the very end keeps on doing the things that please Me—I will give power over the nations.

27   You will rule them with a rod of iron just as My Father gave Me the authority to rule them; they will be shattered like a pot of clay that is broken into tiny pieces.

28   And I will give you the Morning Star!

29   Let all who can hear, listen to what the Spirit says to the churches.

CHAPTER 3

T o the leader of the church in Sardis write this letter: This message is sent to you by the One who has the seven-fold Spirit of God and the seven stars.

I know your reputation as a live and active church, but you are dead.

2   Now wake up! Strengthen what little remains—for even what is left is at the point of death. Your deeds are far from right in the sight of God.

3   Go back to what you heard and believed at first; hold to it firmly and turn to Me again. Unless you do, I will come suddenly upon you, unexpected as a thief, and punish you.

4   Yet even there in Sardis some haven't soiled their garments with the world's filth; they shall walk with Me in white, for they are worthy.

5   Everyone who conquers will be clothed in white, and I will not erase his name from the Book of Life, but I will announce before My Father and His angels that he is Mine.

6   Let all who can hear, listen to what the Spirit is saying to the churches.

*   *   *   *

7   *Write this letter to the leader of the church in Philadelphia:*
This message is sent to you by the One who is holy and true, and has the key of David to open what no one can shut and to shut what no one can open.

8   I know you well: you aren't strong, but you have tried to obey and have not denied My Name: Therefore I have opened a door to you that no one can shut.

9   Note this: I will force those supporting the causes of Satan while claiming to be Mine (but they aren't—they are lying) to fall at your feet and acknowledge that you are the ones I love.

10   Because you have patiently obeyed Me despite the persecution, therefore I will protect you from the time of Great Tribulation and temptation which will come upon the world to test everyone alive.

11   Look, I am coming soon! Hold tightly to the little strength you have—so that no one will take away your crown.

12   As for the one who conquers, I will make him a pillar in the temple of My God; he will be secure, and will go out no more; and I will write My God's Name on him, and he will be a citizen in the city of My God—the New Jerusalem, coming down from heaven from My God; and he will have My new Name inscribed upon him.

13   Let all who can hear, listen to what the Spirit is saying to the churches.

* * * *

14 *Write this letter to the leader of the church in Laodicea:*

This message is from the One who stands firm, the faithful and true Witness (of all that is or was or evermore shall be)*, the primeval source of God's creation:

15 I know you well—you are neither hot nor cold; I wish you were one or the other!

16 But since you are merely lukewarm, I will spit you out of My mouth!

17 You say, "I am rich, with everything I want; I don't need a thing!" And you don't realize that spiritually you are wretched and miserable and poor and blind and naked.

18 My advice to you is to buy pure gold from Me, gold purified by fire—only then will you truly be rich. And to purchase from Me white garments, clean and pure, so you won't be naked and ashamed; and to get medicine from Me to heal your eyes and give you back your sight.

19 I continually discipline and punish everyone I love; so I must punish you, unless you turn from your indifference and become enthusiastic about the things of God.

20 Look! I have been standing at the door and I am constantly knocking. If anyone hears Me calling him and opens the door, I will come in and fellowship with him and he with Me.

21 I will let every one who conquers sit beside Me on My throne, just as I took My place with My Father on His throne when I had conquered.

22 Let those who can hear, listen to what the Spirit is saying to the churches.

CHAPTER 4

Then as I looked, I saw a door standing open in heaven, and the same voice I had heard before, that sounded like a mighty trumpet blast, spoke to me and said,

"Come up here and I will show you what must happen in the future!"

2 And instantly I was, in spirit, there in heaven and saw—oh the glory of it!—a throne and someone sitting on it!

3　Great bursts of light flashed forth from Him as from a glittering diamond, or from a shining ruby, and a rainbow glowing like an emerald encircled His throne.

4　Twenty-four smaller thrones surrounded His, with twenty-four elders sitting on them; all were clothed in white, with golden crowns upon their heads.

5　Lightning and thunder issued from the throne, and there were voices in the thunder. Directly in front of His throne were seven lighted lamps representing the seven-fold Spirit of God.

6　Spread out before it was a shiny crystal sea. Four Living Beings, dotted front and back with eyes, stood at the throne's four sides.

7　The first of these Living Beings was in the form of a lion; the second looked like an ox; the third had the face of a man; and the fourth, the form of an eagle, with wings spread out as though in flight.

8　Each of these Living Beings had six wings, and the central sections of their wings were covered with eyes. Day after day and night after night they kept on saying, "Holy, holy, holy, Lord God Almighty—the One who was, and is, and is to come."

9　And when the Living Beings give glory and honor and thanks to the One sitting on the throne, who lives forever and ever,

10　The twenty-four elders fall down before Him and worship Him, the Eternal Living One, and cast their crowns before the throne, singing,

11　"Oh Lord, You are worthy to receive the glory and the honor and the power, for You have created all things. They were created and çalled into being by Your act of will."

CHAPTER 5

And I saw a scroll in the right hand of the One who was sitting on the throne, a scroll with writing on the inside and on the back, and sealed with seven seals.

2　A mighty angel with a loud voice was shouting out this question: "Who is worthy to break the seals on this scroll, and to unroll it?"

3   But no one in all heaven or earth or from among the dead was permitted to open and read it.

4   Then I wept with disappointment* because no one anywhere was worthy; no one could tell us what it said.

5   But one of the twenty-four elders said to me, "Cease weeping, for look! The Lion of the tribe of Judah, the Root of David, has conquered, and proved Himself worthy to open the scroll and to break its seven seals."

6   I looked and saw a Lamb standing there before the twenty-four elders, in front of the throne and the Living Beings, and on the Lamb were wounds that once had caused His death. He had seven horns and seven eyes, which represent the seven-fold Spirit of God, sent out into every part of the world.

7   He stepped forward and took the scroll from the right hand of the One sitting upon the throne.

8   And as He took the scroll, the twenty-four elders fell down before the Lamb, each with a harp and golden vials filled with incense—the prayers of God's people!

9   They were singing Him a new song with these words: "You are worthy to take the scroll and break its seals and open it; for You were slain, and Your blood has bought people from every nation as gifts for God.

10   And You have gathered them into a kingdom and made them priests of our God; they shall reign upon the earth."

11   Then in my vision I heard the singing of millions of angels surrounding the throne and the Living Beings and the elders:

12   "The Lamb is worthy" (loudly they sang it!) "—the Lamb who was slain. He is worthy to receive the power, and the riches, and the wisdom, and the strength, and the honor, and the glory, and the blessing.

13   And then I heard everyone in heaven and earth, and from the dead beneath the earth and in the sea, exclaiming, "The blessing and the honor and the glory and the power belong to the One sitting on the throne, and to the Lamb forever and ever."

14   And the four Living Beings kept saying, "Amen!" And the twenty-four elders fell down and worshiped Him.

CHAPTER 6

As I watched, the Lamb broke the first seal and began to unroll the scroll. Then one of the four Living Beings, with a voice that sounded like thunder, said, "Come!"

2 I looked, and there in front of me was a white horse. Its rider carried a bow, and a crown was placed upon his head; he rode out to conquer in many battles and win the war.

3 Then He unrolled the scroll to the second seal, and broke it open, too. And I heard the second Living Being say, "Come!"

4 This time a red horse rode out. Its rider was given a long sword and the authority to banish peace and bring anarchy to the earth; war and killing broke out everywhere.

5 When He had broken the third seal, I heard the third Living Being say, "Come!" And I saw a black horse, with its rider holding a pair of balances in his hand.

6 And a voice from among the four Living Beings said, "A loaf of bread for a dollar, or three pounds of barley flour, but there is no olive oil or wine."

7 And when the fourth seal was broken, I heard the fourth Living Being say, "Come!"

8 And now I saw a pale horse, and its rider's name was Death. And there followed after him another horse whose rider's name was Hell. They were given control of one-fourth of the earth, to kill with war and famine and disease and wild animals.

9 And when He broke open the fifth seal, I saw an altar, and underneath it all the souls of those who had been martyred for preaching the Word of God and for being faithful in their witnessing.

10 They called loudly to the Lord and said, "Oh Sovereign Lord, holy and true, how long will it be before You judge the people of the earth for what they've done to us? When will You avenge our blood against those living on the earth?"

11 White robes were given to each of them, and they were told to rest a little longer until their other brothers, fellow servants of Jesus, had been martyred on the earth and joined them.

12   I watched as He broke the sixth seal, and there was a vast earthquake; and the sun became dark like black cloth, and the moon was blood-red.

13   Then the stars of heaven appeared to be falling to earth—like green fruit from fig trees buffeted by mighty winds.

14   And the starry heavens disappeared as though rolled up like a scroll and taken away; and every mountain and island shook and shifted.

15   The kings of the earth, and world leaders and rich men, and high-ranking military officers, and all men great and small, slave and free, hid themselves in the caves and rocks of the mountains,

16   And cried to the mountains to crush them. "Fall on us," they pleaded, "and hide us from the face of the One sitting on the throne, and from the anger of the Lamb,

17   Because the great day of their anger has come, and who can survive it?"

CHAPTER 7

Then I saw four angels standing at the four corners of the earth, holding back the four winds from blowing, so that not a leaf rustled in the trees, and the ocean became as smooth as glass.

2   And I saw another angel coming from the east, carrying the Great Seal of the Living God. And he shouted out to those four angels who had been given power to injure earth and sea,

3   "Wait! Don't do anything yet—hurt neither earth nor sea nor trees—until we have placed the Seal of God upon the foreheads of His servants."

4   How many were given this mark? I heard the number—it was 144,000, out of all twelve tribes of Israel, as listed here:

5	Judah	12,000
	Reuben	12,000
	Gad	12,000
6	Asher	12,000
	Naphtali	12,000
	Manasseh	12,000

7	Simeon	12,000
	Levi	12,000
	Issachar	12,000
8	Zebulun	12,000
	Joseph	12,000
	Benjamin	12,000

9 After this I saw a vast crowd, too great to count, from all nations and provinces and languages, standing in front of the throne and before the Lamb, clothed in white, with palm branches in their hands.

10 And they were shouting with a mighty shout, "Salvation comes from our God upon the throne, and from the Lamb."

11 And now all the angels were crowding around the throne and around the elders and the four Living Beings, and falling face down before the throne and worshiping God.

12 "Amen!" they said. "Blessing, and glory, and wisdom, and thanksgiving, and honor, and power, and might be to our God forever and forever. Amen!"

13 Then one of the twenty-four elders asked me, "Do you know who these are, who are clothed in white, and where they come from?"

14 "No, sir," I replied. "Please tell me."

"These are the ones coming out of the Great Tribulation," he said; "they washed their robes and whitened them by the blood of the Lamb.

15 That is why they are here before the throne of God, serving Him day and night in His temple. The One sitting on the throne will shelter them;

16 They will never be hungry again, nor thirsty, and they will be fully protected from the scorching noontime heat.

17 For the Lamb standing in front of the throne will feed them and be their Shepherd and lead them to the springs of the Water of Life. And God will wipe their tears away."

CHAPTER 8

W hen the Lamb had broken the seventh seal, there was silence throughout all heaven for what seemed like half an hour.

2   And I saw the seven angels that stand before God, and they were given seven trumpets.

3   Then another angel with a golden censer came and stood at the altar; and a great quantity of incense was given to him to mix with the prayers of God's people, to offer upon the golden altar before the throne.

4   And the perfume of the incense mixed with prayers ascended up to God from the altar where the angel had poured them out.

5   Then the angel filled the censer with fire from the altar and threw it down upon the earth; and thunder crashed and rumbled, lightning flashed and there was a terrible earthquake.

6   Then the seven angels with the seven trumpets prepared to blow their mighty blasts.

7   The first angel blew his trumpet, and hail and fire mixed with blood were thrown down upon the earth. One-third of the earth was set on fire so that one-third of the trees were burned, and all the green grass.

8, 9   Then the second angel blew his trumpet, and what appeared to be a huge burning mountain was thrown into the sea, destroying a third of all the ships; and a third of the sea turned red as blood; and a third of the fish were killed.

10   The third angel blew, and a great flaming star fell from heaven upon a third of the rivers and springs.

11   The star was called "Bitterness" because it poisoned a third of all the water on the earth and many people died.

12   The fourth angel blew his trumpet and immediately a third of the sun was blighted and darkened, and a third of the moon and the stars, so that the daylight was dimmed by a third, and the nighttime darkness deepened.

13   As I watched, I saw a solitary eagle flying through the heavens crying loudly, "Woe, woe, woe to the people of the earth because of the terrible things that will soon happen when the three remaining angels blow their trumpets."

CHAPTER 9

Then the fifth angel blew his trumpet and I saw one who was fallen to earth from heaven, and to him was given the key to the bottomless pit.

2 When he opened it, smoke poured out as though from some huge furnace, and the sun and air were darkened by the smoke.

3 Then locusts came from the smoke and descended onto the earth and were given power to sting like scorpions.

4 They were told not to hurt the grass or plants or trees, but to attack those people who did not have the mark of God on their foreheads.

5 They were not to kill them, but to torture them for five months with agony like the pain of scorpion stings.

6 In those days men will try to kill themselves but won't be able to—death will not come. They will long to die—but death will flee away!

7 The locusts looked like horses armored for battle. They had what looked like golden crowns on their heads, and their faces looked like men's.

8 Their hair was long like women's, and their teeth were those of lions.

9 They wore breastplates that seemed to be of iron, and their wings roared like an army of chariots rushing into battle.

10 They had stinging tails like scorpions, and their power to hurt, given to them for five months, was in their tails.

11 Their king is the Prince of the bottomless pit whose name in Hebrew is Abaddon, and in Greek, Apollyon, (and in English, the Destroyer).*

12 One terror now ends, but there are two more coming!

13 The sixth angel blew his trumpet and I heard a voice speaking from the four horns of the golden altar that stands before the throne of God,

14 Saying to the sixth angel, "Release the four mighty demons held bound at the great River Euphrates."

15 They had been kept in readiness for that year and

month and day and hour, and now they were turned loose to kill a third of all mankind.

16 They led an army of 200,000,000 warriors—I heard an announcement of how many there were.

17, 18 I saw their horses spread out before me in my vision; their riders wore fiery-red breastplates, though some were sky-blue and others yellow. The horses' heads looked much like lions', and smoke and fire and flaming sulphur bellowed from their mouths, killing one-third of all mankind.

19 Their power of death was not only in their mouths, but in their tails as well, for their tails were similar to serpents' heads that struck and bit with fatal wounds.

20 But the men left alive after these plagues *still refused to worship God!* They would not renounce their demon-worship, nor their idols made of gold and silver, brass, stone, and wood—which neither see nor hear nor walk!

21 Neither did they change their mind and attitude about all their murders and witchcraft, their immorality and theft.

CHAPTER 10

Then I saw another mighty angel coming down from heaven, surrounded by a cloud, with a rainbow over his head; his face shone like the sun and his feet flashed with fire.

2 And he held open in his hand a small scroll. He set his right foot on the sea and his left foot on the earth,

3 And gave a great shout—it was like the roar of a lion—and the seven thunders crashed their reply.

4 I was about to write what the thunders said when a voice from heaven called to me, "Don't do it. Their words are not to be revealed."

5 Then the mighty angel standing on the sea and land lifted his right hand to heaven,

6 And swore by Him who lives forever and ever, who created heaven and everything in it and the earth and all that it contains and the sea and its inhabitants, that there should be no more delay,

7 But that when the seventh angel blows his trumpet,

then God's veiled plan—mysterious through the ages ever since it was announced by His servants the prophets—will be fulfilled.

8 Then the voice from heaven spoke to me again, "Go and get the unrolled scroll from the mighty angel standing there upon the sea and land."

9 So I approached him and asked him to give me the scroll. "Yes, take it and eat it," he said. "At first it will taste like honey, but when you swallow it, it will make your stomach sour!"

10 So I took it from his hand, and ate it! and just as he had said, it was sweet in my mouth but it gave me a stomach-ache when I swallowed it.

11 Then he told me, "You must prophesy further about many peoples, nations, tribes and kings."

CHAPTER 11

Now I was given a measuring stick and told to go and measure the temple of God, including the inner court where the altar stands, and to count the number of worshipers.

2 "But do not measure the outer court," I was told, "for it has been turned over to the nations. They will trample over the Holy City for forty-two months.

3 And I will give power to My two witnesses to prophesy 1260 days clothed in sackcloth."

4 These two prophets are the two olive trees, and two candlesticks standing before the God of all the earth.

5 Anyone trying to harm them will be killed by bursts of fire shooting from their mouths.

6 They have power to shut the skies so that no rain will fall during the three and a half years they prophesy, and to turn rivers and oceans to blood, and to send every kind of plague upon the earth as often as they wish.

7 When they complete the three and a half years of their solemn testimony, the tyrant who comes out of the bottomless pit will declare war against them and conquer and kill them;

8, 9 And for three and a half days their bodies will be exposed in the streets of Jerusalem (the city fittingly described as "Sodom" or "Egypt")—the very place where their Lord was crucified. No one will be allowed to bury them, and people from many nations will crowd around to gaze at them.

10   And there will be a worldwide holiday—people everywhere will rejoice and give presents to each other and throw parties to celebrate the death of the two prophets who had tormented them so much!

11   But after three and a half days, the spirit of life from God will enter them and they will stand up! And great fear will fall on everyone.

12   Then a loud voice will shout from heaven, "Come up!" And they will rise to heaven in a cloud as their enemies watch.

13   The same hour there will be a terrible earthquake that levels a tenth of the city leaving 7000 dead. Then everyone left will, in their terror, give glory to the God of heaven.

14   The second woe is past, but the third quickly follows:

15   For just then the seventh angel blew his trumpet, and there were loud voices shouting down from heaven, "The kingdom of this world now belongs to our Lord, and to His Christ; and He shall reign forever and ever."

16   And the twenty-four elders sitting on their thrones before God threw themselves down in worship, saying,

17   "We give thanks, Lord God Almighty, who is and was, for now You have assumed Your great power and have begun to reign.

18   The nations were angry with You, but now it is Your turn to be angry with them. It is time to judge the dead, and reward Your servants—prophets and people alike, all who fear Your Name, both great and small—and to destroy those who have caused destruction upon the earth."

19   Then, in heaven, the temple of God was opened and the ark of His covenant could be seen inside. Lightning flashed and thunder crashed and roared, and there was a great hailstorm and the world was shaken by a mighty earthquake.

CHAPTER 12

Then a great pageant appeared in heaven, portraying things to come. I saw a woman clothed with the sun, with the moon beneath her feet, and a crown of twelve stars on her head.

2 She was pregnant and screamed in the pain of her labor, awaiting her delivery.

3 Suddenly a red Dragon appeared, with seven heads and ten horns, and seven crowns on his heads.

4 His tail drew along behind him a third of the stars, which he plunged to the earth. He stood before the woman as she was about to give birth to her child, ready to eat the baby as soon as it was born.

5 She gave birth to a boy who was to rule all nations with a heavy hand, and He was caught up to God and to His throne.

6 The woman fled into the wilderness, where God had prepared a place for her, to take care of her for 1260 days.

7 Then there was war in heaven; Michael and the angels under his command fought the Dragon and his hosts of fallen angels.

8 And the Dragon lost the battle and was forced from heaven.

9 This great Dragon—the ancient serpent called the Devil, or Satan, the one deceiving the whole world—was thrown down onto the earth with all his army.

10 Then I heard a loud voice shouting across the heavens, "It has happened at last! God's salvation and the power and the rule, and the authority of His Christ are finally here; for the Accuser of our brothers has been thrown down from heaven onto earth—he accused them day and night before our God.

11 They defeated him by the blood of the Lamb, and by their testimony; for they did not love their lives but laid them down for Him.

12 Rejoice, oh heavens! you citizens of heaven, rejoice! be glad! But woe to you people of the world, for the Devil has come down to you in great anger, knowing that he has little time."

13 And when the Dragon found himself cast down to

earth, he persecuted the woman who had given birth to the child.

14 But she was given two wings like those of a great eagle, to fly into the wilderness to the place prepared for her, where she was cared for and protected from the Serpent, the Dragon, for three and a half years.

15 And from the Serpent's mouth a vast flood of water gushed out and swept toward the woman in an effort to get rid of her;

16 But the earth helped her by opening its mouth and swallowing the flood!

17 Then the furious Dragon set out to attack the rest of her children—all who were keeping God's commandments and confessing that they belong to Jesus. He stood waiting on an ocean beach.

CHAPTER 13

And now, in my vision, I saw a strange Creature rising up out of the sea. It had seven heads and ten horns, and ten crowns upon its horns. And written on each head were blasphemous names, each one defying and insulting God.

2 This Creature looked like a leopard but had bear's feet and a lion's mouth! And the Dragon gave him his own power and throne and great authority.

3 I saw that one of his heads seemed wounded beyond recovery—but the fatal wound was healed! All the world marveled at this miracle and followed the Creature in awe.

4 They worshiped the Dragon for giving him such power, and they worshiped the strange Creature. "Where is there anyone as great as he?" they exclaimed. "Who is able to fight against him?"

5 Then the Dragon encouraged the Creature to speak great blasphemies against the Lord; and gave him authority to control the earth for forty-two months.

6 All that time he blasphemed God's name and His temple and all those living in heaven.

7 The Dragon gave him power to fight against God's people and to overcome them, and to rule over all nations and language groups throughout the world.

8 And all mankind—whose names were not written down before the founding of the world in the slain Lamb's Book of Life—worshiped the evil Creature.

9 Anyone who can hear, listen carefully:

10 The people of God who are destined for prison will be arrested and taken away; those destined for death will be killed. But do not be dismayed, for here is your opportunity for endurance and confidence.

11 Then I saw another strange animal, this one coming up out of the earth, with two little horns like those of a lamb but a fearsome voice like the Dragon's.

12 He exercised all the authority of the Creature whose death-wound had been healed, whom he required all the world to worship.

13 He did unbelievable miracles such as making fire flame down to earth from the skies while everyone was watching.

14 By doing these miracles, he was deceiving people everywhere. He could do these marvelous things whenever the first Creature was there to watch him. And he ordered the people of the world to make a great statue of the first Creature, who was fatally wounded and then came back to life.

15 He was permitted to give breath to this statue and even make it speak! Then the statue ordered that anyone refusing to worship it must die!

16 He required everyone—great and small, rich and poor, slave and free—to be tattooed with a certain mark on the right hand or on the forehead.

17 And no one could get a job or even buy in any store without the permit of that mark, which was either the name of the creature or the code number of his name.

18 Here is a puzzle that calls for careful thought to solve it. Let those who are able, interpret this code: the numerical values of the letters in his name add to 666!

CHAPTER 14

Then I saw a Lamb standing on Mount Zion in Jerusalem, and with Him were 144,000 who had His Name and His Father's Name written on their foreheads.

2 And I heard a sound from heaven like the roaring

of a great waterfall or the rolling of mighty thunder. It was the singing of a choir accompanied by harps.

3   This tremendous choir—144,000 strong—sang a wonderful new song in front of the throne of God, and before the four Living Beings and the twenty-four elders; and no one could sing this song except these 144,000 who had been redeemed from the earth.

4   For they are spiritually undefiled, pure as virgins, following the Lamb wherever He goes. They have been purchased from among the men on the earth as a consecrated offering to God and the Lamb.

5   No falsehood can be charged against them; they are blameless.

6   And I saw another angel flying through the heavens, carrying the everlasting Good News to preach to those on earth—to every nation, tribe, language and people.

7   "Fear God," he shouted, "and extol His greatness. For the time has come when He will sit as Judge. Worship Him who made the heaven and the earth, the sea and all its sources."

8   Then another angel followed him through the skies saying, "Babylon is fallen, is fallen—that great city—because she seduced the nations of the world and made them share the wine of her intense impurity and sin."

9   Then a third angel followed them shouting, "Anyone worshiping the Creature from the sea* and his statue and accepting his mark on the forehead or the hand.

10   Must drink the wine of the anger of God; it is poured out undiluted into God's cup of wrath. And they will be tormented with fire and burning sulphur in the presence of the holy angels and the Lamb.

11   The smoke of their torture rises forever and ever, and they will have no relief day or night, for they have worshiped the Creature and his statue, and have been tattooed with the code of his name.

12   Let this encourage God's people to endure patiently every trial and persecution, for they are His saints who remain firm to the end in obedience to His commands and trust in Jesus."

13   And I heard a voice in the heavens above me saying, "Write this down: At last the time has come for His martyrs to enter into their full reward. Yes, says the Spirit, they are blest indeed, for now they shall rest from all their

toils and trials; for their good deeds follow them to heaven!"

14 Then the scene changed and I saw a white cloud, and Someone sitting on it who looked like Jesus, who was called "The Son of Man," with a crown of solid gold upon His head and a sharp sickle in His hand.

15 Then an angel came from the temple and called out to Him, "Begin to use the sickle, for the time has come for You to reap; the harvest is ripe on the earth."

16 So the One sitting on the cloud swung His sickle over the earth, and the harvest was gathered in.

17 After that another angel came from the temple in heaven, and he also had a sharp sickle.

18 Just then the angel who has power to destroy the world with fire, shouted to the angel with the sickle, "Use your sickle now to cut off the clusters of grapes from the vines of the earth, for they are fully ripe for judgment."

19 So the angel swung his sickle on the earth and loaded the grapes into the great winepress of God's wrath.

20 And the grapes were trodden in the winepress outside the city, and blood flowed out in a stream 200 miles long and as high as a horse's bridle.

CHAPTER 15

And I saw in heaven another mighty pageant showing things to come: seven angels were assigned to carry down to earth the seven last plagues—and then at last God's anger will be finished.

2 Spread out before me was what seemed to be an ocean of fire and glass, and on it stood all those who had been victorious over the Evil Creature and his statue and his mark and number. All were holding harps of God,

3 And they were singing the song of Moses, the servant of God, and the song of the Lamb:

"Great and marvelous
Are Your doings,
Lord God Almighty.
Just and true
Are Your ways,
Oh King of Ages

4   Who shall not fear,
           Oh Lord,
           And glorify Your Name?
           For You alone are holy.
           All nations will come
           And worship before You,
           For Your righteous deeds
           Have been disclosed."

5   Then I looked and saw that the Holy of Holies of the temple in heaven was thrown wide open!

6   The seven angels who were assigned to pour out the seven plagues then came from the temple, clothed in spotlessly white linen, with golden belts across their chests.

7   And one of the four Living Beings handed each of them a golden flask filled with the terrible wrath of the Living God who lives forever and forever.

8   The temple was filled with smoke from His glory and power; and no one could enter until the seven angels had completed pouring out the seven plagues.

CHAPTER 16

And I heard a mighty voice shouting from the temple to the seven angels, "Now go your ways and empty out the seven flasks of the wrath of God upon the earth."

2   So the first angel left the temple and poured out his flask over the earth, and horrible, malignant sores broke out on everyone who had the mark of the Creature and was worshiping his statue.

3   The second angel poured out his flask upon the oceans, and they become like the watery blood of a dead man; and everything in all the oceans died.

4   The third angel poured out his flask upon the rivers and springs and they became blood.

5   And I heard this angel of the waters declaring, "You are just in sending this judgment, oh Holy One, who is and was,

6   For Your saints and prophets have been martyred and their blood poured out upon the earth; and now, in turn, You have poured out the blood of those who murdered them; it is their just reward."

7 And I heard the angel of the altar say, "Yes, Lord God Almighty, Your punishments are just and true."

8 Then the fourth angel poured out his flask upon the sun, causing it to scorch all men with its fire.

9 Everyone was burned by this blast of heat, and they cursed the name of God who sent the plagues—they did not change their mind and attitude to give Him glory.

10 Then the fifth angel poured out his flask upon the throne of the Creature from the sea,* and his kingdom was plunged into darkness. And his subjects gnawed their tongues in anguish,

11 And cursed the God of heaven for their pains and sores, but they refused to repent of all their evil deeds.

12 The sixth angel poured out his flask upon the great River Euphrates and it dried up so that the kings from the east could march their armies westward without hindrance.

13 And I saw three evil spirits disguised as frogs leap from the mouth of the Dragon, the Creature, and his False Prophet.

14 These miracle-working demons conferred with all the rulers of the world to gather them for battle against the Lord on that great coming Judgment Day of God Almighty.

15 "Take note: I will come as unexpectedly as a thief! Blessed are all who are awaiting Me, who keep their robes in readiness and will not need to walk naked and ashamed."

16 And they gathered all the armies of the world near a place called, in Hebrew, Armageddon—the Mountain of Megiddo.

17 Then the seventh angel poured out his flask into the air; and a mighty shout came from the throne of the temple in heaven, saying, "It is finished!"

18 Then the thunder crashed and rolled, and lightning flashed; and there was a great earthquake of a magnitude unprecedented in human history.

19 The great city of "Babylon" split into three sections, and cities around the world fell in heaps of rubble; and so all of "Babylon's" sins were remembered in God's thoughts, and she was punished to the last drop of anger in the cup of the wine of the fierceness of His wrath.

20 And islands vanished, and mountains flattened out,

21 And there was an incredible hailstorm from heaven;

hailstones weighing a hundred pounds fell from the sky onto the people below, and they cursed God because of the terrible hail.

CHAPTER 17

One of the seven angels who had poured out the plagues came over and talked with me. "Come with me," he said, "and I will show you what is going to happen to the Notorious Prostitute, who sits upon the many waters of the world.

2 The kings of the world have had immoral relations with her, and the people of the earth have been made drunk by the wine of her immorality."

3 So the angel took me in spirit into the wilderness. There I saw a woman sitting on a scarlet animal that had seven heads and ten horns, written all over with blasphemies against God.

4 The woman wore purple and scarlet clothing and beautiful jewelry made of gold and precious gems and pearls, and held in her hand a golden goblet full of obscenities.

5 A mysterious caption was written on her forehead: "Babylon the Great, Mother of Prostitutes and of Idol Worship Everywhere around the World."

6 I could see that she was drunk—drunk with the blood of the martyrs of Jesus she had killed. I stared at her in horror.

7 "Why are you so surprised?" the angel asked. "I'll tell you who she is and what the animal she is riding represents.

8 He was alive but isn't now. And yet, soon, he will come up out of the bottomless pit and go to eternal destruction; and the people of earth, whose names have not been written in the Book of Life before the world began, will be dumbfounded at his reappearance after being dead.

9 And now think hard: His seven heads represent a certain city* built on seven hills where this woman has her residence.

10 They also represent seven kings. Five have already

fallen, the sixth now reigns, and the seventh is yet to come, but his reign will be brief.

11 The scarlet animal that died is the eighth king, having reigned before as one of the seven; after his second reign, he too will go to his doom.

12 His ten horns are ten kings who have not yet risen to power; they will be appointed to their kingdoms for one brief moment, to reign with him.

13 They will all sign a treaty giving their power and strength to him.

14 Together they will wage war against the Lamb, and the Lamb will conquer them; for He is Lord over all lords, and King of kings, and His people are the called and chosen and faithful ones.

15 The oceans, lakes and rivers that the woman is sitting on represent masses of people of every race and nation.

16 The scarlet animal and his ten horns—which represent ten kings who will reign with him—all hate the woman, and will attack her and leave her naked and ravaged by fire.

17 For God will put a plan into their minds, a plan that will carry out His purposes: they will mutually agree to give their authority to the scarlet animal, so that the words of God will be fulfilled.

18 And this woman you saw in your vision represents the great city that rules over the kings of the earth."

CHAPTER 18

After all this I saw another angel come down from heaven with great authority, and the earth grew bright with his splendor.

2 He gave a mighty shout, "Babylon the Great is fallen, is fallen; she has become a den of demons, a haunt of devils and every kind of evil spirit.

3 For all the nations have drunk the fatal wine of her intense immorality. The rulers of the earth have enjoyed themselves with her, and businessmen throughout the world have grown rich from all her luxurious living."

4 Then I heard another voice calling from heaven,

"Come away from her, My people; do not take part in her sins, or you will be punished with her.

5 For her sins are piled as high as heaven and God is ready to judge her for her crimes.

6 Do to her as she has done to you, and more—give double penalty for all her evil deeds. She brewed many a cup of woe for others—give twice as much to her.

7 She has lived in luxury and pleasure—match it now with torments and with sorrows. She boasts, 'I am queen upon my throne. I am no helpless widow. I will not experience sorrow.'

8 Therefore the sorrows of death and mourning and famine shall overtake her in a single day, and she shall be utterly consumed by fire; for mighty is the Lord who judges her."

9 And the world leaders, who took part in her immoral acts and enjoyed her favors, will mourn for her as they see the smoke rising from her charred remains.

10 They will stand far off trembling with fear and crying out, "Alas, Babylon, that mighty city! In one moment her judgment fell."

11 The merchants of the earth will weep and mourn for her, for there is no one left to buy their goods.

12 She was their biggest customer for gold and silver, precious stones, pearls, finest linens, purple silks, and scarlet; and every kind of perfumed wood, and ivory goods and most expensive wooden carvings, and brass and iron and marble;

13 And spices and perfumes and incense, ointment and frankincense, wine, olive oil, and fine flour; wheat, cattle, sheep, horses, chariots, and slaves—and even the souls of men.

14 "All the fancy things you loved so much are gone," they cry, "the dainty luxuries and splendor that you prized so much will never be yours again. They are gone forever."

15 And so the merchants who have become wealthy by selling her these things shall stand at a distance, fearing danger to themselves, weeping and crying.

16 "Alas, that great city, so beautiful—like a woman clothed in finest purple and scarlet linens, decked out with gold and precious stones and pearls!

17 In one moment, all the wealth of the city is gone!"

And all the shipowners and captains of the merchant ships and crews will stand a long way off,

18   Crying as they watch the smoke ascend and saying, "Where in all the world is there another city such as this?"

19   And they will throw dust on their heads in their sorrow and say, "Alas, alas, for that great city! She made us all rich from her great wealth. And now in a single hour all is gone. . . ."

20   But you, oh heaven, rejoice over her fate; and you, oh children of God and the prophets and the apostles! For at last God has given judgment against her for you.

21   Then a mighty angel picked up a boulder shaped like a millstone and threw it into the ocean and shouted, "Babylon, that great city, shall be thrown away as I have thrown away this stone, and she shall disappear forever.

22   Never again will the sound of music be there— no more pianos, saxophones, and trumpets. No industry of any kind will ever again exist there, and there will be no more milling of the grain.

23   Dark, dark will be her nights; not even a lamp in a window will ever be seen again. No more joyous wedding bells and happy voices of the bridegrooms and the brides. Her businessmen were known around the world and she deceived all nations with her sorceries.

24   And she was responsible for the blood of all the martyred prophets and the saints."

CHAPTER 19

After this I heard the shouting of a vast crowd in heaven, "Hallelujah! Praise the Lord! Salvation is from our God. Honor and authority belong to Him alone;

2   For His judgments are just and true. He has punished the Great Prostitute who corrupted the earth with her sin; and He has avenged the murder of His servants."

3   Again and again their voices rang, "Praise the Lord! The smoke from her burning ascends forever and forever!"

4   Then the twenty-four elders and four Living Beings fell down and worshiped God, who was sitting upon the throne, and said, "Amen! Hallelujah! Praise the Lord!"

5   And out of the throne came a voice that said,

"Praise our God, all you His servants, small and great, who fear Him."

6   Then I heard again what sounded like the shouting of a huge crowd, or like the waves of a hundred oceans crashing on the shore, or like the mighty rolling of great thunder, "Praise the Lord. For the Lord our God, the Almighty, reigns.

7   Let us be glad and rejoice and honor Him; for the time has come for the wedding banquet of the Lamb, and His bride has prepared herself.

8   She is permitted to wear the cleanest and whitest and finest of linens." (Fine linen represents the good deeds done by the people of God.)

9   And the angel dictated this sentence to me: "Blessed are those who are invited to the wedding feast of the Lamb." And he added, "God Himself has stated this."

10   Then I fell down at his feet to worship him, but he said, "No! Don't! For I am a servant of God just as you are, and as your brother Christians are, who testify of their faith in Jesus. The purpose of all prophecy and of all I have shown you is to tell about Jesus."

11   Then I saw heaven opened and a white horse standing there; and the One sitting on the horse was named "Faithful and True"—the One who justly punishes and makes war.

12   His eyes were like flames, and on His head were many crowns. A name was written on His forehead,* and only He knew its meaning.

13   He was clothed with garments dipped in blood, and His title was "The Word of God."

14   The armies of heaven, dressed in finest linen, white and clean, followed Him on white horses.

15   In His mouth He held a sharp sword to strike down the nations; He ruled them with an iron grip; and He trod the winepress of the fierceness of the wrath of Almighty God.

16   On His robe and thigh were written this title: "KING OF KINGS AND LORD OF LORDS."

17   Then I saw an angel standing in the sunshine, shouting loudly to the birds, "Come! Gather together for the supper of the Great God!

18   Come and eat the flesh of kings, and captains, and

great generals; of horses and riders; and of all humanity, both great and small, slave and free."

19 Then I saw the Evil Creature gathering the governments of the earth and their armies to fight against the One sitting on the horse and His army.

20 And the Evil Creature was captured, and with him the False Prophet, who could do mighty miracles when the Evil Creature was present—miracles that deceived all who had accepted the Evil Creature's mark, and who worshiped his statue. Both of them—the Evil Creature and his False Prophet—were thrown alive into the Lake of Fire that burns with sulphur.

21 And their entire army was killed with the sharp sword in the mouth of the One riding the white horse, and all the birds of heaven were gorged with their flesh.

CHAPTER 20

Then I saw an angel come down from heaven with the key to the bottomless pit and a heavy chain in his hand.

2 He seized the Dragon—that old Serpent, the Devil, Satan—and bound him in chains for 1,000 years,

3 And threw him into the bottomless pit, which he then shut and locked, so that he could not fool the nations any more until the thousand years were finished. Afterwards he would be released again for a little while.

4 Then I saw thrones, and sitting on them were those who had been given the right to judge. And I saw the souls of those who had been beheaded for their testimony about Jesus, for proclaiming the Word of God, and who had not worshiped the creature or his statute, nor accepted his mark on their foreheads or their hands. They had come to life again and now they reigned with Christ for a thousand years.

5 This is the First Resurrection. (The rest of the dead did not come back to life until the thousand years had ended.)

6 Blessed and holy are those who share in the First Resurrection. For them the Second Death holds no terrors, for they will be priests of God and of Christ, and shall reign with Him a thousand years.

7 When the thousand years end, Satan will be let out of his prison.

8   He will go out to deceive the nations of the world and gather them together, with Gog and Magog, for battle —a mighty host, numberless as sand along the shore.

9   They will go up across the broad plain of the earth and surround God's people and the beloved city of Jerusalem* on every side. But fire from God in heaven will flash down on the attacking armies and consume them.

10   Then the Devil who had betrayed them will again be thrown into the Lake of Fire burning with sulphur where the Creature and False Prophets are, and they will be tormented day and night forever and ever.

11   And I saw a great white throne and the One who sat upon it, from whose face the earth and sky fled away, but they found no place to hide.

12   I saw the dead, great and small, standing before God; and The Books were opened, including the Book of Life. And the dead were judged according to the things written in The Books, each according to the deeds he had done.

13   The oceans surrendered the bodies buried in them; and the earth and the underworld gave up the dead in them. Each was judged according to his deeds.

14   And Death and Hell were thrown into the Lake of Fire. This is the Second Death—the Lake of Fire.

15   And if anyone's name was not found recorded in the Book of Life, he was thrown into the Lake of Fire.

CHAPTER 21

Then I saw a new earth (with no oceans!) and a new sky, for the present earth and sky had disappeared.

2   And I, John, saw the Holy City, the new Jerusalem, coming down from God out of heaven. It was a glorious sight, beautiful as a bride at her wedding.

3   I heard a loud shout from the throne saying, "Look, the home of God is now among men, and He will live with them and they will be His people; yes, God Himself will be among them.

4   He will wipe away all tears from their eyes, and there shall be no more death, or sorrow, or crying, or pain. All of that has gone forever."

5   And the One sitting on the throne said, "See, I am

making all things new!" And then He said to me, "Write this down, for what I tell you is trustworthy and true:

6   It is finished! I am the A and Z—the beginning and the end. I will give to the thirsty the springs of the Water of Life—as a gift!

7   Everyone who conquers will inherit all these blessings, and I will be his God and he will be My son.

8   But cowards who turn back from following me, and those who are unfaithful to Me, and murderers, and those conversing with demons, and idol worshipers and all liars —their doom is in the Lake that burns with fire and sulphur. This is the Second Death."

9   Then one of the seven angels, who had emptied the flasks containing the seven last plagues came and said to me, "Come with me and I will show you the bride, the Lamb's wife."

10   In a vision he took me to a towering mountain peak and from there I watched that wondrous city, the holy Jerusalem, descending out of the skies from God.

11   It was filled with the glory of God, and flashed and glowed like a precious gem, crystal clear like jasper.

12   Its walls were broad and high, with twelve gates guarded by twelve angels. And the names of the twelve tribes of Israel were written on the gates.

13   There were three gates on each side—north, south, east, and west.

14   The walls had twelve foundation stones, and on them were written the names of the twelve apostles of the Lamb.

15   The angel held in his hand a golden measuring stick to measure the city and its gates and walls.

16   When he measured it, he found it was a square as wide as it was long; in fact, it was in the form of a cube, for its height was exactly the same as its other dimensions—1500 miles each way.

17   Then he measured the thickness of the walls and found them to be 216 feet across! (The angel called out these measurements to me, using standard units.)

18   The wall was made of jasper; the city itself was pure transparent gold, like glass!

19   The foundation stones were inlaid with gems.

The first layer* with jasper;
The second with sapphire;

The third with chalcedony;
The fourth with emerald;
The fifth with sardonyx;
20   The sixth layer with sardus;
The seventh with chrysolite;
The eighth with beryl;
The ninth with topaz;
The tenth with chrysoprase;
The eleventh with jacinth;
The twelfth with amethyst.

21   The twelve gates were made of pearls—each gate from a single pearl! And the main street was pure transparent gold, like glass.

22   No temple could be seen in the city, for the Lord God Almighty and the Lamb are worshiped in it everywhere.

23   And the city has no need of sun or moon to light it, for the glory of God and of the Lamb illuminate it.

24   Its light will light the nations of the earth, and the rulers of the world will come and bring their glory to it.

25   Its gates never close: they stay open all day long—and there is no night!

26   And the glory and honor of all the nations shall be brought into it.

27   Nothing evil will be permitted in it—no one immoral or dishonest—but only those whose names are written in the Lamb's Book of Life.

CHAPTER 22

And he pointed out to me a river of pure Water of Life, clear as crystal, flowing from the throne of God and the Lamb,

2   Coursing down the center of the main street. On each side of the river grew Trees of Life, bearing twelve crops of fruit, with a fresh crop each month; the leaves were used for medicine to heal the nations.

3   There shall be nothing in the city which is evil; for the throne of God and of the Lamb will be there, and His servants will worship Him.

4   And they shall see His face; and His name shall be written on their foreheads.

5 And there will be no night there—no need for lamps or sun—for the Lord God will be their light; and they shall reign forever and ever.

*   *   *   *

6, 7 Then the angel said to me, "These words are trustworthy and true: 'I am coming soon!' God who tells His prophets what the future holds has sent His angel to tell you this will happen soon. Blessed are those who believe it and all else written in the scroll."

8 I, John, saw and heard all these things, and fell down to worship the angel who showed them to me;

9 But again he said, "No, don't do anything like that. I too am a servant of Jesus as you are, and as your brothers the prophets are, as well as all those who heed the truth stated in this Book. Worship God alone."

10 Then he instructed me, "Do not seal up what you have written, for the time of fulfillment is near.

11 And when that time comes, all doing wrong will do it more and more; the vile will become more vile; good men will be better; those who are holy will continue on in greater holiness."

12 "See, I am coming soon, and My reward is with Me, to repay everyone according to the deeds he has done.

13 I am the A and Z, the Beginning and the End, the First and Last.

14 Blessed forever are all who are washing their robes, to have the right to enter in through the gates of the city, and to eat the fruit from the Tree of Life.

15 Outside the city are those who have strayed away from God, and the sorcerers and the immoral and murderers and idolaters, and all who love to lie, and do it.

16 I, Jesus, have sent My angel to you to tell the churches all these things. I am both David's Root and his Descendant. I am the bright Morning Star.

17 The Spirit and the bride say, 'Come.' Let each one who hears them say the same, 'Come.' Let the thirsty one come—anyone who wants to; let him come and drink the Water of Life without charge.

18 And I solemnly declare to everyone who reads this book: if anyone adds anything to what is written here, God shall add to him the plagues described in this book.

19   And if anyone subtracts any part of these prophecies, God shall take away his share in the Tree of Life, and in the Holy City just described.

20   He who has said all these things declares: Yes, I am coming soon!"

Amen! Come, Lord Jesus!

21   The grace of our Lord Jesus Christ be with you all. Amen!

THE GOSPEL OF JOHN

The Book of The Revelation ends the New Testament, and for some readers the mysteries of this last book remain the mystery that surrounds Jesus Christ.

Who is He, really?

Another New Testament book written by the author of The Revelation gives some clear answers. It is the Gospel of John. He was the disciple whose early deeds gained him the nickname "Son of Thunder"—and his later character the title "the beloved apostle." This close companion of Jesus reports Jesus' own description of Himself as:

"I am the Bread of Life" (6:35).

"I am the Light of the World" (8:12).

"I am the Gate" (10:9).

"I am the Good Shepherd" (10:19).

"I am the Way—yes, and the Truth and the Life" (14:6).

Here, in the Gospel of John, the reader can meet the man who is also the Son of God, the One who gives eternal life to everyone who believes in Him (3:16).

JOHN

CHAPTER 1

Before anything else existed, there was Christ, with God. He has always been alive and is Himself God.

3 He created everything there is—nothing exists that He didn't make.

4 Eternal life is in Him, and this life gives light to all mankind.

5 His life is the light that shines through the darkness—and the darkness can never extinguish it.

6, 7 God sent John (the Baptist) as a witness so that everyone would know Jesus Christ is the true Light.

8 John himself was not the Light; he was only a witness to identify it.

9 Later on the one who is the true Light arrived to shine on everyone coming into the world.

10 But although He made the world, the world didn't recognize Him when He came.

11, 12 Even in His own land and among His own people, the Jews, He was not accepted. Only a few would welcome and receive Him. But to all who received Him, He gave the right to become children of God. All they needed to do was believe He would save them.

13 All those who believed this were reborn!—not a physical rebirth, resulting from human passion or plan —but from the will of God.

14 And Christ became a human being and lived here on earth among us and was full of loving forgiveness and truth. And some of us have seen His glory—the glory of the only Son of the heavenly Father!

15 John pointed Him out to the people, telling the crowds, "This is the one I was talking about when I said,

'Someone is coming who is greater by far than I am—for He existed long before I did!' "

16 We have all benefited from the rich blessings He brought to us—blessing upon blessing heaped upon us!

17 For Moses gave us only the Law with its rigid demands and merciless justice, while Jesus Christ brought us loving forgiveness as well.

18 No one has ever actually seen God, but of course His only Son has, for He is the companion of the Father and has told us all about Him.

19 The Jewish leaders sent priests and assistant priests from Jerusalem to ask John whether he claimed to be the Messiah.

20 He denied it flatly. "I am not the Christ," he said.

21 "Well then, who are you?" they asked. "Are you Elijah?"

"No," he replied.

"Are you the Prophet?"

"No."

22 "Then who are you? Tell us, so we can give an answer to those who sent us. What do you have to say for yourself?"

23 He replied, "I am a voice from the barren wilderness, shouting as Isaiah prophesied, 'Get ready for the coming of the Lord!' "

24, 25 Then those who were sent by the Pharisees asked him, "If you aren't the Messiah or Elijah or the Prophet, what right do you have to baptize?"

26 John told them, "I merely baptize with water, but right here in the crowd is someone you have never met,

27 Who will soon begin His ministry among you, and I am not fit to be His slave."

28 This incident took place at Bethany, a village on the other side of the Jordan River where John was baptizing.

29 The next day John saw Jesus coming toward Him and said, "Look! This is the Lamb of God who takes away the world's sin!

30 This is the one I was talking about when I said, 'Soon a man far greater than I am is coming who existed long before me!'

31 I didn't know He was the one, but I am here

baptizing with water in order to point Him out to the nation of Israel."

32 Then John told about seeing the Holy Spirit in the form of a dove descending from heaven and resting upon Jesus.

33 "I didn't know He was the one," John said again, "but at the time God sent me to baptize, He told me, 'When you see the Holy Spirit descending and resting upon someone—He is the one you are looking for. He is the one who baptizes with the Holy Spirit.'

34 I saw it happen to this man, and I therefore testify that He is the Son of God."

35 The following day as John was standing with two of his disciples,

36 Jesus walked by. John looked at Him intently and then declared, "See! There is the Lamb of God!"

37 Then two of John's disciples turned and followed Jesus!

38 Jesus looked around and saw them following. "What do you want?" He asked them.

"Sir," they replied, "where do You live?"

39 "Come and see," He said. So they went with Him to the place where He was staying and were with Him from about four o'clock that afternoon until the evening.

40 (One of these men was Andrew, Simon Peter's brother.)

41 Andrew then went to find his brother Peter and told him, "We have found the Messiah!"

42 And he brought him to Jesus. Jesus looked intently at Peter for a moment and then said, "You are Simon, John's son—but you shall be called Peter, the Rock!"

43 The next day Jesus decided to go to Galilee. He found Philip and told him, "Come with Me."

44 (Philip was from Bethsaida, Andrew and Peter's home town.)

45 Then Philip went off to look for Nathanael and told him, "We have found the Messiah!—the very person Moses and the prophets told about! His name is Jesus, the son of Joseph from Nazareth!"

46 "Nazareth!" exclaimed Nathanael, "Can anything good come from there?"

"Just come and see for yourself," Philip declared.

47 As they approached, Jesus said, "Here comes an honest man—a true son of Israel!"

48 "How do you know what I am like?" Nathanael demanded.

And Jesus replied, "I could see you under that fig tree before Philip found you!"

49 Nathanael replied, "Sir, You are the Son of God —the King of Israel!"

50 Jesus asked him, "Do you believe all this just because I told you I had seen you under the fig tree? You will see greater proofs than this!

51 You will even see heaven open and the angels of God coming back and forth to Me, the Man of Glory."

CHAPTER 2

Two days later Jesus' mother was a guest at a wedding in the village of Cana in Galilee,

2 And Jesus and His disciples were invited too.

3 The wine supply ran out during the festivities, and Jesus' mother came to Him with the problem.

4 "I can't help you now," He said. "It isn't yet My time for miracles."

5 Then His mother told the servants, "Do whatever He tells you!"

6 Six stone waterpots were standing there; they were used for Jewish ceremonial purposes and held perhaps 20 to 30 gallons each.

7, 8 Jesus told the servants to fill them to the brim with water. When this was done He said, "Dip some out and take it to the master of ceremonies."

9 When the master of ceremonies tasted the water (that was now wine!) not knowing where it had come from (though of course the servants did), he called the bridegroom over.

10 "This is wonderful stuff!" he said. "You're different from most hosts! Usually they give out the best wine first; and afterwards when everyone is full and doesn't care, then they bring out the less expensive brands! But you have kept the best for the last!"

11 This miracle at Cana in Galilee was Jesus' first

public demonstration of His heaven-sent power. And His disciples believed that He really was the Messiah.

12 After the wedding He left for Capernaum for a few days with His mother, brothers, and disciples.

13 It was time for the Jewish Passover celebration, and Jesus went to Jerusalem.

14 In the Temple area He saw merchants selling cattle, sheep, and doves for sacrifices, and money changers behind their counters.

15 Jesus made a whip from some ropes and chased them all out, and drove out the sheep and oxen, scattered the money changers' coins over the floor and turned over their tables!

16 Then going over to the men selling doves, He told them, "Get these things out of here! Don't turn My Father's House into a market!"

17 Then His disciples remembered this Old Testament prophecy: "Concern for God's House will be My undoing!"

18 "What right have You to order them out?" the Jewish leaders demanded. "If You have this authority from God, show us a miracle to prove it."

19 "All right," Jesus replied, "this is the miracle I will do for you: Destroy this Sanctuary and in three days I will raise it up!"

20 "What!" they exclaimed. "It took 46 years to build this Temple, and You can do it in three days?"

21 But by "this Sanctuary" He meant His body.

22 After He came back to life again, the disciples remembered His saying this and realized that what He had quoted from the Old Testament really did refer to Him and had come true!

23 Because of the miracles He did in Jerusalem at the Passover celebration, many people were convinced that He was indeed the Messiah.

24, 25 But Jesus didn't trust them, for He knew mankind to the core. No one needed to tell Him how changeable human beings are.

CHAPTER 3

After dark one night a Jewish religious leader named Nicodemus, a member of the sect of the Pharisees, came for an interview with Jesus. "Sir," he said, "we all know that God has sent You to teach us. Your miracles are proof enough of this."

3 Jesus replied, "With all the earnestness I possess I tell you this: Unless you are born again, you can never get into the Kingdom of God."

4 "Born again!" exclaimed Nicodemus. "What do You mean? How can an old man go back into his mother's womb and be born again?"

5 Jesus replied, "What I am telling you so earnestly is this: Unless one is born of water and the Spirit, he cannot enter the Kingdom of God.

6 Men can only reproduce human life, but the Holy Spirit gives you new life from heaven,

7 So don't be surprised at My statement that you must be born again!

8 Just as you can hear the wind but can't tell where it comes from or where it will go next, so it is with the Spirit! We do not know on whom He will next bestow this life from heaven."

9 "What do You mean?" Nicodemus asked.

10, 11 Jesus replied, "You, a respected Jewish teacher, and yet you don't understand these things? I am telling you what I know and have seen—and yet you won't believe Me.

12 But if you don't even believe Me when I tell you about such things as these happening here among men, how can you possibly believe if I tell you what is going on in heaven?

13 For only I, the Man of Heaven, have come to earth and will return to heaven again.

14 And as Moses in the wilderness lifted up the image of a bronze serpent on a pole, even so must I be lifted up upon a pole

15 So that anyone who believes in Me will have eternal life.

16 For God loved the world so much that He gave

His only Son so that anyone who believes in Him will not perish but have eternal life.

17   God did not send His Son into the world to condemn the world, but to save it.

18   There is no eternal doom awaiting those who are trusting Him to save them. But those who don't trust Him have already been tried and condemned for not believing in the only Son of God.

19   Their sentence is based on this fact: that the Light from heaven came into the world, but they loved their former darkness more than the Light, for their deeds were evil.

20   They hated the heavenly Light because they wanted to sin in the darkness. They stayed away from that Light for fear their sins would be exposed and they would be punished.

21   But those doing right come gladly to the Light to let everyone see that they are doing what God wants them to."

*   *   *   *   *

22   Afterwards Jesus and His disciples left Jerusalem and stayed for a while in Judea and baptized people there.

*   *   *   *   *

23, 24   John the Baptist was not yet in prison. He was baptizing at Aenon, near Salim, because there was plenty of water there.

25   One day someone began an argument with John's disciples, telling them that Jesus' baptism was best.

26   So they came to John and said, "Master, the man you met on the other side of the Jordan River—the one you said was the Messiah—He is baptizing too, and everybody is going over there instead of coming here to us."

27   John replied, "God in heaven appoints each man's work.

28   My work is to prepare the way for that man so that everyone will go to Him. You yourselves know how plainly I told you that I am not the Messiah. I am here to prepare the way before Him—that is all.

29 The crowds will naturally go to the main attraction*—the bride will go where the bridegroom is! A bridegroom's friends rejoice with him. I am the bridegroom's friend, and I am filled with joy at His success.

30 He must become greater and greater, and I must become less and less.

31 He has come from heaven and is greater than anyone else. I am of the earth, and my understanding is limited to the things of earth.

32 He tells what He has seen and heard, but how few believe what He tells them!

33, 34 Those who believe Him discover that God is a fountain of truth! For this one—sent by God—speaks God's words, for God's Spirit is upon Him without measure or limit.

35 The Father loves this man because He is His Son, and God has given Him everything there is.

36 And all who trust Him—God's Son—to save them have eternal life; those who don't believe and obey Him shall never see heaven, but the wrath of God remains upon them."

CHAPTER 4

When the Lord knew the Pharisees had heard about the greater crowds coming to Him than to John to be baptized and to become His disciples—(though Jesus Himself didn't baptize them, but His disciples did)—

3 He left Judea and returned to the province of Galilee.

4 He had to go through Samaria on the way,

5, 6 And around noon as He approached the village of Sychar, He came to Jacob's Well, located on the parcel of ground Jacob gave to his son Joseph. Jesus was tired from the long walk in the hot sun and sat wearily beside the well.

7 Soon a Samaritan woman came to draw water, and Jesus asked her for a drink.

8 He was alone at the time as His disciples had gone into the village to buy some food.

9 The woman was surprised that a Jew would ask a "despised Samaritan" for anything (usually they won't

even speak to them!), and she remarked about this to Jesus.

10   He replied, "If you only knew what a wonderful gift God has for you, and who I am, you would ask Me for some *living* water!"

11   "But You don't have a rope or a bucket," she said, "and this is a very deep well! From where would you get this living water?

12   And besides, are you greater than our ancestor Jacob? How can you offer better water than this which he himself enjoyed, along with his sons and cattle?"

13   Jesus replied that people soon became thirsty again after drinking that water.

14   "But the water I give them," He said, "becomes a perpetual spring within them, watering them forever with eternal life."

15   "Please, sir," the woman said, "give me some of that water! Then I'll never be thirsty again and won't have to make this long trip out here every day."

16   "Go and get your husband," Jesus told her.

17   "But I'm not married," the woman replied.

"All too true!" Jesus said,

18   "For you have had five husbands, and you aren't even married to the man you're living with now! You couldn't have spoken a truer word!"

19   "Sir," the woman said, "You must be a prophet!

20   But say, tell me, why is it you Jews insist that Jerusalem is the only place of worship, while we Samaritans claim it is here (at Mount Gerazim*), where our ancestors worshiped?"

21-24   Jesus replied, "The time is coming, Ma'am, when we will no longer be concerned about whether to worship the Father here or in Jerusalem! For it's not *where* we worship that counts, but *how* we worship—is our worship spiritual and real? Do we have the Holy Spirit's help? For God is Spirit, and we must have His Spirit's help to worship as we should. The Father wants this kind of worship from us. But you Samaritans know so little about Him, worshiping blindly, while we Jews know all about Him, for salvation comes to the world through the Jews."

25   The woman said, "Well, at least I know that the

Messiah will come—the one they call Christ—and when He does, He will explain everything to us."

26　Then Jesus told her, "I am the Messiah!"

27　Just then His disciples arrived. They were surprised to find Him talking to a woman, but none of them asked Him why, or what they had been discussing.

28　Then the woman left her waterpot beside the well and went back to the village and told everyone, "Come and meet a man who told me everything I ever did! Can this be the Messiah?"

29　So the people came streaming from the village to see Him.

31　Meanwhile, the disciples were urging Jesus to eat.

32　"No," He said, "I have some food you don't know about!"

33　"Who brought it to Him?" the disciples asked among themselves.

34　Then Jesus explained: "My nourishment comes from doing the will of God who sent Me and finishing His work.

35　Do you think the work of harvesting will not begin until the summer ends four months from now? Look around you! Vast fields of human souls are ripening all around us and are ready now for reaping.

36　The reapers will be paid good wages and will be gathering eternal souls into the granaries of heaven! What joys await the sower and the reaper, both together!

37　For it is true that one sows and someone else reaps.

38　I sent you to reap where you didn't sow; others did the work, and you received the harvest!"

39　Many from that Samaritan village believed He was the Messiah because of the woman's report, "He told me everything I ever did!"

40　So when they saw Him at the well, they begged Him to stay at their village; and He did for two days.

41　While He was there teaching them, many others believed.

42　Then they said to the woman, "Now we believe because we have heard Him ourselves, not just because of what you told us. He is indeed the Savior of the world."

43   At the end of the two days' stay He went on into
Galilee.

44   For, as Jesus used to say, "A prophet is honored
everywhere but in his own country!"

45   And sure enough, the Galileans welcomed Him
with open arms, for they had been in Jerusalem at the
Passover celebration and had seen some of His miracles.

46, 47   In the course of His journey through Galilee
He arrived at the town of Cana, where He had turned
the water into wine. While He was there, a government
official in the city of Capernaum, whose son was very sick,
heard that Jesus had come from Judea and was traveling
in Galilee. This man went over to Cana, found Jesus, and
begged Him to come to Capernaum with him and heal
his son, who was now at death's door.

48   Jesus asked, "Won't any of you believe in Me
unless I do more and more miracles?"

49   The official pled, "Sir, please come now before
my child dies."

50   Then Jesus told him, "Go back home. Your son is
healed!" And the man believed Jesus and started home.

51   While he was on his way, some of his servants
met him with the news that all was well—his son had re-
covered!

52   He asked them when the lad had begun to feel
better, and they replied, "Yesterday afternoon at about
one o'clock his fever was gone!"

53   Then the father realized it was the same moment
that Jesus had told him, "Your son is healed." And the
officer and his entire household believed that Jesus was
the Messiah.

54   This was Jesus' second miracle in Galilee after
coming from Judea.

CHAPTER 5

Afterwards Jesus returned to Jerusalem for one of the
Jewish religious holidays.

2   Inside the city near the Sheep Gate was Bethesda
Pool, with five covered platforms or porches surrounding
it.

3   Crowds of sick folks—lame, blind, or with para-

lyzed limbs—lay on the platforms (waiting for a certain movement of the water,

4 For an angel of the Lord came from time to time and disturbed the water, and the first person to step down into it afterwards was healed!)

5 One of the men lying there had been sick for 38 years.

6 When Jesus saw him and knew how long he had been ill, He asked him, "Would you like to get well?"

7 "I can't," the sick man said, "for I have no one to help me into the pool at the movement of the water. Someone else always gets in ahead of me while I am trying to get there."

8 Jesus told him, "Stand up, roll up your sleeping mat and go on home!"

9 Instantly, the man was healed! He rolled up the mat and began walking! But it was on the Sabbath when this miracle was done.

10 So the Jewish leaders objected They said to the man who was cured, "You can't work on the Sabbath! It's illegal to carry that sleeping mat!"

11 "The man who healed me told me to," was his reply.

12 "Who said such a thing as that?" they demanded.

13 The man didn't know, and Jesus had disappeared into the crowd.

14 But afterwards Jesus found him in the Temple and told him, "Now you are well; don't sin as you did before,* or something even worse may happen to you."

15 Then the man went to find the Jewish leaders, and told them it was Jesus who had healed him.

16 So they began harassing Jesus as a Sabbath breaker.

17 But Jesus replied, "My Father constantly does good,* and I'm following His example!"

18 Then the Jewish leaders were all the more eager to kill Him because in addition to disobeying their Sabbath laws, He had spoken of God as His Father, thereby making Himself equal with God.

19 Jesus replied, "The Son can do nothing by Himself. He does only what He sees the Father doing, and in the same way.

20 For the Father loves the Son, and tells Him every-

thing He is doing; and the Son will do far more awesome miracles than this man's healing!

21 He will even raise from the dead anyone He wants to, just as the Father does.

22 And the Father leaves all judgment of sin to His Son,

23 So that everyone will honor the Son, just as they honor the Father. But if you refuse to honor God's Son, whom He sent to you, then you are certainly not honoring the Father.

24 I say emphatically that anyone who listens to My message and believes in God who sent Me has eternal life, and will never be damned for his sins, but has already passed out of death into life.

25 And I solemnly declare that the time is coming, in fact, it is here, when the dead shall hear My voice—the voice of the Son of God—and those who listen shall live.

26 The Father has life in Himself, and has granted His Son to have life in Himself,

27 And to judge the sins of all mankind because He is the Son of Man.

28 Don't be so surprised! Indeed the time is coming when all the dead in their graves shall hear the voice of God's Son,

29 And shall rise again—those who have done good, to eternal life; and those who have continued in evil, to judgment.

30 But I pass no judgment without consulting the Father. I judge as I am told. And My judgment is absolutely fair and just, for it is according to the will of God who sent Me and is not merely My own!

31 When I make claims about Myself they aren't believed,

32, 33 But someone else, yes, John the Baptist,* is making these claims for Me. You have gone out to listen to his preaching, and I know that all he says about Me is true!

34 But the truest witness I have is not from a man, though I have reminded you about John's witness so that you will believe in Me and be saved.

35 John shone brightly for a while, and you benefited and rejoiced,

36 But I have a greater witness than John. I refer to the miracles I do; these have been assigned Me by the Father, and they prove that the Father has sent Me.

37 And the Father Himself has also testified about Me, though not appearing to you personally, or speaking to you directly.

38 But you are not listening to Him, for you refuse to believe Me—the one sent to you with God's message.

39 You search the Scriptures, for you believe they give you eternal life. And the Scriptures point to Me!

40 Yet you won't come to Me so that I can give you this life eternal!

41, 42 Your approval or disapproval means nothing to Me, for as I know so well, you don't have God's love within you.

43 I know because I have come to you representing My Father and you refuse to welcome Me, though you readily enough receive those who aren't sent from Him, but represent only themselves!

44 No wonder you can't believe! For you gladly honor each other, but you don't care about the honor that comes from the only God!

45 Yet it is not I who will accuse you of this to the Father—Moses will! Moses, on whose laws you set your hopes of heaven.

46 For you have refused to believe Moses. He wrote about Me, but you refuse to believe him, and so you refuse to believe in Me.

47 And since you don't believe what he wrote, no wonder you don't believe Me either."

CHAPTER 6

After this, Jesus crossed over the Sea of Galilee (also known as the Sea of Tiberias).

2-5 And a huge crowd (many of them pilgrims on their way to Jerusalem for the annual Passover celebration) were following Him wherever He went, to watch Him heal the sick. So when Jesus went up into the hills and sat down with His disciples around Him, He soon saw a great multitude of people climbing the hill, looking for

Him. Turning to Philip He asked, "Philip, where can we buy bread to feed all these people?"

6 (He was testing Philip, for He already knew what He was going to do!)

7 Philip replied, "It would take a fortune to begin to do it!"

8, 9 Then Andrew, Simon Peter's brother, spoke up. "There's a youngster here with five barley loaves and a couple of fish! But what good is that with all this mob?"

10 "Tell everyone to sit down," Jesus ordered. And all of them (the approximate count of the men only was 5,000) sat down on the grassy slopes.

11 Then Jesus took the loaves and gave thanks to God and passed them out to the people. Afterwards He did the same with the fish. And everyone had all he wanted.

12 "Now gather the scraps," Jesus told His disciples, "so that nothing is wasted."

13 And twelve baskets were filled with the leftovers!

14 When the people realized what a great miracle had happened, they exclaimed, "Surely, He is the Prophet we have been expecting!"

15 Jesus saw that they were ready to take Him by force and make Him their king, so He went higher into the mountains alone.

16 That evening His disciples went down to the shore to wait for Him there.

17 But as darkness fell and Jesus still hadn't come back, they got into the boat and headed across the lake toward Capernaum.

18, 19 But soon a gale swept down upon them as they rowed, and the sea grew very rough. They were three or four miles out when suddenly they saw Jesus walking toward the boat! They were terrified,

20 But He called out to them and told them not to be afraid.

21 Then they were willing to let Him in, and immediately the boat was where they were going!

22, 23 The next morning, back across the lake, crowds began gathering on the shore, waiting to see Jesus.* For they knew that He and His disciples had come over together and that the disciples had gone off in their boat, leaving Him behind. Several small boats from Tiberias were nearby,

24 So when the people saw that Jesus wasn't there, or His disciples, they got into the boats and went across to Capernaum to look for Him.

25 When they arrived and found Him, they said, "Sir, how did You get here?"

26 Jesus replied, "The truth of the matter is that you want to be with Me because I fed you, not because you believe in Me.

27 But you shouldn't be so concerned about perishable things like food. No, spend your energy seeking the eternal life that I the Man from Heaven can give you. For God the Father has sent Me for this very purpose."

28 They replied, "What should we do to satisfy God?"

29 Jesus told them, "This is the will of God, that you believe in the one He has sent."

30, 31 They replied, "You must show us more miracles if You want us to believe You are the Messiah. Give us free bread every day, like our fathers had while they journeyed through the wilderness! As the Scriptures say, 'Moses gave them bread from heaven.' "

32 Jesus said, "Moses didn't give it to them! My Father did.* And now He offers you true Bread from heaven.

33 The true Bread is a Person—the one sent by God from heaven, and He gives life to the world."

34 "Sir," they said "give us that Bread every day of our lives!"

35 Jesus replied, "I am the Bread of Life! No one coming to Me will ever be hungry again! Those believing in Me will never thirst!

36 But the trouble is, as I have told you before, you haven't believed even though you have seen Me.

37 But some will come to Me—those the Father has given Me—and I will never, never reject them.

38 For I have come here from heaven to do the will of God who sent Me, not to have My own way!

39 And this is the will of God, that I should not lose even one of all those He has given Me, but that I should raise them to eternal life at the Last Day!

40 For it is My Father's will that everyone who sees

His Son and believes on Him should have eternal life, and that I should raise him at the Last Day."

41 Then the Jews began to murmur against Him because He claimed to be the Bread from heaven.

42 "What?" they exclaimed. "Why, He is merely Jesus, the son of Joseph, whose father and mother we know. What is this He is saying, that He came down from heaven?"

43 But Jesus replied, "Don't murmur among yourselves about My saying that!

44 For no one can come to Me unless the Father who sent Me draws him to Me, and at the Last Day I will bring them all back to life.

45 As it is written in the Scriptures, 'They shall all be taught of God.' Those the Father speaks to, who learn the truth from Him, will be attracted to Me.

46 (Not that anyone actually sees the Father, for only I have seen Him.)

47 How earnestly I tell you this—anyone who believes in Me already has eternal life!

48 Yes, I am the Bread of Life!

49 There was no real life* in that bread from the skies, which was given to your fathers in the wilderness, for they all died.

50, 51 But there is such a thing as Bread from heaven giving eternal life to everyone who eats it! And I am that Living Bread that came down out of heaven. Anyone eating this Bread shall live forever; this Bread is My flesh, given to redeem humanity."

52 Then the Jews began arguing with each other about what He meant. "How can this man give us His flesh to eat?" they asked.

53 So Jesus said it again, "With all the earnestness I possess I tell you this: Unless you eat the flesh of the Man of Glory* and drink His blood, you cannot have eternal life within you.

54 But anyone who eats My flesh and drinks My blood has eternal life, and I will raise him at the Last Day.

55 For My flesh is the true food, and My blood is the true drink.

56 Everyone who eats My flesh and drinks My blood is in Me, and I in him.

57 I live by the power of the living Father who sent Me, and in the same way, those who partake of Me shall live because of Me!

58 I am the true Bread from heaven; and anyone who eats this Bread shall live forever, and not die as your fathers did—though they ate bread from heaven."

59 (He preached the above sermon in the synagogue in Capernaum.)

60 Even His disciples said, "This is very hard to understand. Who can tell what He means?"

61 Jesus knew within Himself that His disciples were complaining and said to them, "Does *this* offend you?

62 Then what will you think if you see Me, the Son of Mankind, return to heaven again?

63 Only the Holy Spirit gives eternal life. Those born only once (the physical birth) will never receive this gift. But now I have told you how to get this true spiritual life.

64 But some of you don't believe Me." (For Jesus knew from the beginning who didn't believe, and the one who would betray Him.)

65 And He remarked, "That is what I meant when I said that no one can come to Me unless the Father attracts him to Me."

66 At this point many of His disciples turned away and deserted Him.

67 Then Jesus turned to The Twelve and asked, "Are you going too?"

68 Simon Peter replied, "Master, to whom shall we go? You alone have the words that give eternal life,

69 And we believe them and know You are the holy Son of God."

70 Then Jesus said, "I chose the twelve of you, and one is a devil."

71 (He was speaking of Judas, son of Simon Iscariot, one of The Twelve, who would betray Him.)

CHAPTER 7

After this Jesus went to Galilee, going from village to village, for he wanted to stay out of Judea, where the Jewish leaders were plotting His death.

2   But soon it was time for the Tabernacle Ceremonies, one of the annual Jewish holidays,

3   And Jesus' brothers urged Him to go to Judea for
the celebration. "Go where more people can see Your
miracles!" they scoffed.

4   "You can't be famous when You hide like this! If
You're so great, prove it to the world!"

5   For even His brothers didn't believe in Him.

6   Jesus replied, "It is not the right time for Me to
go now. But you can go any time and it will make no
difference,

7   For the world can't hate you; but it does hate Me
because I accuse it of sin and evil.

8   You go on, and I'll come later when it is the right
time."

9   So He remained in Galilee.

10   But after His brothers had left for the celebration,
then He went too, though secretly, staying out of the
public eye.

11   The Jewish leaders tried to find Him at the celebration and kept asking if anyone had seen Him.

12   There was a lot of discussion about Him among
the crowds. Some said, "He's a wonderful man," while
others said, "No, He is duping the public."

13   But no one had the courage to speak out for Him
in public for fear of reprisals from the Jewish leaders.

14   But midway through the festival, Jesus went up
to the Temple and preached openly.

15   The Jewish leaders were surprised when they
heard Him. "How can He know so much when He's never
been to our schools?" they asked.

16   So Jesus told them, "I'm not teaching you My
own thoughts, but those of God who sent Me.

17   If any of you really determines to do God's will,
then you will certainly know whether My teaching is from
God or is merely My own.

18   Anyone presenting his own ideas is looking for
praise for himself, but anyone seeking to honor the one
who sent him is a good and true person.

19   None of *you* obeys the laws of Moses! So why
pick on *Me* for breaking them? Why kill Me for this?

20   The crowd replied, "You're out of Your mind!
Who's trying to kill You?"

21, 22, 23 Jesus replied, "I worked on the Sabbath by healing a man, and you were glad!* You work on the Sabbath too—when you obey Moses' law of circumcision (actually, this tradition is older than the Mosaic law), for if the correct time for circumcising your children falls on the Sabbath, you go ahead and do it, as you should. So why should I be condemned for making a man completely well on the Sabbath?

24 Think this through and you will see that I am right."

25 Some of the people who lived there in Jerusalem (and knew what was going on*) said among themselves, "Isn't this the man they are trying to kill?

26 But here He is, preaching in public, and they say nothing to Him. Can it be that our leaders have learned after all that He really is the Messiah?

27 But how could He be? For we know where this man was born; when Christ comes, He will just appear and no one will know where He comes from."

28 So Jesus, in a sermon in the Temple, called out, "Yes, you know Me and where I was born and raised, but I am the representative of one you don't know, and He is Truth.

29 I know Him because I was with Him, and He sent Me to you."

30 Then the Jewish leaders sought to arrest Him; but no hand was laid on Him, for God's time had not yet come.

31 Many among the crowds at the Temple believed on Him. "After all," they said, "what miracles do you expect the Messiah to do that this man hasn't done?"

32 When the Pharisees heard that the crowds were in this mood, they and the chief priests sent officers to arrest Jesus.

33 But Jesus told them, "Not yet!* I am to be here a little longer. Then I shall return to the one who sent Me.

34 You will search for Me but not find Me. And you won't be able to come where I am!"

35 The Jewish leaders were puzzled by this statement. "Where is He planning to go?" they asked. "Maybe He is thinking of leaving the country and going as a

missionary among the Jews in other lands or maybe even to the Gentiles!

36 What does He mean about our looking for Him and not being able to find Him, and, 'You won't be able to come where I am'?"

37 On the last day, the climax of the holidays, Jesus shouted to the crowds, "If anyone is thirsty, let him come to Me and drink.

38 For the Scriptures declare that rivers of living water shall flow from the inmost being of anyone who believes in Me."

39 (He was speaking of the Holy Spirit, who would be given to everyone believing in Him; but the Spirit had not yet been given because Jesus had not yet returned to His glory in heaven.)

40 When the crowds heard Him say this, some of them declared, "This man surely is the prophet who will come just before the Messiah."

41, 42 Others said, "He is the Messiah." Still others, "But He *can't* be! Will the Messiah come from *Galilee?* For the Scriptures clearly state that the Messiah will be born of the royal line of David, in *Bethlehem,* the village where David was born."

43 So the crowd was divided about Him.

44 And some wanted Him arrested, but no one touched Him.

45 The Temple police who had been sent to arrest Him returned to the chief priests and Pharisees. "Why didn't you bring Him in?" they demanded.

46 "He says such wonderful things!" they mumbled. "We've never heard anything like it."

47 "So you also have been led astray?" the Pharisees mocked.

48 "Is there a single one of us Jewish rulers or Pharisees who believes He is the Messiah?

49 These stupid crowds do, yes; but what do they know about it? A curse upon them anyway!"

50 Then Nicodemus spoke up. (Remember? He was the Jewish leader who came secretly to interview Jesus.)

51 "Is it legal to convict a man before he is even tried?" he asked.

52 They replied, "Are you a wretched Galilean too?

Search the Scriptures and see for yourself—no prophets will come from Galilee!"

53 Then the meeting broke up and everybody went home.

CHAPTER 8

Jesus returned to the Mount of Olives.

2 Early the next morning He came again to the Temple. A crowd soon gathered, and He sat down and talked to them.

3 As He was speaking, the Jewish leaders and Pharisees brought a woman caught in adultery and placed her out in front of the staring crowd.

4 "Teacher," they said to Jesus, "this woman was caught in the very act of adultery.

5 Moses' law says to kill her. What about it?"

6 They were trying to trap Him into saying something they could use against Him. But Jesus stooped down and wrote in the dust with His finger.

7 They kept demanding an answer, so He stood up again and said, "All right, hurl the stones at her until she dies. But only he who never sinned may throw the first!"

8 Then He stooped down again and wrote some more in the dust.

9 And the Jewish leaders slipped away one by one, beginning with the eldest, until only Jesus was left in front of the crowd with the woman.

10 Then Jesus stood up again and said to her, "Where are your accusers? Didn't even one of them condemn you?"

11 "No, sir," she said.

And Jesus said, "Neither do I. Go and sin no more."

12 Later, in one of His talks, Jesus said to the people, "I am the Light of the world. So if you follow Me, you won't be stumbling through the darkness, for living light will flood your path."

13 The Pharisees replied, "You are boasting—and lying!"

14 Jesus told them, "These claims are true even though I make them concerning Myself. For I know

where I came from and where I am going, but you don't know this about Me.

15 You pass judgment on Me without knowing the facts. I am not judging you now;

16 But if I were, it would be an absolutely correct judgment in every respect, for I have with Me the Father who sent Me.

17 Your laws say that if two men agree on something that has happened, their witness is accepted as fact.

18 Well, I am one witness, and My Father who sent Me is the other."

19 "Where is Your Father?" they asked.

Jesus answered, "You don't know who I am, and so you don't know who My Father is. If you knew Me, then you would know Him too."

20 Jesus made these statements while in the section of the Temple known as the treasury. And He was not arrested, for His time had not yet run out.

21 Later He said to them again, "I am going away; and you will search for Me, and die in your sins. And you cannot come where I am going."

22 The Jews asked, "Is He planning suicide? What does He mean, 'You cannot come where I am going'?"

23 Then He said to them, "You are from below; I am from above. You are of this world; I am not.

24 That is why I said that you will die in your sins; for unless you believe that I am the Messiah, the Son of God, you will die in your sins."

25 "Tell us who You are," they demanded.

He replied, "I am the one I have always claimed to be.

26 I could condemn you for much and teach you much, but I won't, for I say only what I am told to by the one who sent Me; and He is Truth."

27 But they still didn't understand that He was talking to them about God.

28 So Jesus said, "When you have killed the Man of Glory, then you will realize that I am He and that I have not been telling you My own ideas, but have spoken what the Father taught Me.

29 And He who sent Me is with Me—He has not deserted Me—for I always do those things that are pleasing to Him."

30, 31 Then many of the Jewish leaders who heard

Him say these things began believing Him to be the Messiah. Jesus said to them, "You are truly My disciples if you live as I tell you to,

32 And you will know the truth, and the truth will set you free."

33 "But we are descendants of Abraham," they said, "and have never been slaves to any man on earth! What do You mean, 'set free'?"

34 Jesus replied, "You are slaves to sin, every one of you.

35 And slaves don't have rights in their master's home, but the Son has every right there is!

36 So if the Son sets you free, you will indeed be free—

37 Even though You are descendants of Abraham! And yet some of you are trying to kill Me because My message does not find a home within your hearts.

38 I am telling you what I saw when I was with My Father. But you are following the advice of *your* father."

39 "Our father is Abraham," they declared.

"No!" Jesus replied, "for if he were, you would follow his good example.

40 But instead you are trying to kill Me—and all because I told you the truth I heard from God. Abraham wouldn't do a thing like that!

41 No, you are obeying your *real* father when you act that way."

They replied, "We were not born out of wedlock—our true Father is God Himself."

42 Jesus told them, "If that were so, then you would love Me, for I have come to you from God. I am not here on My own, but He sent Me.

43 Why can't you understand what I am saying? It is because you are prevented from doing so!

44 For you are children of your father the Devil, and you love to do the evil things he does. He was a murderer from the beginning and a hater of truth—there is not an iota of truth in him. When he lies, it is perfectly normal; for he is the father of liars.

45 And so when I tell the truth, you just naturally don't believe it!

46 Which of you can truthfully accuse Me of one

single sin? No one!* And since I am telling you the truth, why don't you believe Me?

47 Anyone whose Father is God listens gladly to the words of God. Since you don't, it proves you aren't His children."

48 "You Samaritan! Foreigner! Devil!" the Jewish leaders snarled. "Didn't we say all along You were possessed by a demon?"

49 "No," Jesus said, "I have no demon in Me. For I honor My Father—and you dishonor Me.

50 And though I have no wish to make Myself great, God wants this for Me and judges (those who reject Me.)*

51 With all the earnestness I have I tell you this—no one who obeys Me shall ever die!"

52 The leaders of the Jews said, "Now we know You are possessed by a demon. Even Abraham and the mightiest prophets died, and yet You say that obeying You will keep a man from dying!

53 So You are greater than our father Abraham, who died? And greater than the prophets, who died? Who do You think You are?"

54 Then Jesus told them this: "If I am merely boasting about Myself, it doesn't count. But it is My Father —and you claim Him as your God—who is saying these glorious things about Me.

55 But you do not even know Him. I do. If I said otherwise, I would be as great a liar as you! But it is true—I know Him and fully obey Him.

56 Your father Abraham rejoiced to see My day. He knew I was coming and was glad."

57 *The Jewish leaders*: "You aren't even 50 years old—sure, You've seen Abraham!"

58 *Jesus*: "The absolute truth is that I was in existence before Abraham was even born!"

59 At that point the Jewish leaders picked up stones to kill Him. But Jesus was hidden from them, and walked past them and left the Temple.

CHAPTER 9

As he was walking along, He saw a man blind from birth.

2 "Master," His disciples asked Him, "why was this man born blind? Was it a result of his own sins or those of his parents?"

3 "Neither," Jesus answered. "But to demonstrate the power of God.

4 All of us must quickly carry out the tasks assigned us by the one who sent Me, for there is little time left before the night falls and all work comes to an end.

5 But while I am still here in the world, I give it My light."

6 Then He spat on the ground and made mud from the spittle and smoothed the mud over the blind man's eyes,

7 And told him, "Go and wash in the Pool of Siloam" (the word "Siloam" means "Sent"). So the man went where he was sent and washed and came back seeing!

8 His neighbors and others who knew him as a blind beggar asked each other, "Is this the same fellow—that beggar?"

9 Some said yes, and some said no. "It can't be the same man," they thought, "but he surely looks like him!"

But the beggar said, "I *am* the same man!"

10 Then they asked him how in the world he could see. What had happened?

11 And he told them, "A man they call Jesus made mud and smoothed it over my eyes and told me to go to the Pool of Siloam and wash off the mud. I did, and I can see!"

12 "Where is He now?" they asked.

"I don't know," he replied.

13 Then they took the man to the Pharisees.

14 (Now as it happened, this all occurred on a Sabbath.)

15 Then the Pharisees asked him all about it. So he told them how Jesus had smoothed the mud over his eyes, and when it was washed away, he could see!

16 Some of them said, "Then this fellow Jesus is not from God, because He is working on the Sabbath!"

Others said, "But how could an ordinary sinner do such miracles?" So there was a deep division of opinion among them.

17 Then the Pharisees turned on the man who had been blind and demanded, "This man who opened your eyes—who do you say He is?"

"I think He must be a prophet sent from God," the man replied.

18 The Jewish leaders wouldn't believe he had been blind, until they called in his parents

19 And asked them, "Is this your son? Was he born blind? If so, how can he see?"

20 His parents replied, "We know this is our son and that he was born blind,

21 But we don't know what happened to make him see, or who did it. He is old enough to speak for himself. Ask him!"

22, 23 They said this in fear of the Jewish leaders who had announced that anyone saying Jesus was the Messiah would be excommunicated.

24 So for the second time they called in the man who had been blind and told him, "Give the glory to God, not to Jesus, for we know He is an evil person."

25 "I don't know whether He is good or bad," the man replied, "But I know this: *I was blind, and now I see!*"

26 "But what did He do?" they asked. "How did He heal you?"

27 "Look!" the man exclaimed. "I told you once; didn't you listen? Why do you want to hear it again? Do you want to become His disciples too?"

28 Then they cursed him and said, "You are His disciple, but we are disciples of Moses.

29 We know God has spoken to Moses, but as for this fellow, we don't know anything about Him."

30 "Why, that's very strange!" the man replied. "He can heal blind men, but you don't know anything about Him!

31 Well, God doesn't listen to evil men, but He has open ears to those who worship Him and do His will.

32 Since the world began, there has never been anyone who could open the eyes of someone born blind.

33 If this man were not from God, He couldn't do it."

34 "You illegitimate bastard, you!" they shouted. "Are you trying to teach *us*?" And they threw him out.

35 When Jesus heard what had happened, He found the man and said, "Do you believe in the Messiah?"

36 The man answered, "Who is He, sir, for I want to."

37 "You have seen Him," Jesus said, "and He is speaking to you!"

38 "Yes, Lord," the man said, "I believe!" And he worshiped Jesus.

39 Then Jesus told him, "I have come into the world to give sight to those who are spiritually blind and to show those who think they see that they are blind."

40 The Pharisees who were standing there asked, "Are you saying we are blind?"

41 "If you were blind, you wouldn't be guilty," Jesus replied. "But your guilt remains because you claim to know what you are doing."

CHAPTER 10

Anyone refusing to walk through the gate into a sheep-fold, who sneaks over the wall, must surely be a thief!

2 For a shepherd comes through the gate!

3 The gatekeeper opens the gate for him, and the sheep hear his voice and come to him; and he calls his own sheep by name and leads them out.

4 He walks ahead of them; and they follow him, for they recognize his voice.

5 They won't follow a stranger, but will run from him, for they don't recognize his voice."

6 Those who heard Jesus use this illustration didn't understand what He meant,

7 So He explained it to them. "I am the Gate for the sheep," He said.

8 "All others who came before Me are thieves and robbers. But the true sheep did not listen to them.

9 Yes, I am the Gate. Those who come in by way of

the Gate will be saved and will go in and out and find green pastures.

10 The thief's purpose is to steal, kill and destroy. My purpose is to give eternal life—abundantly!

11 I am the Good Shepherd. The Good Shepherd lays down His life for the sheep.

12 A hired man will run when he sees a wolf coming, and will leave the sheep, for they aren't his and he isn't their shepherd. And so the wolf leaps on them and scatters the flock.

13 The hired man runs because he is hired and has no real concern for the sheep.

14 I am the Good Shepherd and know My own sheep, and they know Me,

15 Just as My Father knows Me and I know the Father; and I lay down My life for the sheep.

16 I have other sheep, too, in another fold. I must bring them also, and they will heed My voice; and there will be one flock with one Shepherd.

17 The Father loves Me because I lay down My life that I may have it back again.

18 No one can kill Me without My consent—I lay down My life voluntarily. For I have the right and power to take it again. For the Father has given Me this right."

19 When He said these things, the Jewish leaders were again divided in their opinions about Him.

20 Some of them said, "He has a demon or else is crazy. Why listen to a man like that?"

21 Others said, "This doesn't sound to us like a man possessed by a demon! Can a demon open the eyes of blind men?"

*   *   *   *   *

22, 23 It was winter, and Jesus was in Jerusalem at the time of the Dedication Celebration. He was at the Temple, walking through the section known as Solomon's Cloister

24 The Jewish leaders surrounded Him and asked, "How long are You going to keep us in suspense? If you are the Messiah, tell us plainly."

25 "I have already told you, and you didn't believe

Me," Jesus replied. "The proof is in the miracles I do in the name of My Father.

26　But you don't believe Me because you are not part of My flock.

27　My sheep recognize My voice, and I know them, and they follow Me.

28　I give them eternal life, and they shall never perish. No one shall snatch them away from Me,

29　For My Father has given them to Me, and He is more powerful than anyone else, so no one can kidnap them from Me.

30　I and the Father are one."

31　Then again the Jewish leaders picked up stones to kill Him.

32　Jesus said, "At God's direction I have done many a miracle to help the people. For which one are you killing Me?"

33　They replied, "Not for any good work, but for blasphemy; You, a mere man, have declared Yourself to be God."

34, 35, 36　"In your own Law it says that men are gods!" He replied. "So if the Scripture (which cannot be untrue) speaks of those as gods, to whom the message of God came, do you call it blasphemy when the one sanctified and sent into the world by the Father says, 'I am the Son of God'?

37　Don't believe Me unless I do miracles of God.

38　But if I do, believe them even if you don't believe Me! Then you will become convinced that the Father is in Me, and I in the Father."

39　Once again they started to arrest Him. But He walked away and left them

40　And went beyond the Jordan River to stay near the place where John was first baptizing.

41　And many came to Him there. "John didn't do miracles," they remarked, "but all his predictions concerning this man have come true."

42　And many came to the decision that He was the Messiah.

CHAPTER 11

Do you remember Mary, who poured the costly perfume on Jesus' feet and wiped them with her hair? Well, her brother Lazarus, who lived in Bethany with his sisters Mary and Martha, was sick.

3 So the two sisters sent a message to Jesus telling Him, "Sir, your good friend is very, very sick."

4 But when Jesus heard about it, He said, "The purpose of his illness is not death, but for the glory of God. I, the Son of God, will receive glory from this situation."

5 Although Jesus was very fond of Martha, Mary and Lazarus,

6 He stayed where He was for the next two days and made no move to go to them.

7 Finally, after the two days, He said to His disciples, "Let's go to Judea."

8 But His disciples objected. "Master," they said, "only a few days ago the Jewish leaders in Judea were trying to kill You. Are You going there again?"

9 Jesus replied, "There are 12 hours of daylight every day, and during every hour of it a man can walk safely and not stumble.

10 Only at night is there danger of a wrong step, because of the dark."

11 Then He said, "Our friend Lazarus has gone to sleep, but now I will go and waken him!"

12, 13 The disciples, thinking Jesus meant Lazarus was having a good night's rest, said, "That means he is getting better!" But Jesus meant Lazarus had died.

14 Then He told them plainly, "Lazarus is dead.

15 And for your sake, I am glad I wasn't there, for this will give you another opportunity to believe in Me. Come, let's go to him."

16 Thomas (nicknamed "The Twin") said to his fellow disciples, "Let's go too—and die with Him."

17 When they arrived at Bethany, they were told that Lazarus had already been in his tomb for four days!

18 Bethany was only a couple of miles down the road from Jerusalem,

19 And many of the Jewish leaders had come to pay

their respects and to console Martha and Mary on their loss.

20 When Martha got word that Jesus was coming, she went to meet Him. But Mary stayed at home.

21 Martha said to Jesus, "Sir, if You had been here, my brother wouldn't have died.

22 And even now it's not too late, for I know that God will bring my brother back to life again, if You will only ask Him to."

23 Jesus told her, "Your brother will come back to life again."

24 "Yes," Martha said, "when everyone else does, on Resurrection Day."

25 Jesus told her, "I am the one who raises the dead and gives them life again. Anyone who believes in Me, even though he dies like anyone else, shall live again.

26 He is given eternal life for believing in Me and shall never perish. Do you believe this, Martha?"

27 "Yes, Master," she told Him. "I believe You are the Messiah, the Son of God, the one we have so long awaited."

28 Then she left Him and returned to Mary and calling her aside from the mourners told her, "He is here and wants to see you."

29 Mary left immediately to go to Him.

30 Now Jesus had stayed outside the village, at the place where Martha met Him.

31 When the Jewish leaders, who were at the house trying to console Mary, saw her hastily leave, they assumed she was going to Lazarus' tomb to weep; so they followed her.

32 When Mary arrived where Jesus was, she fell down at His feet, saying, "Sir, if You had been here, my brother would still be alive."

33 When Jesus saw her weeping and the Jewish leaders wailing with her, He was moved with indignation and deeply troubled.

34 "Where is he buried?" He asked them.

They told Him, "Come and see."

35 Tears came to Jesus' eyes.

36 "They were close friends," the Jewish leaders said. "See how much He loved him."

37, 38 But some said, "This fellow healed a blind

man—why couldn't He keep Lazarus from dying?" And again Jesus was moved with deep anger. Then they came to the tomb. It was a cave with a heavy stone rolled across its door.

39   "Roll the stone aside," Jesus told them.

But Martha, the dead man's sister, said, "By now the smell will be terrible, for he has been dead four days."

40   "But didn't I tell you that you will see a wonderful miracle from God if you believe?" Jesus asked her.

41   So they rolled the stone aside. Then Jesus looked up to heaven and said, "Father, thank You for hearing Me.

42   (You always hear Me, of course, but I said it because of all these people standing here, so that they will believe You sent Me.)"

43   Then He shouted, "Lazarus, come out!"

44   And Lazarus came—bound up in the gravecloth, his face muffled in a head swath. Jesus told them, "Unwrap him and let him go!"

45   And so at last many of the Jewish leaders who were with Mary and saw it happen, finally believed on Him!

46   But some went away to the Pharisees and reported it to them.

47   Then the chief priests and Pharisees convened a council to discuss the situation. "What are we going to do?" they asked each other, "for this man certainly does miracles.

48   If we let Him alone, the whole nation will follow Him—and then the Roman army will come and kill us and take over the Jewish government."

49   But one of them, Caiaphas, who was High Priest that year, said, "You stupid idiots—

50   Let this one man die for the people—why should the whole nation perish?"

51   This prophecy (that Jesus should die for the entire nation) came from Caiaphas in his position as High Priest—he didn't think of it by himself, but was inspired to say it.

52   It was a prediction that Jesus' death would not be for Israel only, but for all the children of God scattered around the world.

53   So from that time on the Jewish leaders began plotting Jesus' death.

54 Jesus now stopped His public ministry and left Jerusalem; he went to the edge of the desert to the village of Ephraim and stayed there with His disciples.

55 The Passover, a Jewish holy day, was near, and many country people arrived in Jerusalem several days early so that they could go through the cleansing ceremony before the Passover began.

56 They wanted to see Jesus, and as they gossiped in the Temple, they asked each other, "What do you think? Will He come for the Passover?"

57 Meanwhile the chief priests and Pharisees had publicly announced that anyone seeing Jesus must report Him immediately so that they could arrest Him.

CHAPTER 12

Six days before the Passover ceremonies began, Jesus arrived in Bethany where Lazarus was—the man He had brought back to life.

2 A banquet was prepared in Jesus' honor. Martha served, and Lazarus sat at the table with Him.

3 Then Mary took a jar of costly perfume made from essence of nard, and anointed Jesus' feet with it and wiped them with her hair. And the house was filled with fragrance.

4 But Judas Iscariot, one of His disciples—the one who would betray Him—said,

5 "That perfume was worth a fortune! It should have been sold and the money given to the poor!"

6 (Not that he cared for the poor, but he was in charge of the disciples' funds and often dipped into them for his own use!)

7 Jesus replied, "Let her alone. She did it in preparation for My burial.

8 You can always help the poor, but I won't be with you very long!"

9 When the ordinary people of Jerusalem heard of His arrival, they flocked to see Him and also to see Lazarus—the man who had come back to life again.

10 Then the chief priests decided to kill Lazarus too,

11 For it was because of him that many of the Jewish

leaders had deserted and believed in Jesus as their Messiah.

12 The next day, the news that Jesus was on the way to Jerusalem swept through the city, and a huge crowd of Passover visitors

13 Took palm branches and went down the road to meet him, shouting, "The Savior! God bless the King of Israel! Hail to God's Ambassador!"

14 Jesus rode along on a young donkey, fulfilling the prophecy that said,

15 "Don't be afraid of your King, people of Israel, for He will come to you meekly, sitting on a donkey's colt!"

16 At the time, His disciples didn't realize that this was a fulfillment of prophecy; but after Jesus returned to His glory in heaven, they noticed how many prophecies of Scripture had come true before their eyes.

17 And those in the crowd who had seen Jesus call Lazarus back to life were telling all about it.

18 In fact, that was why so many went out to meet Him—because they had heard about this mighty miracle.

19 Then the Pharisees said to each other, "We've lost. Look—the whole world has gone after Him!"

20 Some Greeks who had come to Jerusalem to attend the Passover

21 Paid a visit to Philip, who was from Bethsaida, and said, "Sir, we want to meet Jesus."

22 Philip told Andrew about it, and they went together to ask Jesus.

23, 24 Jesus replied that the time had come for Him to return to His glory in heaven, and that "I must fall and die like a kernel of wheat that falls between the furrows of the earth. Unless I die, I will be alone—a single seed. But My death will produce many new wheat kernels—a plentiful harvest of new lives.

25 If you love your life down here—you will lose it! If you despise your life down here—you will exchange it for eternal glory!

26 If these Greeks want to be My disciples, tell them to come and follow Me, for My servants must be where I am. And if they follow Me, the Father will honor them.

27 Now My soul is deeply troubled. Shall I pray,

'Father, save Me from what lies ahead'? But that is the very reason why I came!

28   Father, bring glory and honor to Your name."

Then a voice spoke from heaven saying, "I have already done this, and I will do it again."

29   When the crowd heard the voice, some of them thought it was thunder, while others declared an angel had spoken to Him.

30   Then Jesus told them, "The voice was for your benefit, not Mine.

31   The time of judgment for the world has come— and the time when Satan* the prince of this world, shall be cast out.

32   And when I am lifted up (on the cross*), I will draw everyone to Me."

33   He said this to indicate how He was going to die.

34   "Die?" asked the crowd. "We understood that the Messiah would live forever and never die. Why are You saying He will die? What Messiah are You talking about?"

35   Jesus replied, "My light will shine out for you just a little while longer. Walk in it while you can, and go where you want to go before the darkness falls, for then it will be too late for you to find your way.

36   Make use of the Light while there is still time; then you will become sons of Light." After saying these things, Jesus went away and was hidden from them.

37   But despite all the miracles He had done, most of the people would not believe He was the Messiah.

38   This is exactly what Isaiah the prophet had predicted: "Lord, who will believe us? Who will accept God's mighty miracles as proof?"

39   But they couldn't believe, for as Isaiah also said:

40   "God has blinded their eyes and hardened their hearts so that they can neither see nor understand nor turn to Me to heal them."

41   Isaiah was referring to Jesus when he made this prediction, for he had seen a vision of the Messiah's glory.

42   However, even many of the Jewish leaders believed Him to be the Messiah but wouldn't admit it to anyone because of their fear that the Pharisees would excommunicate them from the synagogue,

43 For they loved the praise of men more than the praise of God.

* * * * *

44 Jesus shouted to the crowds, "If you trust Me, you are really trusting God.

45 For when you see Me, you are seeing the one who sent Me.

46 I have come as a Light to shine in this dark world, so that all who put their trust in Me will no longer wander in the darkness.

47 If anyone hears Me and doesn't obey Me, I am not his judge—for I have come to save the world and not to judge it.

48 But all who reject Me and My message will be judged at the Day of Judgment by the truths I have spoken.

49 For these are not My own ideas, but I have told you what the Father said to tell you,

50 And I know His instructions give eternal life; so whatever He tells Me to say, I say!"

CHAPTER 13

Jesus knew on the evening of Passover Day that it would be His last night on earth before returning to His Father. During supper the Devil had already suggested to Judas Iscariot (Simon's son) that this was the night to carry out his plan to betray Jesus. Jesus knew that the Father had given Him everything and that He had come from God and would return to God. And how He loved His disciples!

4 So He got up from the supper table, took off His robe, wrapped a towel around His loins,

5 Poured water into a basin, and began to wash the disciples' feet and to wipe them with the towel He had around Him.

6 When He came to Simon Peter, Peter said to Him, "Master, You shouldn't be washing our feet like this!"

7 Jesus replied, "You don't understand now why I am doing it; some day you will."

8 "No," Peter protested, "You shall never wash my feet!"

"But if I don't, you can't be My partner," Jesus replied.

9 Simon Peter exclaimed, "Then wash my hands and head as well—not just my feet!"

10 Jesus replied, "One who has bathed all over needs only his feet washed to be entirely clean! Now you are clean—but that isn't true of everyone here."

11 For Jesus knew who would betray Him. That is what He meant when He said, "Not all of you are clean."

12 After washing their feet, He put on His robe again and sat down and asked, "Do you understand what I was doing?

13 You call Me 'Master' and 'Lord,' and you do well to say it, for it is true.

14 And since I, the Lord and Teacher, have washed your feet, you ought to wash each other's feet.

15 I have given you an example to follow: do as I have done to you.

16 How true it is that a servant is not greater than his master! Nor is the messenger more important than the one who sends him.

17 You know these things—now do them! That is the path of blessing.

18 I am not saying these things to all of you; I know so well each one of you I chose. The Scripture declares, 'One who eats supper with Me will betray Me,' and this will soon come true.

19 I tell you this now so that when it happens, you will believe on Me.

*   *   *   *   *

20 Truly, anyone welcoming the Holy Spirit,* whom I will send, is welcoming Me. And to welcome Me is to welcome the Father who sent Me."

*   *   *   *   *

21 Now Jesus was in great anguish of spirit and exclaimed, "Yes, it is true—one of you will betray Me."

22 The disciples looked at each other, wondering whom He could mean.

23   I was sitting next to Jesus at the table, being His closest friend,

24   And Simon Peter motioned to me to ask Him who it was who would do this terrible deed.

25   So I turned and asked Him, "Lord, who is it?"

26   He told me, "It is the one I honor by giving the bread dipped in the sauce." And when He had dipped it, He gave it to Judas, son of Simon Iscariot.

27   And when he had eaten it, Satan entered into him. Then Jesus told him, "Hurry—do it now."

28   None of the others at the table knew what Jesus meant.

29   Some thought that since Judas was their treasurer, Jesus was telling him to go and pay for the food or to give some money to the poor.

30   Judas left at once, going out into the night.

31   As soon as Judas left the room, Jesus said, "My time has come; the glory of God will soon surround Me— and God shall receive great praise because of all that happens to Me.

32   And God shall give Me His own glory, and this so very soon.

33   Dear, dear children, how brief are these moments before I must go away and leave you! Then, though you search for Me, you cannot come to Me—just as I told the Jewish leaders.

34   And so I am giving a new commandment to you now—love each other just as much as I love you.

35   Your strong love for each other will prove to the world that you are My disciples."

36   Simon Peter said, "Master, where are You going?" And Jesus replied, "You can't go with Me now; but you will follow Me later."

37   "But why can't I come now?' he asked, "for I am ready to die for You."

38   Jesus answered, "Die for Me? No—three times before the cock crows tomorrow morning, you will deny that you even know Me!"

CHAPTER 14

Don't be upset. Trust God—and trust Me.

1, 2, 3　There are many homes up there where My Father lives, and I am going to get them ready for your coming! When they are all ready, I will come back and get you and take you with Me; then you will be where I am. I would tell you plainly if this were not so.

4　And you know how to get where I am going."

5　"No, we don't," Thomas said. "We don't even know where You are going—how can we know the way?"

6　Jesus told him, "I am the Way—yes, and the Truth and the Life. No one can get to the Father except by means of Me.

7　If you had known who I am, then you would have known who My Father is! From now on you know Him— and have seen Him!"

8　Philip said, "Sir, show us the Father and we will be satisfied."

9　Jesus replied, "Don't you even yet know who I am, Philip, even after all this time I have been with you? Anyone who has seen Me has seen the Father! So why are you asking to see Him?

10　Don't you believe that I am in the Father and the Father is in Me? The words I say are not My own, but are from my Father who lives in Me! And He does His work through Me.

11　Just believe it—that I am in the Father and the Father is in Me. Or else believe it because of the mighty miracles you have seen Me do.

12, 13　In solemn truth I tell you, anyone believing in Me shall do the same miracles I have done, and even greater ones, because I am going to be with the Father. You can ask Him for *anything*, using My name, and I will do it, for this will bring praise to the Father because of what I, the Son, will do for you.

14　Yes, ask *anything*, using My name, and I will do it!

15, 16　If you love Me, obey Me; and I will ask the Father and He will give you another Comforter, and He will never leave you!

17   He is the Holy Spirit, the Spirit who leads into all truth. The world at large cannot receive Him, for it isn't looking for Him and doesn't recognize Him. But you do, for He lives with you now and some day shall be in you!

18   No, I will not abandon you or leave you orphans in the storm—I will come to you!

19   In just a little while I will be gone from the world, but I will still be present with you. For I will live again —and you will too.

20   When I come back to life again, you will know that I am in My Father, and you in Me, and I in you.

21   The one who obeys Me is the one who loves Me; and because he loves Me, My Father will love him; and I will too, and I will reveal Myself to him."

22   Judas (not Judas Iscariot, but His other disciple with that name) said to Him, "Sir, why are You going to reveal Yourself only to us disciples and not to the world at large?

23   Jesus replied, "Because I will only reveal Myself to those who love Me and obey Me. The Father will love them too, and We will come to them and live with them.

24   But the world neither loves Me nor obeys Me. And remember, I am not making up this answer to your question! It is the answer given by the Father who sent Me.

25   I am telling you these things now while I am still with you.

26   But when the Father sends the Comforter to represent Me—and by the Comforter I mean the Holy Spirit —He will teach you much more as well as remind you of everything I Myself have told you.

27   I am leaving you with a gift—peace of mind and heart! And the peace I give isn't fragile like the peace the world gives! So don't be troubled or afraid.

28   Remember what I told you—I am going away, but I will come back to you. If you really love Me, you will be very happy for Me, for now I can go to the Father, who is greater than I am.

29   I have told you these things before they happen so that when they do, you will believe (in Me)*

30   I don't have much more time to talk to you, for the

evil prince of this world is on the way. He has no power over Me,

31 But I will freely do what the Father requires of Me so that the world will know that I love the Father. Come, let's be going."

CHAPTER 15

I am the true Vine, and My Father is the Gardener. 2 He lops off every branch that doesn't produce. And those that bear fruit He prunes for even larger crops.

3 He has already tended you by pruning you back for greater strength and usefulness by means of the commands I gave you.

4 Take care to live in Me, and let Me live in you. For a branch can't produce fruit when severed from the vine! Nor can you be fruitful apart from Me.

5 Yes, I am the Vine; you are the branches. Whoever lives in Me and I in him shall produce a large crop of fruit. For apart from Me you can't do a thing.

6 If anyone separates from Me, he is thrown away like a useless branch, withers and is gathered into a pile with all the others and burned.

7 But if you stay in Me and obey My commands, you may ask any request you like, and it will be granted!

8 My true disciples produce bountiful harvests. This brings great glory to My Father.

9 I have loved you even as the Father has loved Me. Live within My love.

10 When you obey Me, you are living in My love, just as I obey My Father and live in His love.

11 I have told you this so you will be filled with My joy. Yes, your cup of joy will overflow!

12 I demand that you love each other as much as I love you!

13 And here is how to measure it—the greatest love is when a person lays down his life for his friends;

14 And you are My friends if you obey Me.

15 I no longer call you slaves, for a master doesn't confide in his slaves; now you are My friends, proved by the fact that I have told you everything the Father told Me.

16 You didn't choose Me! I chose you! I appointed you to go and produce lovely fruit always, so that no matter what you ask for from the Father, using My name, He will give it to you.

17 I demand that you love each other,

18 For you get enough hate from the world! But then, it hated Me before it hated you!

19 The world would love you if you belonged to it; but you don't—for I chose you to come out of the world, and so it hates you!

20 Do you remember what I told you? 'A slave isn't greater than his master!' Since they persecuted Me, naturally they will persecute you. And if they listened to Me, they will listen to you!

21 The people of the world will persecute you because you belong to Me, for they don't know God, who sent Me.

22 They would not be guilty unless I had come and spoken to them. But now they have no excuse for their sin.

23 Anyone hating Me is also hating My Father.

24 If I hadn't done such mighty miracles among them, they would not be counted guilty. But as it is, they saw these miracles and yet they hated both of us—Me and My Father.

25 This has fulfilled what the prophets said (concerning the Messiah), 'They hated Me without reason.'

26 But I will send you the Comforter—the Holy Spirit, the source of all truth. He will come to you from the Father, and will tell you all about Me.

27 And you also must tell everyone about Me, because you have been with Me from the beginning."

CHAPTER 16

I have told you these things so that you won't be staggered by all that lies ahead.*

2 For you will be excommunicated from the synagogue, and indeed the time is coming when those who kill you will think they are doing God a service.

3 This is because they have never known the Father or Me.

4 Yes, I'm telling you these things now so that when they happen, you will remember I warned you. I didn't tell you earlier since I would still be with you for a while.

5 But now I am going away to the one who sent Me; and none of you is interested in the purpose of My going—none seems to wonder why.

6 Instead you are only filled with sorrow.

7 But the fact of the matter is that it is best for you that I go away, for if I don't, the Comforter won't come. If I do, He will—for I will send Him to you.

8 And when He has come, He will convince the world of its sin, and of the availability of God's goodness, and of deliverance from judgment.

9 Its sin is unbelief in Me;

10 There is righteousness available because I go to the Father and you shall see Me no more;

11 There is deliverance from judgment because the prince of this world has already been judged.

12 Oh, there is so much more I want to tell you, but you can't understand it all now.

13 When the Holy Spirit, who is truth, comes, He shall guide you into all truth, for He will not be presenting His own ideas but passing on to you what He has heard. He will tell you about the future.

14 He shall praise Me and bring Me great honor by showing you My glory.

15 All the Father's glory is Mine; this is what I mean when I say that He will show you My glory.

16 In just a little while I will be gone, and you will see Me no more; but just a little while after that, and you will see Me again!"

17, 18 "Whatever is He saying?" some of His disciples asked. "What is this about 'going to the Father'? We don't know what He means!"

19 Jesus realized they wanted to ask Him, so He said, "Are you asking yourselves what I mean?

20 Truly I tell you, the world will rejoice over what is going to happen to Me, and you will weep. But your weeping shall suddenly be turned to wonderful joy (when you see Me again*).

21 It will be the same joy as that of a woman in labor when her child is born—her anguish gives place to rapturous joy and the pain is forgotten.

22   You have sorrow now, but I will see you again and then you will rejoice; and no one can rob you of that joy.

23   At that time you won't need to ask Me for anything, for you can go directly to the Father and ask Him, and He will give you what you ask for because you use My name.

24   You haven't tried this before, but begin now. Ask, using My name, and you will receive and your cup of joy will overflow.

25   I have spoken of these matters very guardedly, but the time will come when this will not be necessary and I will tell you plainly all about the Father.

26   Then you will present your petitions over My signature. And I won't need to ask the Father to grant you these requests,

27   For the Father Himself loves you dearly because you love Me and believe that I came from the Father.

28   Yes, I came from the Father into the world and will leave the world and return to the Father."

29   "At last You are speaking plainly," His disciples said, "and not in riddles.

30   Now we understand that You know everything and don't need anyone to tell You anything. From this we believe that You came from God."

31   "Do you finally believe this?" Jesus asked.

32   "But the time is coming—in fact, it is here—when you will be scattered, each one returning to his own home, leaving Me alone. Yet I will not be alone, for the Father is with Me.

33   I have told you all this so that you will have peace of heart and mind. Here on earth you will have many trials and sorrows; but cheer up, for I have overcome the world."

CHAPTER 17

When Jesus had finished saying all these things, He looked up to heaven and said, "Father, the time has come. Reveal the glory of Your Son so that He can give the glory back to You.

2   For You have given Him authority over every man

and woman in all the earth. He gives eternal life to each one You have given Him.

3 And this is the way to have eternal life—by knowing You, the only true God, and Jesus Christ, the one You sent to earth!

4 I brought You glory here on earth by doing everything You told Me to.

5 And now, Father, reveal My glory as I stand in Your presence, the glory We shared before the world began.

6 I have told these men all about You. They were in the world, but then You gave them to Me. Actually, they were always Yours, and You gave them to Me; and they have obeyed You.

7 Now they know that everything I have is a gift from You,

8 For I have passed on to them the commands You gave Me; and they took them and know of a certainty that I came down to earth from You, and they believe You sent Me.

9 My plea is not for the world, but for these You have given Me, because they belong to You.

10 And all of them, since they are Mine, belong to You; and You have given them back to Me, with everything else of Yours, and so they are My glory!

11 Now I am leaving the world, and leaving them behind, and coming to You. Holy Father, keep them in Your own care—all those You have given Me—so that they will be united just as We are, with none missing.

12 During My time here I have kept safe within Your family all of these You gave to Me. I guarded them so that not one perished, except the son of hell, as the Scriptures foretold.

13 And now I am coming to You. I have told them many things while I was with them so that they would be filled with My joy.

14 I have given them Your commands. And the world hates them because they don't fit in with it, just as I don't.

15 I'm not asking you to take them out of the world, but to keep them safe from Satan's power.

16 They are not part of this world any more than I am.

17   Make them pure and holy through teaching them Your words of truth.

18   As You sent Me into the world, I am sending them into the world,

19   And I consecrate Myself to meet their need for growth in truth and holiness.

20   I am not praying for these alone, but also for all future believers who will come to Me because of their testimony.

21   My prayer for all of them is that they will be of one heart and mind, just as You and I are, Father—that just as You are in Me and I am in You, so they will be in Us.

22   I have given them the glory You gave Me—the glorious unity of being one, as We are—

23   I in them and You in Me, all being perfected into one—so that the world will know You sent Me and will understand that You love them as much as You love Me.

24   Father, I want them with Me—these You've given Me—so they can see My glory. You gave Me the glory because You loved Me before the world began!

25   O righteous Father, the world doesn't know You, but I do; and these disciples know You sent Me.

26   And I have revealed You to them, and will keep on revealing You so that the mighty love You have for Me may be in them, and I in them."

CHAPTER 18

After saying these things Jesus crossed the Kidron ravine with His disciples and entered a grove of olive trees.

2   Judas, the betrayer, knew this place, for Jesus had gone there many times with His disciples.

3   The chief priests and Pharisees had given Judas a squad of soldiers and police to accompany him. Now, with blazing torches, lanterns and weapons, they arrived at the olive grove.

4, 5   Jesus fully realized all that was going to happen to Him. Stepping forward to meet them He asked, "Who are you looking for?"

"Jesus of Nazareth," they replied.

"I am He," Jesus said.

6   And as He said it, they all fell backwards to the ground!

7   Once more He asked them, "Who are you searching for?"

And again they replied, "Jesus of Nazareth."

8   "I told you I am He," Jesus said; "and since I am the one you are after, let these others go."

9   He did this to carry out the prophecy He had just made, "I have not lost a single one of those You gave Me . . ."

10   Then Simon Peter drew a sword and slashed off the right ear of Malchus, the High Priest's servant.

11   But Jesus said to Peter, "Put your sword away. Shall I not drink from the cup the Father has given Me?"

12   So the Jewish police with the soldiers and their lieutenant arrested Jesus and tied Him.

13   First they took Him to Annas, the father-in-law of Caiaphas, the High Priest that year.

14   (Caiaphas was the one who told the other Jewish leaders, "Better that one should die for all.")

15   Simon Peter followed along behind, as did another of the disciples who was acquainted with the High Priest. So that other disciple was permitted into the courtyard along with Jesus,

16   While Peter stood outside the gate. Then the other disciple spoke to the girl watching at the gate, and she let Peter in.

17   The girl asked Peter, "Aren't you one of Jesus' disciples?"

"No," he said, "I am not!"

18   The police and the household servants were standing around a fire they had made, for it was cold. And Peter stood there with them, warming himself.

19   Inside, the High Priest began asking Jesus about His followers and what He had been teaching them.

20   Jesus replied, "What I teach is widely known, for I have preached regularly in the synagogue and Temple; I have been heard by all the Jewish leaders and teach nothing in private that I have not said in public.

21   Why are you asking Me this question? Ask those who heard Me. You have some of them here. They know what I said."

22 One of the soldiers standing there struck Jesus with his fist. "Is that the way to answer the High Priest?" he demanded.

23 "If I lied, prove it," Jesus said. "Should you hit a man for telling the truth?"

24 Then Annas sent Jesus, bound, to Caiaphas the High Priest.

25 Meanwhile as Simon Peter was standing by the fire, he was asked again, "Aren't you one of His disciples?"

"Of course not," he replied.

26 But one of the household slaves of the High Priest —a relative of the man whose ear Peter had cut off—asked, "Didn't I see you out there in the olive grove with Jesus?"

27 Again Peter denied it. And immediately a rooster crowed.

28 Jesus' trial before Caiaphas ended in the early hours of the morning; next he was taken to the palace of the Roman governor. His accusers wouldn't go in themselves for that would "defile" them, they said, and they wouldn't be allowed to eat the Passover lamb.

29 So Pilate, the governor, went out to them and asked, "What is your charge against this man? What are you accusing Him of doing?"

30 They replied, "We wouldn't have brought Him to you if He weren't a criminal!"

31 "Then take Him away and judge Him yourselves by your own laws," Pilate told them.

"But we want Him crucified," they said, "and your approval is required."

32 (This fulfilled Jesus' prediction concerning the method of His execution.)

33 Then Pilate went back into the palace and called for Jesus to be brought to him, "Are you the King of the Jews?" he asked Him.

34 " 'King' as *you* use the word or as the *Jews* use it?" Jesus asked.

35 "Am I a Jew?" Pilate retorted. "Your own people and their chief priests brought You here. Why? What have You done?"

36 Then Jesus answered, "I am not an earthly king. If I were, My followers would have fought when I was arrested by the Jewish leaders. But My Kingdom is not of the world."

37 Pilate replied, "But You are a King then?" "Yes," Jesus said. "I was born for that purpose. And I came to bring truth to the world. All who love the truth are My followers."

38 "What is truth?" Pilate exclaimed. Then he went out again to the people and told them, "He is not guilty of any crime.

39 But you have a custom of asking me to release someone from prison each year at Passover. So if you want me to, I'll release the 'King of the Jews.' "

40 But they screamed back, "No! Not this man, but Barabbas!" (Barabbas was a robber.)

CHAPTER 19

Then Pilate laid open Jesus' back with a leaded whip,

2 And the soldiers made a crown of thorns and placed it on His head and robed Him in royal purple.

3 Then they bowed* low before Him. "Hail, 'King of the Jews!' " they mocked, and struck Him with their fists.

4 Pilate went outside again and said to the Jews, "I am going to bring Him out to you now, but understand clearly that I find Him NOT GUILTY."

5 Then Jesus came out wearing the crown of thorns and the purple robe. And Pilate said, "Behold the man!"

6 At sight of Him the chief priests and Jewish officials began yelling, "Crucify! Crucify!"

"*You* crucify Him," Pilate said. "I find Him NOT GUILTY."

7 They replied, "By our laws He ought to die because He called Himself the Son of God."

8 When Pilate heard this, he was more frightened than ever.

9 He took Jesus back into the palace again and asked Him, "Where are You from?" But Jesus gave no answer.

10 "You won't talk to me?" asked Pilate. "Don't you realize that I have the power to release You or to crucify You?"

11 Then Jesus said, "You would have no power at all over Me unless it were given to you from above! So those who brought Me to you have the greater sin."

12 Then Pilate tried to release Him, but the Jewish leaders told him, "If you release this man, you are no friend of Caesar's. Anyone who declares himself a king is a rebel against Caesar."

13 At these words Pilate brought Jesus out to them again and sat down at the judgment bench on the stone-paved platform.

14 It was now about noon of the day before Passover. And Pilate said to the Jews, "Here is your King!"

15 "Away with Him," they yelled. "Away with Him —crucify Him!"

"What? Crucify your King?" Pilate asked.

"We have no king but Caesar," the chief priests shouted back.

16 Then he gave Jesus to them to crucify Him.

17 So they had Him at last, and He was taken out of the city, carrying His cross, to the place known as "The Skull" (in Hebrew, "Golgotha").

18 There they crucified Him and two others with Him, one on either side with Jesus between them.

19 And Pilate posted a sign above Him reading, "JESUS OF NAZARETH, THE KING OF THE JEWS."

20 The place where Jesus was crucified was near the city; and the signboard was written in Hebrew, Latin and Greek, so that many people read it.

21 Then the chief priests said to Pilate, "Change it from 'The King of the Jews' to '*He said,* I am King of the Jews.'"

22 Pilate replied, "What I have written, I have written. It stays exactly as it is."

23, 24 When the soldiers had crucified Jesus, they put his garments into four piles, one for each of them. But they said, "Let's not tear up His robe" (for it was seamless). "We'll throw dice to see who gets it." This fulfilled the Scripture that says, "They divided My clothes among them, and cast lots for My robe" (Psalm 22: 18).

25 And that is what they did.

Standing near the cross, were Jesus' mother, Mary, His aunt, the wife of Cleopas, and Mary Magdalene.

26 When Jesus saw His mother standing beside me— His close friend—He said to her, "He is your son."

27 And to me He said, "She is your mother!" And from then on I took her into my home.

28 Jesus knew that everything was now finished and to fulfill the Scriptures said, "I'm thirsty."

29 A jar of sour wine was sitting there, so a sponge was soaked in it and put on a hyssop branch and held up to His lips.

30 When Jesus had tasted it, He said, "It is finished," and bowed His head and dismissed His spirit.

31 The Jewish leaders didn't want the victims hanging there the next day, which was the Sabbath (and a very special Sabbath at that, for it was the Passover), so they asked Pilate to order the legs of the men broken, to hasten death; then their bodies could be taken down.

32 So the soldiers came and broke the legs of the two men crucified with Jesus;

33 But when they came to Him, they saw that He was dead already, and they didn't break His legs.

34 However, one of the soldiers pierced His side with a spear, and blood and water flowed out.

35 I saw this all myself and have given an accurate report so that you also can believe.

36, 37 The soldiers did this in fulfillment of the Scripture that says, "Not one of His bones shall be broken," and, "They shall look on Him they pierced."

38 Afterwards Joseph of Arimathea, who had been a secret disciple of Jesus for fear of the Jewish leaders, boldly asked Pilate for permission to take Jesus' body down; and Pilate told him to go ahead. So he came and took away His body.

39 Nicodemus (the man who had come to Jesus at night) came too, bringing a hundred pounds of embalming ointment made from myrrh and aloes.

40 Together they wrapped Jesus' body in a long linen cloth saturated with the spices, as is the Jewish custom of burial.

41 The place of crucifixion was near a grove of trees, where there was a new tomb, never used before.

42 And so, because of the need for haste before the Sabbath, and because the tomb was close at hand, they laid Him there.

CHAPTER 20

E arly Sunday morning, while it was still dark, Mary
Magdalene came to the tomb and found that the stone
was rolled aside from the entrance.

2 She ran and found Simon Peter and me and said,
"They have taken the Lord's body out of the tomb, and
I don't know where they have put Him!"

3, 4 We ran to the tomb to see; I outran Peter and
got there first

5 And stooped and looked in and saw the linen cloth
lying there, but I didn't go in.

6 Then Simon Peter arrived and went on inside. He
also saw the cloth lying there,

7 With the swath that had covered Jesus' head, rolled
up in a bundle and lying at the side.

8 Then I* went in, too, and saw, and believed (that
He had risen*)—

9 For until then we hadn't realized that the Scriptures
said He would come to life again!

10 We went on home,

11 And by that time Mary (had returned*) to the
tomb and was standing outside crying. And as she wept,
she stooped and looked in

12 And saw two white-robed angels sitting at the
head and foot of the place where the body of Jesus had
lain.

13 The angels asked her, "Why are you crying?"

She replied, "Because they have taken away my Lord,
and I don't know where they have put Him."

14 She glanced over her shoulder and saw someone
standing behind her. It was Jesus, but she didn't recognize Him!

15 "Why are you crying?" He asked her. "Who are
you looking for?"

(She thought He was the gardener.) "Sir," she said,
"if you have taken Him away, tell me where you have put
Him, and I will go and get Him."

16 "Mary!" Jesus said. She turned toward Him.

"Master!" she exclaimed.

17 "Don't touch Me," He cautioned, "for I haven't

yet ascended to the Father. But go find My brothers and tell them that I ascend to My Father and your Father, My God and your God."

18 Mary Magdalene found the disciples and told them, "I have seen the Lord!" Then she gave them His message.

19 That evening the disciples were meeting behind locked doors, in fear of the Jewish leaders, when suddenly Jesus was standing there among them! After greeting them

20 He showed them His hands and side. And how wonderful was their joy as they saw their Lord!

21 He spoke to them again and said, "As the Father has sent Me, even so I am sending you."

22 Then He breathed on them, and told them, "Receive the Holy Spirit!

23 If you forgive anyone's sins, they are forgiven. If you refuse to forgive them, they are unforgiven."

24 One of the disciples, Thomas ("The Twin"), was not there at the time with the others.

25 So they kept telling him, "We have seen the Lord!"

But he replied, "I won't believe it unless I see the nail wounds in His hands—and put my fingers into them—and place my hand into His side!"

26 Eight days later the disciples were together again, and this time Thomas was with them. The doors were locked; but suddenly, as before, Jesus was standing among them and greeting them!

27 Then He said to Thomas, "Put your finger into My hands! Put your hand into My side! Don't be faithless any longer! Believe!"

28 "My Lord and my God." Thomas said.

29 Then Jesus told him, "You believe because you have seen Me. But blessed are those who haven't seen Me and believe anyway!"

30, 31 Jesus' disciples saw Him do many other miracles besides the ones told about in this book, but these are recorded so that you will believe that He is the Messiah, the Son of God, and that believing in Him you will have Life.

CHAPTER 21

Later Jesus appeared again to the disciples beside the Lake of Galilee. This is how it happened:

2 A group of us were there—Simon Peter, Thomas ("The Twin"), Nathanael (from Cana, in Galilee), my brother James and I and two other disciples.

3 Simon Peter said, "I'm going fishing."

"We'll come too," we all said. We did, but caught nothing all night.

4 At dawn we saw a man standing on the beach but couldn't see who it was.

5 He called, "Any fish, boys?"

"No," we replied.

6 Then He said, "Throw out your net on the right-hand side of the boat, and you'll get plenty of them!" So we did, and couldn't draw in the net because of the weight of the fish; there were so many!

7 Then I said to Peter, "It is the Lord!" At that, Simon Peter put on his tunic (for he was stripped to the waist) and jumped into the water (and swam ashore).

8 The rest of us stayed in the boat and dragged the loaded net to shore, about 300 feet away.

9 When we got there, we saw that a fire was kindled and fish were frying over it, and there was bread.

10 "Bring some of the fish you've just caught," Jesus said.

11 So Simon Peter went out and pulled the net ashore. He counted 153 large fish; and yet the net hadn't torn!

12 "Now come and have some breakfast!" Jesus said; and none of us dared ask Him if he really was the Lord, for we were quite sure of it.

13 Then Jesus went around serving us the bread and fish.

14 This was the third time Jesus had appeared to us since His return from the dead.

15 After breakfast Jesus said to Simon Peter, "Simon, son of John, are you more of a friend to Me than these others?"

"Yes," Peter replied, "You know how much I really love You."

"Then feed My lambs," Jesus told him.

16 Jesus repeated the question: "Simon, son of John, are you *really* a friend of Mine?"

"Yes, Lord," Peter said, "You know how deeply I love You!"

"Then take care of My sheep," Jesus said.

17 Once more He asked him, "Simon, son of John, *do you really* love Me deeply?"

Peter was grieved at the way Jesus asked the question this third time. "Lord, You know my heart; You know I do," he said.

Jesus said, "Then feed My little sheep.

18 When you were young, you were able to do as you liked and go wherever you wanted to; but when you are old, you will stretch out your hands and others will direct you and take you where you don't want to go."

19 Jesus said this to let him know what kind of death he would die to glorify God. Then Jesus told him, "Follow Me."

20 Peter turned around and saw the disciple Jesus loved following (the one who had leaned around at supper that time to ask Jesus, "Master, which of us will betray You?").

21 Peter asked Jesus, "What about him, Lord? What sort of death will he die?"

22 Jesus replied, "If I want him to live until I return, what is that to you? *You* follow Me."

23 So the rumor spread among the brotherhood that that disciple wouldn't die! But that isn't what Jesus said! He only said, "If I want him to live until I come, what is that to you?"

24. .*I am that disciple!* I saw these events and have recorded them here. And we all know that my account of these things is accurate.

25 And I suppose that if all the other events in Jesus' life were written, the whole world could hardly contain the books!